Black American
Street Life

Black American Street Life

South Philadelphia, 1969–1971

Dan Rose

upp

University of Pennsylvania Press
Philadelphia • 1987

University of Pennsylvania Press
Conduct and Communication Series

Erving Goffman and Dell Hymes, *Founding Editors*
Dell Hymes, Gillian Sankoff, and Henry Glassie, *General Editors*

*A complete listing of the books in this series
appears at the back of this volume*

Library of Congress Cataloging-in-Publication Data

Rose, Dan.
  Black American street life: South Philadelphia, 1969-1971/Dan
Rose.
  p. cm.—(University of Pennsylvania Press conduct and
communication series)
  Bibliography: p.
  Includes index.
  ISBN 0-8122-8071-7.   ISBN 0-8122-1245-2 (pbk.)
  1. Afro-Americans—Pennsylvania—Philadelphia—Social life and
customs. 2. Afro-Americans—Pennsylvania—Philadelphia—Social
conditions. 3. South Philadelphia (Philadelphia, Pa.)—Social life
and customs. 4. South Philadelphia (Philadelphia, Pa.)—Social
conditions. 5. Philadelphia (Pa.)—Social conditions.
6. Philadelphia (Pa.)—Social life and customs. 7. Rose, Dan.
I. Title. II. Series.
F158.9N4R67 1987
974.8'1100496073—dc19   87-17830
                                                              CIP

and
Emma

Contents

List of Illustrations

Photographs

Figures

if my
house burns down, open my face
& you will be amazed

Ishmael Reed (1971)

1. Knowing Ourselves

I heard the pounding of the basketball echo off the boarded-up school building. Three high-school boys played on an abandoned pad of concrete. There was no net for the rim, and sometimes the ball fell through the hoop so cleanly there was the illusion it had missed altogether.

I stopped and watched and felt like playing, partly because they could use another man to make opposing teams with two each. I asked if I could play and one of them said, Yeah. So he and I were one of the teams.

I was staying in the youth hostel in Fairmount Park, the large expanse of grass and trees that lies on either side of Philadelphia's Schuylkill River. I had just hauled part of my library and household goods to Philadelphia from Madison, Wisconsin. My wife, Karen, was to come out on the next trip. Through the University of Pennsylvania I had received a dissertation grant to study the everyday life of Afro-Americans. On this warm September Saturday I had been walking through an old section of the city along Lombard Street in South Philadelphia where black people had historically lived; now I was dribbling the ball and deciding whether to pass off or drive in for a layup.

My teammate and the other two were *playing* at playing ball; I was caught up in a double game. My partner might try an impossible move and lose the ball, or he might try the same daring feint and succeed. Either way the three of them laughed and commented and talked to one another, and I had trouble picking up what they were saying. Some of the moves they were trying were so exaggerated and risky that none of us had any hope they would work. I was alert to differences between the way I had grown up playing

In an uneasy compromise with history I have not capitalized the word *black* in this book. In 1969 I heard the word used exclusively as a pejorative by the men and women with whom I associated. I have written the word here without caps as it was used then. At present it is customary to capitalize it since it has largely replaced Negro and Afro-American in common usage.

in the white American middle class of small midwestern towns and the way the game was played in urban, black Philadelphia. The first difference was a big one. At home we had always gone by the rule that when your team makes a basket, the other team gets the ball.

In Philadelphia it was just the opposite. I passed off to my team-mate, he made the shot, and *we kept the ball*. This game, new to me, was called *Make it, take it*. With these rules, the team that started making shots could get on a roll and win without ever losing the ball. The rule was disconcerting to me and had the effect of making the game more intense—you had to be better on defense to block the other team's shot, and you had to get the ball in order to stop their momentum and start your own. At the same time there was all that incentive to make your own shot because you had the ball again immediately.

They were playing at playing, and I could not quite push myself into the style of what they were saying and doing. One of the main differences between their kind of play and mine was that they obscured the score so no one could keep track of the amount by which a team was winning or losing. That little byplay always kept the margin of difference between the two scores small, but I was pretty sure my man and I were winning by a good bit.

Playing basketball while growing up, my friends and I had learned how to work on our shots. We would first practice a jump shot from the keyhole, then stand and pump in free throws, and after that try two-handed or one-handed shots from various fixed positions on the floor. Then we would practice dribbling, first driving to the left using the left hand, next driving the other way with the right. Each fake, each type of shot—whether jump shot, set shot, or layup—was a single Cartesian piece. We only assembled the pieces when we started a game.

For my Philadelphia teammate and our two opponents, it was, conceptually, a different game. There were no discrete moves, no special, bracketed shots. It was as if the game was a continuous flow from the beginning to the end; the entire repertoire of adventurous tactics—dribbling, driving, shooting, passing, faking, running a play—formed an unbroken performance, sometimes successful, sometimes not. It did not particularly matter. The score was no longer paramount; instead, the emphasis was on performing when one received the ball, not as an isolated *star*, but within an organic flow of self and other, ball and basket, depending on the opportunities of the very instant.

I felt in my first contact with the men in the basketball game that I was in a zone of American life that revealed cultural differences separating us. Our dialects were different, our styles of playing the game were different, the rules were different, and the kind of humor on the court was different.

After the game, we walked to a mom-and-pop grocery store and bought sodas. We talked for a while; then I walked on to continue exploring the narrow streets. What struck me most vividly was that the game was a single, continuously improvised performance. Everything was experimental; nothing was reduced to parts. While we in white middle-class America assembled a game from components, my brief teammates never broke the game down. They played in a flowing stream from the minute they walked onto the court.

Ethnography

Over distances far greater than that from Madison to Philadelphia, travel writers search for otherness, motivated by the desire for the distinctively different and the exotic. Within the continental United States, there is a muted, perhaps inverted, version of this search for otherness: it is called *seeing America.*

SEE THE U.S.A.
IN YOUR CHEVROLET

That General Motors Corporation television ad captured the American summer vacation spirit to help mass market automobiles.

Travel within, rather than travel outside, one's country tends to be less exotic merely because it *is* one's own country, an extension, somehow, of what we take for granted. To travel within, to draw close to our distinctive versions of our own national identity, is a form of auto-ethnography, or reflexive ethnography, part of the postmodern experience of self-examination. True, one can create the exotic from the most mundane, like writing a piece for an airline magazine based on observations at the local laundromat, using various literary devices—nostalgia, irony, novelty, humor, parody, exaggeration, or comparison. But within a country as culturally complex and densely textured as the United States, there are ways of life that at once disconnect a group of people from their neighbors and yet allow them to firmly partake in the national identity—

the way first-generation working-class Ukrainians in a mixed-ethnic, urban neighborhood distance themselves from the others despite attempting to become "American," for example.

The study of one's own society is for anthropologists a special challenge. Cultural anthropologists have been leaving the continental United States each year by the hundreds to live in such geographically and culturally remote regions as the Amazon basin, the New Guinea highlands, the African rain forest, the Kalahari desert. By travel to the remote and intrinsically exotic outposts, anthropologists have displaced parts of their own identities in some vital way and taken up, to varying degrees, the interests of peoples very unlike themselves. Catholic, Jewish, Protestant, and Mormon social scientists, or Anglo-American, Afro-American, Spanish-American, Italian-American, or Polish-American social scientists, instead of investing their egos and scholarly thought in their own cultural-national-religious traditions, assimilate those of others. Anthropologists, folklorists, or sociologists displace their identities through their inquiry into the lives of humans who usually perceive the world very differently than they do themselves.

Methods that anthropologists evolved for studying forms of life culturally remote from themselves have been turned back on their own society. The resulting ethnography tends to affect an ethnographer's identity differently than the lifelong examination of a Pacific island people or Latin American Indians. It was said of Rousseau that he took personally all that happened politically to France; self and country were joined in his identity. Something like this may well happen on the cultural plane to ethnographers who study within their own country. Through ethnographic inquiry one's identity is displaced, but perhaps the displacement is less extreme for those who study at home. Here the exploration of the other becomes a more intensive exploration of an extended self.

A reflexive ethnography is like travel in one's own country in that the anthropologist—or cultural journalist, for that matter—looks to other humans as varieties of the *self* rather than as varieties of the *other*. To put it conversely, if one studies peoples in Ecuador who recently hunted heads, there is much more a tendency (as well as a literary legacy) to think of them as culturally distant from oneself rather than as a component of one common social destiny.

Anthropologists have tended to think about peoples culturally and geographically distant rather than ones whose identity is culturally close to their own. The entire field bears this character and carefully sustains it. A reflexive ethnography challenges anthropology by reversing this tendency, since it is based on travel within the social, political, and national space the ethnographer grew up in and continuously inhabits.

My purpose is not to make the familiar exotic but to add to the familiarity the reader already has with black America. My prose complements the imagery currently available on television situation comedies, in the writings of black novelists and poets and social scientists, in black popular music, and in the work of Afro-Americanists.

This book nonetheless makes demands on the reader. It is just one fragment of near-contemporary life, which when joined with other such fragments as each of us possesses, nonetheless refuses to add up to a whole. The text's design is in part a function of the way I conducted fieldwork, how I finally chose to live with black people. The reader must prove indulgent because the book constantly finds generalization impossible. It will become clear in the discussion of research method how intensive and spatially constrained was the universe I studied—the playing, living, and working space at one end of a city block.

I make no attempt to let my experiences there stand synecdochically for black life in America, or even for all inner-city life. Philadelphia may resemble Harlem, but the nature of a comparison of the two depends on what cut through the flow of time and space we happen to make, or what level of generalization can be mustered. At the more general levels an assertion and its opposite too often seem equally plausible, and I find it necessary to resist generalizing about black life from my two years living in one locality of a single American city. Readers can absorb what is written here into their own experiences, using it as another fragment among those constituting their knowledge of the country.

Among those doing ethnography, there has evolved an interest in writing books that intimately address the people with whom they worked. The ethnographies of these authors exemplify the point that anthropologists displace their identities and take up the identities of those with whom they have lived. Richard Price (1983), for example, collected oral history from and for the Saramakas, as well as for anthropological and historical scholars; Henry Glassie (1982), collecting every story in Ballymenone, conducted his study for later generations. Their ethnographic texts were constructed to loop through the scholarly community back to the people who provided the information.

The ethnography of ourselves is not looped, in the sense that, because it is about us, we all can have more or less ready access to it; the distance between the observer and the observed is thus shortened. A specular ethnography is not so much about us as individuals as it is about us as members of a culturally differentiated nation. Reflexive ethnography is another way of making us more available to ourselves.

• • •

The continuous performance on the basketball court that I observed while playing the game with the three other men was like other black pickup games that I watched. There may also be an unbroken cultural seam joining the neighborhood ball court and field to their respective professional sports. In the competition of professional football Gale Sayers used a cultural play world to unify dance with the moves of a football running back.

In high school I had a close friend, Vern Breakfield (he still is one of my best friends). We played in the same backfield together and did everything together. Break was the extrovert and I was the introvert of the act. He liked to dance and go out with girls and jive a lot, and I always hung back and listened to the music.

One time Break taught me a dance called the Run-Around. It's where you put one foot forward, sway from side to side—a kind of five-and-go swing. Well, I never used it on the dance floor, but one day we were playing West Side High and I was on defense and I intercepted a pass. I took the ball away from this guy and put one step forward, chopped my step, put another step forward, swayed from side to side—and stepped out sixty yards for the touchdown.

I came back to the sidelines so happy. "Did you see me do it, Break, did you see me do it?"

"Yeah, I saw it." Break muttered, "My God almighty, the Run-Around." He was so mad. "Man, here I teach you this stuff to do on the dancing floor and I get you to a party and you won't even do it. You get to the game, do it, and go sixty yards for a touchdown."

The thing was I didn't know what I was doing out there. I was just doing it. (Sayers 1972:15–16)

The choreography of the dance floor was unconsciously transported to a sporting event as if all performances were one. The two symbolic forms, dance and football, were joined at a level outside awareness, and, amazingly, that performance was closely read from the sidelines by a discriminating viewer.

Entry

Philadelphia is the most fertile single source of antiques in America. The age of the city, its size, and its conservativeness make for a richness that buyers of estates, antique dealers, and knowledgeable collectors appreciate. On the Ninth, Tenth, and Eleventh street blocks of Pine Street, just south of Center City, are more than thirty antique shops, some wholesale, others retail, that service a national and international clientele.

Pine Street has belonged to both black and white worlds since 1790. In 1969, black men drove trucks and loaded and unloaded antiques for white shop-owners. North of Pine, a residential area abutting the Pennsylvania Hospital had once housed Philadelphia's white elite; it was still white. South of Pine, Lombard Street had historically been a black residential area but was beginning to gentrify as young, professional white couples moved into inexpensive housing.

Sandwiched between Lombard, with its changing complexion, and Antique Row on Pine was a tiny street named Waverly. It was wide enough for a nineteenth-century horse-drawn wagon but not for a 1962 Buick Electra 225. Old black people lived on Waverly; some had been there all their lives. It was an enclosed miniature of black public space.

Karen and I moved into an apartment on Clinton, a block from Waverly, and I began to explore systematically the area W. E. B. DuBois had studied intensively for fifteen months in 1896–97. When DuBois conducted his sociological survey on a postdoctoral fellowship at the University of Pennsylvania, the Seventh Ward was a long, narrow political jurisdiction that was bounded by Seventh Street on the east and the Schuylkill River on the west. It housed at that time a fifth of Philadelphia's black population and was considered the historic center of Negro Philadelphia. Clinton, Waverly, Pine, and Lombard Streets were included in the ward.

DuBois's ([1899] 1967) book, *The Philadelphia Negro*, was reissued in 1967 with a new introduction by E. Digby Baltzell, a sociologist

1. Waverly Street. The tiny row houses are on the right as one looks east on Waverly. In the foreground is a man's two-wheel cart, licensed by the city, which he used to pick up trash to sell. (Photograph by the author)

of the upper class and a member of the sociology department at the University of Pennsylvania. Baltzell noted how the black population of Philadelphia had increased dramatically since DuBois's study, and he documented the growing alienation of white from black throughout the city.

In 1967 Baltzell was writing during one of the more turbulent periods of America's violent history. Three years earlier Philadelphia had witnessed a riot, an armed confrontation between black residents and police in North Philadelphia. The face-off between populace and police served to fragment the solidarity of the black community, which was once represented to whites by the National Association for the Advancement of Colored People (NAACP). I was shown by a black schoolteacher, who was reared in North Philadelphia, where I as a white fieldworker should never go. He made an elaborate three-page map to illustrate his point. North Philadelphia was to be avoided. This directed me, as a result, toward South Philadelphia.

The year 1969 seemed to promise few remedies for the social forces unleashed in the country by rapid economic growth, the demand by blacks for fuller public participation, and the protest against the war in Vietnam. The 1960s were closing to the release of the report by the National Commission on the Causes and Prevention of Violence (1969). It had been a violent and anguished decade. In 1968 Martin Luther King, Jr., was assassinated, and rioting erupted in 125 American cities. King's recent assassination was raw in the national memory, and it was against this memory that we moved with more than a little concern to Philadelphia.

As I began full-scale fieldwork in October 1969, I carried DuBois's book with me as a conversational gambit, for I was walking into unknown cultural and political territory. Television had shown to white Americans the marches and the aftermath of rioting. Less visible were the legislative, judicial, and electoral victories that were transforming America for both black and white. For most white Americans the black areas of the city, sources of danger and fear, were to be avoided.

Behind Pine Street, Waverly was a thin, straight ribbon of shadow. I walked west down the narrow granite-cobbled street. Small, two-story houses were on my left. Sitting on the marble steps, old black people seemed to disregard me. I felt as if I were both carefully watched and invisible simultaneously. Unlike in a small midwestern town, there was no attempt at greeting. Ahead, where Waverly met Tenth Street, I could see a group of men about my age standing and sitting in casual conversation. I decided that I would stop and talk with them, using my book to engage them in a conversation.

I pictured myself in the tradition of male fieldworkers who studied street-corner society or men's groups. The classic example of reflexive ethnography was William Foote Whyte's *Street Corner Society* (1955). The more recent models of white men studying black men were Elliot Liebow's *Tally's Corner* (1967) and Ulf Hannerz's *Soulside* (1969). On Iseminger Street, several blocks away from where I was walking, Roger Abrahams had moved in eleven years earlier and collected texts of black verbal performances.

Now here's a story, a story of old,
When men were men and women were bold.
It was back in a town that was peaceful and quiet
When one lonely night a man came walking down the
    street. . . .

(Kid) (in Abrahams 1966:166)

He titled his book *Deep Down in the Jungle* (1966), a reference to the black area so named by its inhabitants that he, and later I, studied.

Social scientists initiate contact with people they study using a form of social engagement Sartre called *bad faith*. In bad faith encounters, one or both members have disguised interests that reach beyond the moment of sociality. Social scientists engage others in bad faith, mentally prepared by the narratives of their science, in large part socialized by the texts written by professors and colleagues. The experiences they have are preprogrammed. Heidegger was eloquent on the point: "Basic concepts determine the way in which we get an understanding beforehand of the area of subject-matter underlying all the objects a science takes as its theme, and all positive investigation is guided by this understanding" (1962: 30). The language of the scholarly works is designed to structure what the investigator is to learn from the conversations and observations of fieldwork.

For example, in formulating his study of black men, Liebow asked the sociological question, Why are these men not working? A large literature as well as personal interests contributed to his research agenda. In contrast to Liebow, I wanted to ask an anthropological question, What are these people doing? It was a weekday, and at the end of Waverly Street I saw men sharing a bottle. Liebow would want to know why they were unemployed; I wanted to know what the circle of conversationalists was accomplishing.

I was about to talk with men I did not know, my mind mediated by the authorities of texts by which I would understand their behavior. I was also carrying a book by a black man, a kind of talisman to guarantee safe passage and mark my sacred status as an ethnographer. The subfields of the social sciences I had stored in thought were almost all concerned with the social *event*. My assumptions concerning the life of people were informed from reading the literatures of culture and personality, ethnomethodology, ethnoscience, face-to-face interaction, social psychology, and sociolinguistics, the complex of theories associated with microsociology (Knorr-Cetina and Cicourel 1981).

My acquaintance with black America was acquired through television, magazines, and newspapers, and I read the anthropological literature on blacks, sociological books and articles, and then current novels and poetry by black authors.

Ethnographers have more in mind than their socialization, as students, to a massive library which legitimizes their field of speciality. Like other fieldworkers, I read poetry and fiction in the field. The summer prior to fieldwork I was immersed in the fragmented world of the *roman nouveau*. Fictions affect field experience too. Faulkner had a profound effect on Renato Rosaldo, for example, who in his first book wrote a standard social organization account of the Philippine Ilongot. On rethinking his field experience and, perhaps, recalling the social history of fictional Yoknapatawpha County, he rewrote the Ilongot's own social history, making it closer to what he had heard them tell him (1980:17n).

In addition to the science of social activity, we inevitably carry with us into fieldwork the poetics of human life. Our own poetics of investigation becomes unconsciously fused with the imponderabilia of everyday life, extensive portions of which we then struggle to reclaim. The reclamations, diggings in the strata of the self, are like an arrangement of archaeologists' shards. These are realized as communication through textualization and become a contribution to the body of knowledge, the literature. In our disciplines we are critics of one another's subjectivities and objectifications in engaging the world. The internal dialogue of the ethnographer is between the scientific literature and the poetics we have also read and that we powerfully feel. With these sensibilities we engage the people we study. The subjectivities of others we encounter with our own; we capture and inscribe them within our disciplinary discourse (Rose 1986).

• • •

As I walked down Waverly I was ready with an expectant smile as I looked at one old man sitting on his worn marble front steps, but he did not look at me. Behind him the door to his small row house was open. I could see through the house, which was one room deep. In back, there was a lush splash of green, rampant, untrimmed vegetation growing on another, but no longer inhabited, tiny street behind.

I was rehearsing in my mind what I would say to the men at the end of the block, but now, as I came closer, I tried to anticipate their reactions to me. As I drew up to their circle I greeted them. As if in some small surprise, a few returned my greeting, but as I slowed, they made no further moves. I asked if I might join them, that I was planning to write a book on the area. Showing them DuBois's book, I explained that he had studied the ward at the end of the last century. The man standing next to me said he had heard of DuBois.

The topic switched away from DuBois and me, and I became, in a conversational sense this time, invisible again. Men dropped by until there were seven of us standing there. Each of them knew the others, and they used their nicknames to address one another. By doing so they introduced themselves to me.

Most men talked directly with Al, nicknamed Capone. He balled up his fist and tried to see how close he could come to tagging Johnny without hitting him, a game of intimidation. Johnny crouched as if to fight back in the mock boxing drama. Al suddenly came too close or seemed, even in play, too invincible, and Johnny abruptly dropped the game.

Sitting on the stoop of the windowless abandoned house in front of which we were gathered was a handsome, delicate featured man, withdrawn, drinking from a bottle in a brown paper bag. His nickname was Trip. A police car went by and there was talk about *the man*. After the cruiser passed, a tall man wearing cowboy boots and a ten-gallon hat ducked into the small space to join us, pretending by his exaggerated motions that he was eluding the police. He had a cigarette in his hand. In the shadow of Waverly Street he emptied the tobacco from one end and replaced it with a piece of hash. Then he crinkled the paper to hold it there and lit the cigarette.

2. Trip. The picture shows Trip with the houses of Waverly Street behind him. (Photograph by the author)

Trip said he was drinking a mixture of wine and whiskey. DB (Dancing Bartender) was sipping whiskey straight from a bottle wrapped in a brown bag. One of the other men asked for a drink, and Al said, "Don't give him a drink, he's shaking like a whore in church." They kept kidding him, offering antagonistic opinions on whether or not someone should offer him a sip. Finally they all agreed he needed a drink. Trip's bottle was passed around; when it was handed to me, I took a nip and passed it on.

A man, walking a little oddly, came up to where we were standing; he was retarded. Al kidded gently with him, asking him how old he would be on his birthday. He hesitated and then said he was going to be either twenty-four or thirty. Al laughed and said, "Every year I have to tell you how old you are." Then Al asked him, "What month is your birthday?" As if drawing the words from a distant place the man slowly answered,

January

February

March

April

May

June

July

August

September

October

December

January

My birthday is February.

Despite his mental slowness, he was included warmly in the play.

Tex left just as abruptly as he had arrived, his cigarette finished. Trip, still sitting on the marble stoop, solemnly asked each one, "Who was that?"

Each one he turned to answered, "That's your brother."

"Why did you ask who he was?" Al asked.

Trip replied, pointing his chin in my direction, "I just wanted him to know he was my brother."

Before I left I learned that I was with the 410 Gang. I did not know what *gang* meant, but I assumed it was a territorially based male group that protected a certain geographical area with weapons. When that assumption turned out to be faulty, I tried to replace it with others. I came to believe that some of the men in the loosely knit group had grown up together, that the group had added on and sloughed off members, and that the real core of the group was Al and Trip. Al was confrontational, Trip was remote. They were a balanced pair at the middle of a network of men who spent time and created an imaginative leisure life around the 410 Bar and the Ninth and Rodman Bar.

The 410 Bar, their home base, was age-graded; almost all the men were between twenty-five and thirty-five years of age. At the periphery of the 410 Gang (from my point of view) were women—lovers, sisters, wives, mothers—who would for one reason or another show up at the bar to see someone or have a drink.

The gang's leisure times were a continuous string of self-produced entertainments and dramatic confrontations—between one another and between themselves and the police. The intense dramatic recreations were interspersed with pickup work along Antique Row: moving furniture, driving a truck, or painting a local

3. 410 Bar. This building is now a townhouse, and white people have colonized this section of the city. (Photograph by the author)

landlord's apartment or a shop. If one kind of life had precedence over the other, leisure dramaturgy claimed more serious attention than did furniture loading.

With one another the men were alternately extremely sensitive to the last nuance of gesture or tone, praise or slight, and engaged in litigation through hostile and angry confrontation. Waverly Street, the 410 Bar, the small streets and bars and rented rooms and apartments they knew—these constituted an intimate, inward-looking space that I at times crashed ignorantly into. Balanced with what I considered a phenomenal awareness of interpersonal nuance were a physical toughness and lack of revealed fear, close to abandon. Play could escalate to fateful encounters, banter could become challenge, and one's character might suddenly be on the line. Trip told me later, in the bar one night, that he and the others had collectively thrown their knives away. They did not want to hurt each other, he explained. Although the men had arrived at that point with one another, some of them like Tex, who was the most flagrantly individualized, aggressive, and confrontational, remained apart.

The next day I returned to Tenth and Waverly. I had responded to Al and Trip and felt they could help me learn my way into their social life. At the corner I entered the 410 Bar. The front had once been green, but now in its soft decay it absorbed more light than it reflected. The paint had the appearance of a finely ground green vegetable powder ready to liquify and run off in the next rain. I plunged into the bar in slow motion, waiting for my eyes to get used to the darkness. The place was deserted. No, there was a bartender. He was sitting behind the far end of the bar, only his very very black head visible from the doorway when my eyes adjusted to the gloom. He did not get up immediately, and that lengthening pause gave me all the time in the world, too much time. I could have gone anywhere in the narrow barroom—to the tables, three of them without adequate chairs, or to the bar with its high, thin wooden stools.

I ordered a beer and the bartender rose, rinsed a glass, and wordlessly tapped the beer. He wiped the counter with a dirty sopping rag and set the glass down. Several brown roaches investigated the phenomenon, found nothing, and moved on. The beer was cool and the glass sweat, leaving a pool on the counter. Then the door opened and a wizened old black woman walked in. The door whizzed shut on a spring behind her and she went up to the bar, opening her coin purse. Without an exchange of words the bartender brought her a shot of whiskey, which she paid for with coins. Taking her excess change, she turned, walked behind me, and stood in front of the blue and red Wurlitzer jukebox reading the selections. The bartender stood immobile watching her, his face almost lost in the fading light of the afternoon, which filtered in only at the transoms of the two bar doors. He was short, very robust, his hair processed and gleaming, waved over his head. His skin shown like oil, and shafts of light split off it where the light hit.

The music burst out. It beat. The words were clear and the melody in a minor key. For me this was another world, pulsing in rhythms that eluded my sensibilities, dominating the room, filling all the space, overtaking the rundownness and decay. The shriveled woman began to dance to the song, head down, eyes closed, her arms and legs and body and head articulate and numb in the always changing flow of movement. I began to count the bottles beside the gray mirror crazed with age. I examined the labels for clues of familiarity, anything that would remind me of where I was, what I was doing. I read everything in the room, the ancient calendar, the warped paper sign declaring that minors would not be served.

I ordered a second beer. The music stopped and the woman stood at the bar, too small to crawl up on the stool. Then I went to the bathroom. It was nearly impossible to tell which of the two indistinctly marked doors was the one I wanted, so I took the second one. When I came out there were four more people in the room, opposite the bar at a middle table. Slightly away from the table sat a twenty-five- or thirty-year-old man with a sports car driver's cap on. He had no hair, and he was white. His parents, about fifty years old, sat at the table. No one was talking. I recognized the fourth person from the day before. It was Al. He was standing, bent over the woman, kissing her deliberately on the cheek. Just as deliberately he kissed the other cheek over and over. His one arm was on the chair behind her. The other hand tilted her face for his passionless, measured kisses.

I was ignored by the six people. There was no way of breaking into the dramas—the isolated dance, the silent quartet against the wall. I finished the second beer and left the bar.

After walking more, I returned to the apartment on Clinton Street and attempted in the early evening to miniaturize in the field notes the events in the 410 that afternoon. Already it seemed too complex, too much was unknown. The whole thing would require time and involvement before I could grasp with any real understanding all that lay behind such simple appearing phenomena.

Covert Inquiry

In 1969 the Public Health Service funded a Center for Urban Ethnography at the University of Pennsylvania, grant number PHS 17216 01. The purpose in making the grant was to address our lack of knowledge of minorities in American cities, and especially the black experience. Funding was earmarked for study of the causes of rioting, and it was hoped that ethnography could be used to demystify contemporary urban life. The director of the center was John Szwed; Erving Goffman and Dell Hymes were associate directors. My initial correspondence had been with Goffman, and at the end of the first full month of fieldwork he invited Karen and me to his house to review and evaluate our situation.

Karen and I sat in blue leather chairs at his house in Society Hill and sipped beer while we talked. He asked how we were doing, and I explained that I was making friends at a bar with a mainly black clientele which was located in the historic center of black Philadelphia. I said that I expected to pursue their networks and expand my awareness of their way of life. Goffman knew that my interest was in the way people are aware of their own society, for

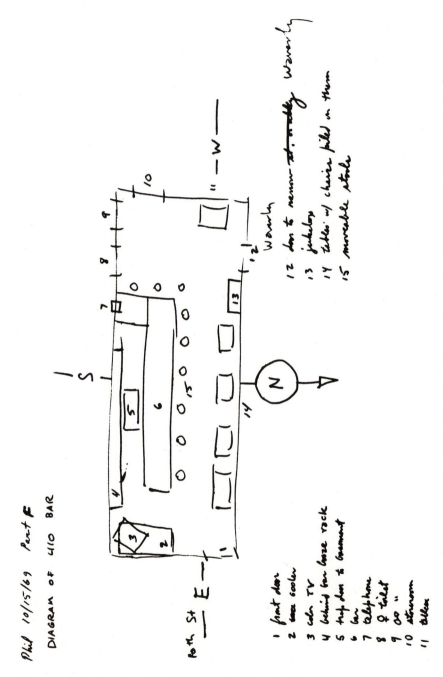

Figure 1. Line drawing of the 410 Bar, taken from the field notes.

I had proposed that my doctoral dissertation research be a study of peoples' own awareness of their social structure. For blacks that meant inner-city life as well as the rest of America.

I did not mention to Goffman that through family members I had met black leaders in two of the largest midwestern cities during the summer and had discussed my proposed Philadelphia research project with them. That midwestern segment of urban leadership, it turned out, had ties through friendship and business with people of comparable status in Philadelphia and gave me an introduction to the Philadelphia group.

In our talks both in the Midwest and in Philadelphia I witnessed the extreme toughness of the black men who had to face the explosive racial situation at that time in the northern cities. A number of white observers were becoming aware of the growing polarization between black and white communities and the rapid evolution of a new sense of power for blacks within the city. Black leaders found, in the wake of the civil rights advances, that they could organize public marches, effectively boycott white retail businesses, or disrupt government. The new leaders and their new constituencies owed little to the established city politicians, seemingly nothing to the NAACP, and apparently not much to other vintage Negro associations such as the church. The political forces unleashed by the Reverend Martin Luther King and others plunged directly into the heart of the cities where no other movement had gone before; they captured the imagination and following of the poor, those on welfare, the unemployed, the underemployed, and the young.

I did not want to study the activists directly and am convinced that it would have been nearly impossible. A month before the evening talk with Goffman I had met several times with the Philadelphia acquaintances of my midwestern contacts. The welcome was neither warm nor encouraging; indeed it was antagonistic, wary, evasive, and confrontational by turn, and I decided to shift attention toward a far less politicized and polarized living and working environment. Although I was far from feeling at home, I felt I could live and work more effectively with the men of the 410 Bar and their extended networks than I could with the politically engaged and resistant men who on occasion pointed to the rifle prominently propped in the corner of the office when they talked about their dealings with whites.

Meeting with one part of the Philadelphia black political leadership forced me to face in a matter of hours the brute fact before hidden to me, that American race relations could be a raw and violent frontier. Like others, I had grown up blinded to the realities and like most of us, I preferred other images. All too often we talk ourselves out of dealings across those wounding lines altogether.

When Karen and I walked into Goffman's house we both had our own ideas of how to conduct ethnography. Karen had thought I ought to get a job in a black area, and I had resisted that notion because I wanted explicitly to sit down and talk with people about their way of life, ask questions, and benefit from whoever was willing to contribute to and shape my research. Since we were living in a house Karen had chosen on a beautiful street in an all-white neighborhood, it seemed that there was a tacit agreement between us that she would pursue work on her master's thesis while I walked in to conduct the study. I preferred to live among blacks, and Karen felt that we could move to a black residential area once we understood the geography of the city better and had made some friends in the black community.

Goffman turned from me after I told him about what I was doing and asked Karen what her professional interests were. She told him about her musical training, that she had played bassoon in the college orchestra and had very successfully taught vocal music. She and I had both been in graduate school full time the year before fieldwork. She was working toward the completion of her master's degree and for the thesis was pursuing research on the use of percussion in the music of Bela Bartok. I wanted her to be able to work in Philadelphia and sought to help by agreeing to live on Clinton Street. My own best interest would have been better served by immediately residing in a black neighborhood with everyone knowing that I was an anthropologist there to study their way of life.

I am certain that Goffman was not satisfied with the way my fieldwork was progressing, and he began to sketch in a research scenario vastly different than the one I envisioned. He had conducted his doctoral research on a Shetland Island and wanted that kind of pristine isolation and resultant immersion for us. He began to talk about how we might creatively manage our identities in order to engage ourselves directly with the black community with little or no outside white contact. Karen, he said, could have come to Philadelphia to study music. It is a musical city and no one would have a problem with that explanation. He portrayed my role as one of dropping out of school to follow her here, taking a job in a black person's establishment, and living in a black neighborhood. He further urged that we not mention that we were studying anyone, since the job I took would be an excellent cover through which I could get to the stuff of everyday life—"how people shave in the morning," he said; how the most mundane things are done. There could be no living in two worlds in this shift of identities and locations. "You will be taken for hippies," he told us, and I had to admire the bold way he limned our possible futures. What he was proposing was that we become undercover agents for scientific purposes.

My immediate response was negative. There seemed no way that I could justify taking a covert identity. At Wisconsin the civil rights movement and protest against the Vietnam War had politicized the student body, and my own politics were closer to those of the Students for a Democratic Society and the Democratic party than to any other party or political action group. Among the anthropology students there was an explicit desire to decolonize the field, to become forthright in dealing with peoples we might study, and above all to make anthropology relevant to the political needs of the times. We were moving toward a discursive democracy of inquiry where we and the people we studied were to be engaged equally and the identities of persons we lived with were to be protected from any political repercussions our studies might possibly cause.

Karen and I did not share the same political perspectives; she was far more politically conservative and considered herself a Rockefeller Republican. Her response to Goffman, nevertheless, came as a profound surprise; she told him she agreed with him and thought that both she and I ought to get jobs and live and work in one of the black neighborhoods. I was stunned because it meant she would give up her academic work and lead the life of an undercover operative for anthropology.

I was inwardly enraged that Karen would side with Goffman against me in front of him and that she would so easily abandon her own studies to throw herself into a field in which she had previously shown no interest. And yet Goffman's brilliant portrayal of our identities and his desire that we be wholly caught up in black peoples' ways of life were intellectually compelling. The challenge to draw close to others, to collapse our identities insofar as possible into theirs, struck me directly and I opened myself to it. With Karen in the field there would be two engaged in the research rather than one.

As I sat there I quickly developed an idea of what I might do; the image of a hole-in-the-wall auto repair shop that I had seen in

South Philadelphia came to mind, and I was certain I had the resourcefulness to live and work on the street. Although I could not then reconcile my feelings of conflict, anger, and resentment, I told Goffman that we would do it.

Inexplicably, I wanted to demonstrate that this mode of research could be done and done well. In retrospect, living that way proved far more difficult than I could have imagined, and I would not do covert research again. I cannot yet justify it with my professional and personal ethics. In addition, living under cover caused great personal anguish. It made a difficult personal situation, given the climate of race relations at that time, far worse. I was continuously anxious, not merely afraid of some surprise discovery, because unlike Goffman and Karen I lacked the desire and ability to play the role of actor, which would conceal a primary part of my personal identity, that of anthropologist.

When conducting his doctoral dissertation research on the Shetland Islands, Goffman did not reveal that he was a sociology graduate student. Thus, it was in his methodological repertoire to feign a persona for purposes of inquiry. My immediate response to these methods was entirely negative, for I wanted to conduct field research openly.

In the end I agreed that there were advantages in covert research, particularly its intensity and its intimate, mimetic personal involvements. That I assented may be partly attributed to reading I had done in graduate school, particularly about the ethnographic research strategy that had been proposed by Ward Goodenough. Until 1969 Goodenough had made the most important theoretical contribution to ethnographic research since Malinowski, and I wanted to conduct ethnography within his guidelines. Goodenough had written in 1957, "As I see it, a society's culture consists of whatever it is one has to know or believe in order to operate in a manner acceptable to its members, and do so in any role that they accept for any one of themselves." I certainly wished to follow the intimate form of inquiry that he had formulated, and I wanted the results that came from close ethnographic description: "Ethnographic description, then, requires methods of processing observed phenomena such that we can inductively construct a theory of how our informants have organized the same phenomena. It is the theory, not the phenomena alone, which ethnographic description aims to present" (Goodenough 1964:36).

As a result of our conversation with Goffman, Karen and I chose for study a black residential area several blocks south of that studied by DuBois and Abrahams. I worked for a black man in an auto repair shop, and we lived in a second- and third-story apartment next door. Our street, a residential one that also had commercial establishments, was a part of South Philadelphia, which itself was made up of numerous ethnic enclaves: black, Irish, Italian, Jewish, Lithuanian, and others. Our neighbors were nearly all black, and we associated exclusively with them. Our lives, mine especially, were circumscribed by fear. Whether the fear was rational or irrational, I do not know. Neither of us was damaged, and no one broke into our apartment. Indeed, we came to be taken for granted as a presence on the street during the two years we lived there. I usually wore my mechanic's uniform, which had my name embroidered on the left breast.

•   •   •

In the cultural sciences our deepest anxieties are stirred by covert inquiry. To act secretively in gathering information, it is argued, deceives the people who host us, and this deception and its potential discovery make it possible that our successors at a field site will find themselves unwelcome. The lack of access that would result from discovery is the greatest fear among scientists, for inquiry would become impossible. Our ethical debates often mask the pragmatics of the field situation. We are explicit because we wish to return and engage freely in research, not because deception is itself unequivocally unethical.

Covert research has been much discussed in the sociological literature (Bulmer 1982) and has been in general disfavor among American anthropologists. Neither the folklorists nor the students of American civilization, both of whom use ethnographic methods, have been prominent in the debates. The sociological discourse on the ethics of secret participation has been marked by the polarized positions of those for versus those against. The value of the knowledge acquired openly or under disguise, however, has not been systematically compared. I would like to touch briefly on the nature of knowledge acquired through the covert inquiry I conducted.

From Malinowski (1922) forward, the field methods of ethnographers have been relatively uniform if not always explicit. The anthropologist entered a local community with Western paraphernalia, built or moved into a residence, and began to take censuses, elicit genealogies, and interview interpreters and loquacious neighbors.

Knowledge gained by these intrusive means was documented immediately in field journals. The notes entered were made up of the answers to direct questions, for interrogation was the rational, fruitful means by which knowledge was acquired. In addition, the anthropologist, equipped with pencil and paper, observed ceremonial and work life, taking notes during the course of the unfolding action. When the anthropologist participated in a ceremony, he or she committed a record of the involvement to writing as soon as possible after the event. The more rational fieldworkers spent hours arranging field notes into categories, interrogating their own data according to the particular set of interests they had acquired through the literature, seminars, and conversations with faculty while in graduate school. Drafting an article while in the field was a way of immediately uncovering where more data were needed. By working up field notes, an anthropologist could identify gaps and at the next opportunity ask the relevant persons the questions necessary to fill in what was missing from the record.

Historically the ethnographic text was the consummate source of field method for the graduate student, and it was thus the natural product of such methods. One conducted fieldwork in order to write ethnography; the method of directed inquiry determined the way one filled out the categorical scheme of the text (Goodenough 1961:12). In covert work one cannot acquire knowledge by the use of the interrogative form. There is no census taking, no elicitation of a genealogy; there are no extended, directed interviews, no preestablished categories acquired from reading ethnographies that have been fashioned to inform that type of inquiry. In covert operations ethnographers have to take what they can get, whenever they can get it, within the natural flow of events, not as ethnographers but as persons who have arranged to be there for some entirely ordinary and local reasons. Questions foreshorten time. Answers, when given, allow one to learn something about the organization of life without having to live it. Bourdieu has remarked on what happens in the traditional interrogative mode of social research.

> The cancelling out of the practical functions of temporal guide-marks that results from the context of interrogation and from scientific recording is the hidden condition of cumulating and seriating the aggregate of the oppositions which can be produced in relation to different universes of discourse, that is, with different functions. By cumulating information which is not and cannot always be mastered by any single inform-

ant—at any rate, never on the instant—the analyst wins the *privilege of totalization* (thanks to the power to *perpetuate* that writing and all the various techniques for recording give him, and also to the abundant time he has for analysis). He thus secures the means of apprehending the logic of the system which a partial or discrete view would miss; but by the same token, there is every likelihood that he will overlook the change in status to which he is subjecting practice and its products, and consequently that he will insist on trying to answer questions which are not and cannot be questions for practice, instead of asking himself whether the essential characteristic of practice is not precisely the fact that it excludes such questions. (Bourdieu 1977:106)

The ethnographer working clandestinely has to live in order to acquire information. What is maddening is that in secret inquiry knowledge is developed at the same slow pace as the flow of local life, in Bourdieu's term, practice. It virtually takes a lifetime to absorb the knowledge of life in a covert manner. Obviously, then, temporalities are extremely different in covert and overt forms of information acquisition. While engaged in fieldwork I suffered from two major anxieties: one, that I would not be able to acquire enough information for an ethnographic account, and two, that the information would not be appropriate to ethnographic description as it was then constituted. As a result I requested from the center an extended stay in the field, which was granted. To some extent, the anxieties of *not enough* and *not appropriate* would probably confront any ethnographer trained at that time in American and British anthropological models of social organization.

Ethnographic texts of the last sixty years and the more recent writings on field methods do not prepare the investigator for living as his or her neighbors do, though it may have been done often enough, and for working alongside fellow laborers in order to acquire data. The ultimate frustration is that one's data as it is gathered, one's field notes as they are entered, do not have the essential literary contour or organizational echo of the ethnographic monograph. Field notes from clandestine inquiry may well be textual orphans in the corpus of earlier ethnographic writing.

The knowledge derived from covert work is intense, intensely local, personal, and centered in individuals one knows and events one has lived through with them. One becomes alert to redundancy, replays of the same forms of human behavior on different occasions, the obscure but firm rules governing the form of mundane relations, situations, and activities. The investigator must seek settings that will yield a great deal of information, secretly force conversations back toward the categories of *Notes and Queries* (Royal Anthropological Institute 1951), or else give up that particular moment and decide to look back later for what lay concealed within it.

I took down all field notes from memory at the end of the day, typing them on an old typewriter I bought at a pawn shop and kept in a room with a table and chair on the third floor of the apartment. My full graduate student library had to remain in storage during the field stay, so I kept only a few books with me, including Martin Heidegger's *Being and Time* (1962) and two volumes of Alfred Schutz's *Collected Papers* (1962). They too were in the third-floor room with the typewriter, table, and chair. I carried Schutz's books into South Philadelphia because I was interested in how he considered the social world to be built up of intersubjective acts. When I knew I was to be working in an auto repair shop I took Heidegger along because he was one of the few thinkers who understood humanity as living within the everyday world by means of equipment. I felt his notions of being-in-the-world would be useful for understanding the life of mechanics in a repair shop, that seemingly endless and greasy manipulation of the quotidian. Heidegger became an informant by means of a book, a philosophical treatise established on some of the most deeply held Western assumptions. Along with numerous other published sources, such as the anthropological readings of graduate school, his *Being and Time* served to both illuminate and obstruct what I experienced while working in the repair shop and living on the street. My field notes revealed the kind of knowledge I acquired for ethnographic purposes from covert field research: documentation of individual persons, social occasions, users of space, the awesome materiality of everyday life in an auto repair shop—tools, nuts, bolts, grease, autos, clothes, oil, tires, and so on—and the give-and-take between persons, the discourses of the quotidian, the laconic stories and customers' requests—asking for tools, money, repairs; offers of stolen goods; chances to play the numbers, grievances, debates. I would be lying under an automobile pulling a transmission, the stench of scorched transmission fluid cauterizing my senses, and a customer would come in to talk with Telemachus, the man I worked for and with. I could not hear all that was said:

—— a fifty nine Buick...

—— bring it down Monday...

—— tow it...

—— wife said she'd...

Do I emerge from under the auto and feign the need for a 9/16 wrench, interrupting my work in order to stand near Telemachus and his prospective customer and listen to their negotiations below or above the sound of Smoky Robinson and the Miracles on the radio? Or do I merely wait for the chance occurrence—say, three or four minutes a day—when customer, Telemachus, and I are together? No wonder I did not think that my field notes conformed to those of my graduate school friends. What do I write in my field notes from overhearing partial strips of human interaction, half a phone conversation, only the loudest words of an irate customer with a CB (*comeback*, an auto that did not remain repaired)? And if my field notes are different, what will the dissertation look like, and then the articles, the subsequent book, the career?

The usual, explicit ethnographic fieldwork, organized around the interests of the ethnographer, fractures the discourse and flow of the mundane course of action (Clifford 1983:125). Anthropological category, elicited through the interrogative mode, dominates the ethnographer's speech (Frake 1964:132–45). The fieldwork is accomplished in order that a text recognizable as ethnography can be efficiently and quickly written. Covert ethnography cannot fracture time through questions whose answers satisfy categories. The disguised investigators must retrospectively query the uninterrupted occasions they and their cohorts have lived through; the anthropological a priori has been suspended in favor of the contingency within the flow of life. Time stretches out in the tedium of the ordinary, unbroken by the pointed inquiries of scientific concern. Knowledge so derived is assembled after the fact; it emerges more reluctantly from the background, from the haze of minutiae and the opaqueness that drenches all moments. There is no explicit ethnographic textual form that organizes the flow of field experiences on the day they happen. The clarity that the received corpus conveyed to ethnographic workers is not available.

This text is a document in which there is at best a compromised congruity between written ethnographic form and the mode of hidden inquiry awash in the quotidian. I am going to place Telemachus in the foreground, because he was the person I associated with most closely during the two years of fieldwork. Anecdotes and analyses flow from him and swirl around him, but this is not a life history. Again the form of inquiry eludes the demands of the genre, for I could hardly elicit a life history without arousing his suspicion as to why I would want to know so much about *him*. I could not in the fashion of genial fieldwork (Rabinow 1977:152–53) educate him about the kind of information I desired. It was equally impossible to play the game, with him or anyone else, of "Let's be intellectuals together and explore the *episteme* of your culture"—at least not as a mechanic, often working ten hours a day.

Associated with the problem of knowing in covert inquiry is that of the role of the observer and the identity of the person doing research. My identity, according to my daily round and my uniform, was that of mechanic, a white person from the midwestern United States, a hippy, underemployed, educated but not streetwise, perhaps avoiding the law, maybe engaged in illegal activity, perhaps taking a break to *get himself together*. The nature of this identity was a function of the complex of available personas of the time (such as hippy), my fixed attributes (my front), and the experiences of the people living nearby. As far as I know only one of the men I associated closely with did *not* have a prison record. I should add that asking questions, for scientific or any other purposes, was exceptional behavior, and it is probably just as well I did not try to do so. In public men conducted sociable talk by trading first-person narrations, this exchange of stories revealing the interests and activities of each participant. Questions, either polite or penetrating, were not a part of their ordinary speech genres. It seemed on long acquaintance that questions or even disguised interrogative sentences would have met with a suspicious, even hostile, resistance. In my attributed identity as one who may have had, and indeed did have, something to hide, I was not asked, nor was Karen, why we were there. It was assumed that there were any number of plausible reasons for our presence.

In authoring this book, the greatest problem has been determining the framework or format, the blend of genres in which to write. I found no exact models and so have sought what was aesthetically satisfying. One model for my choice of genre is Michel Leiris's four-volume autobiography (Bree 1980; Leiris 1986); the idea would be to treat the field experience as a succession of moments in a longer history of the self. Leiris became an ethnographer in order to escape the excesses of subjectivism, but the autobiographical mode seems to collapse self and other in ways the genre cannot handle. In addition to the difficulties of selecting an appropriate genre, the main limitations of this book are that it is based on research that was done for the dissertation, that the research was blatantly covert, and that my location was strictly circumscribed by an auto repair shop and a street with a locally fixed set of resources for my identity.

Despite the restrictions, I attempted to manipulate what happened, not by invoking the identity of a professional social scientist, but by mimesis, doing as exactly as possible what others did; by attending any event open and available, as when tickets to cabarets or picnics were sold on the street; by strictly identifying with blacks; and by becoming a recognizable fixture on the street, a mechanic-handyman who hustled for pickup work.

Conducting research while in disguise had several major effects on me. I wished never to study within such a restricted environment again, and I wished to turn my research toward more expansive vistas, away from the smaller scale of the study of face-to-face interaction (Goffman 1959:22ff.). These were personal reactions. Professionally the experience forced me to question the method and to deconstruct ethnographic practice. The intensity of real-time, secret observation—intense perhaps because I was in an American city—made me question the assumptions of the literature on face-to-face encounters and particularly the central notion of event or situation. In brief, I came to think that the event as a unit of analysis did violence to the lived reality of everyday life and distorted rather than revealed the temporal grounds of interaction and social life.

This book bears little resemblance to the dissertation, and it took fifteen years to write it. The length of time from leaving fieldwork in August 1971 to writing the book in 1986 was largely due to the emotional power that the negative field experience exerted over me. Whenever I sat down to write an ethnographic account during the fifteen years, sometimes as narrative, other times as fiction, I would turn away in frustration and despair. I am certain that my response to the field notes and my long avoidance of them was a result of the pain of covert research and the unsorted emotions that attend interracial relations in this country. Why I have finished the book now after this period of time I cannot say.

2. La Vie Quotidienne

While the aim of the fieldwork was the study of everyday life, it cannot be said that this was the source of method. The idea was to immerse myself as much as possible in the stream of the ordinary and the mundane in order to acquire the point of view of others. The method was ethnographic and so relied, as vexing as the method was and has become, on documenting details and assembling from them a larger understanding. Part of my purpose in studying black Americans in this way was a direct response to the social conditions of the times and to the acknowledged poverty of knowledge about black peoples' life in America. Clifford Geertz, in a conference transcript recorded after the presentation of a number of papers on *The Negro American*, confirmed what many were then thinking: " 'The Negro population,' '*the* Negro American,' is not conceptually differentiated enough by us. We do not have enough grasp of the differentiation—culturally, structurally, and so on—of the Negro population from within, the internal view of it" (1966:297).

By studying everyday life in detail, employing ethnography, the internal viewpoint could be more fully revealed. The stereotypes of that period, the 1960s, particularly those perpetrated by psychology with its view of blacks as pathological and by sociology with its labeling of blacks as socially deviant, demanded remedy. In a *Harper's* interview, Ralph Ellison warned what the impact of the sociological version of black life might be on the black self-image.

This is tricky terrain, because today the sociologists are up to their necks in politics and have access to millions of governmental dollars, which, I'm afraid, have been secured at the cost of propagating an image of the Negro condition which is apt to destroy our human conception of ourselves just at the moment when we are becoming politically free. Those who buy this image are surely in trouble, no matter the money it brings. (1984:399)

Writing in 1972 and directing his comments toward white students of black life, John Szwed asked that

we "desegregate" anthropology, giving Afro-Americans the best we can as observers of human cultural capacity and achievement. If we treat Afro-Americans without political posturing, the hidden assumptions, and smuggled motives, I am convinced that their cultural accomplishments will not need the spurious defenses and the eleventh-hour apologies that we have been in the habit of offering in the name of research. (1972:172)

Within the Modern movement that largely defined European and American cultural life in the twentieth century, philosophers and others including social scientists and historians identified everyday life as a subject of inquiry. The philosophers contrasted scientific and philosophical modes of thought while the social scientists aimed to describe the vernacular. From philosophy the idea of everyday life as a theme of research dispersed and joined existing interest in American and French cultural sciences. Phenomenology became ethnomethodology in the United States, and in France it was transformed by Sartre into existentialism, which influenced structuralism, the social sciences, rural sociology, sociology, and anthropology. Social scientists study little other than everyday life, although they do not examine the mundane from a field called *everyday life*. Scholarly interest in the ordinary has grown, and some of the best work has been done by the social historians.

Edmund Husserl's *Ideas* ([1913] 1962), in which he distinguished between the natural and the theoretical standpoints, and his later formulation of the *Lebenswelt* confirmed his influence among first philosophers, then social scientists. Husserl's phenomenology opened for later investigation the rationalities of the quotidian and intersubjectivity. In his initial statement, he characterized everyday life on spatio-temporal coordinates and described how we as humans in the natural standpoint subjectively experience the world.

Husserl seemed especially alive to the destabilization of experience in daily life that resulted from the growth of scientific thought. The connection between the mode of scientific thought and the ordinary layman's thinking was identified as central to inquiry. It remains unclear in the recent literature where the everyday left off and the scientific or theoretical consciousness began, and there has been a failure to address what this dichotomy means. That scientists shop for groceries on their way home from the lab raises the issue of where one rationality ends and the other takes effect. Given that scientists are subject to management and themselves become managers of scientific projects, the question arises, Is the management of science within the realm of science or the realm of the everyday, or does it inhabit some third space of rationality? Although I have made no explicit efforts to answer these questions, this work has been informed by phenomenological thought.

•   •   •

When I entered the field, sociologists had studied fleeting encounters in American public life but had not elaborated theories that addressed the establishment of long-term relationships built up from the moments in face-to-face interaction. Anthropologists, by contrast, had studied people bonded over long periods of time, indeed, took long-term bonding for granted. The genealogical method, which enabled them to derive structurally stable kinship relations, was the accepted means for studying interactively established continuities. My interests fell somewhere between the sociologists and the anthropologists. I wanted to know how persons in face-to-face encounters built up ties over relatively long periods of time, the practical bases of their *relationships*.

Despite the limitations that living covertly placed on my ability to investigate people's ties to one another, such a study was my continual preoccupation. In searching for the basis of my concerns, I had looked to philosophy. The *Monadology* of Leibniz had not provided a way of understanding human social bonds, as if the monads could be mapped to social individuals. Whitehead's atomistic metaphysics expressed in *Process and Reality*, with its bipolar actual entities connected to other actual entities through prehensions, forming societies, was not useful to me. I could not from Whitehead's vocabulary translate either to my own social experience or to ethnographic inquiry. Even Rousseau's discussion of the social contract, more useful for understanding the body politic than interpersonal interactions, was quickly emended by Levi-Strauss with Mauss's idea of exchange (Levi-Strauss 1974:315). During the field investigation I was self-consciously preoccupied with the *practices* by which relationships were built up and dissolved. It was the leitmotif of my research.

I have in front of me a file box of notecards from the first year of fieldwork, which began in September 1969 and extended through August 1970. I see the neat rows of cards, indexed initially by the month, and time seems contained, like a mind full of carefully ordered memories here replicated as if memories were purely sequential.

As I read through the cards, a complex documentary unfolds like a movie, moving me backward and forward in a reverie. Through memory I am thrust into the middle of the action, and I pass through a dozen holographic stories. I can read and reread again and again, evoking absent moments and the people I lived with—their gestures, poses, conversations, activities. The notecards represent a captured swath of time, seized from a particular point of view. I cannot write of it in the way I am reliving it now in my mind as I read. I can imagine what I lived through but cannot fictionalize the experiences as would a novelist. Giving pseudonyms is difficult. People were their names. I can shape the reader's access to what I experienced, but I cannot take many liberties with the experience itself; it is simply there, weighty, full, larger than I am. I can dominate, through selection, what you are reading but not my witnessing. My witnessing dominated me, caught me up; it propelled me along the lines of what was there, and who those people were, but at the same time it fused with who I was, what my interests were—interests, even my least awareness, shaped by reading I had done in the social science literature.

From selections in the box of cards I draw profiles, evoke persons, and reconstruct biographies or occasions within the larger temporal scaffolding around fieldwork. The act of representation is itself vulnerable, subject to question and uncertainties. Representation claims for itself a voice in the competition of cultural discourse.

I was compelled by my own trained preoccupations to study social bonding, but nearly every anthropologist who engages in fieldwork has more than a single interest, even though secondary interests are not often contained in dissertation research proposals and do not always find expression. One of my interests was the social dimensions of space. When I requested an extension of my grant from the Center for Urban Ethnography I was asked to give a paper. Additional funding would be based on the vote of the directors and invited guests. My paper, entitled "Social Space," began to outline the spaces of street life.

I was preoccupied by the study of social organization but almost unconsciously was captivated by the mysterious spatial orders of the bar, the workplace, the household, and the street. From my present vantage point, years later, I am more interested in the spatial order than the kinship or social networks. In any case covert research made systematic pursuit of kindreds virtually impossible.

Kinship studies are based on the rhetoric of interrogation. On reflection, it is clear that nearly every moment was in some way spatially constrained. I wrote in a field note that I felt I was always having to act, as if each space were a different stage, requiring that I play a role in addition to the covert one I needed to sustain. I did not enjoy my role-playing, for I am no actor, and perhaps that heightened my awareness, even while it frustrated me because I could not perform according to the norms of the street.

We cannot in advance of a field situation know what we will find, what the people will be like in relation to ourselves, or who we might become in relation to them. There is a subtle and profound chemistry, a fusion of sensibilities, an assimilation of sorts, even during a relatively short stay. We know that our perceptions will be shaped by our reading and by conversations with colleagues and, perhaps, with people from the area we are to study. But we cannot predict, from such early, innocent contact, what we will come away with and what will seem momentous or relevant, if we truly allow ourselves to be spoken to as responsive humans. It is curious that the very books and articles that we necessarily rely upon to shape experience can block it instead. Our way of life may conflict with theirs or may well obscure what we can learn. We can remain unaware that one culture is systematically interfering with another, and so inadvertently deceive ourselves and our readers. Sure, we come away with some reasonably accurate awareness, but what have we missed or obscured? As ethnographers we can only place ourselves in the way of understanding and make the effort to comprehend the peoples' form of life. My point is in part that, without living with the people we study, we cannot know how they structure their everyday life. Our initial preparation may not prepare us adequately; our ways of thinking and being may occlude knowing. Given the ways cultures work, we can assume that much of how we think will indeed cloud our representations of the ways others lead their lives.

In the effort to capture everyday life we can, following Husserl, employ the coordinates of space and time. For Western thinkers that strategy is intuitively reasonable or self-evident. Martin Heidegger, who was Husserl's student, pushed the phenomenological investigation of being into everyday life and began not with time or space but with being-in-the-world. If I had followed Heidegger's lead I would have understood everyday life much differently; I would have looked to the world of work, itself a Western notion. I was interested in some of the same questions as Heidegger, but the way he formulated them hid their relevance to the interior perspective of street life.

In *Being and Time*, Heidegger outlined the project of phenomenological understanding, in part by rejecting the history of ontology. He argued that the ontological questions of the past had obscured the question of being. We, he wrote, are the subject of the question of being. To clarify his search, he discounted the advances of the positive sciences and dismissed anthropology, psychology, and especially biology as useless for ontological inquiry. The idea of being, which the social sciences translated as the ideas of the self, interested me, and in a field note that I wrote the first week I worked in the auto repair shop, I asked what the idea of the human was among the people I was studying. This is the anthropological question turned back upon the objects of inquiry; it does not ask, What is human? in some objective, depersonalized, decultured way, but rather asks, What do the people I am with think it is to be human? Heidegger ruled out the possibility of asking a culturally relative question and in so doing presumed that a culturally positioned person such as himself could ask the question appropriate for all times and places, and for all diverse humanity.

The reason I could not follow Heidegger, and by following Heidegger I mean pursuing our inherited Western beliefs in the primacy of human labor as defining everyday life, was that he placed the restricted question of being and everyday life in the same frame of investigation. Being-in-the-world, he explained at the beginning, is conducted by our *dealings*. We and our life on the earth are essentially expressed by how we manipulate the environment. Shifting the philosophers' attention, with regard to epistemology, from the historic emphasis on visual perception to dealings, he wrote, "The kind of dealing which is closest to us is as we have shown, not a bare perceptual cognition, but rather that kind of concern which manipulates things and puts them to use; and this has its own kind of 'knowledge' " (Heidegger 1962:95). Heidegger transferred our thought from perceptual cognition to those largely unconscious immediate relationships with what is closest to us. At the same time he plunged us into the world of labor. The manipulation of gear and tools by which he typifies being-in-the-world reifies what has happened in the West during the industrial revolution of the nineteenth and twentieth centuries but hardly holds for all humanities' indwelling in everyday life *from their standpoint*.

It is here that, instructive as Heidegger is, we must part company in order to get on with the ethnographic quest. In large part the aim of ethnography, and its finest achievement, is to represent insofar as possible the point of view of the members of other cultures. This effort precedes and makes possible cultural relativism. If I am to ask what the everyday life of black people I lived with was like, then I must begin from within their conception of the everyday, not my own. I must ask the more fundamental question at the same time: Does the notion of everyday life map to what happens in the street or in the house? At best my own ideas must serve as a scaffolding that can be at least partly disassembled as I gain knowledge. I must ask, as I did early in fieldwork, how the people I lived with viewed the human within life on the street, not whether they achieved the human according to my definition or that found in the literature.

Life on the street was not like Heidegger's romantic world of a craftsman's tools handily set near an alpine hut. Even the ideas of an eight-hour day and the forty-hour work week, which we now view as the standard and which the postmodern individual resists or subverts, does not capture the world of everyday that I found and experienced. Like Adam I wanted to name, not the animals, but the inner life of the street; I wanted to find a quasi-holistic word or phrase that would help me possess for thought the microscopic cultural zone I lived in from day to day. If I could name what I felt, I could bestow coherence on the box of field notes and on the two years I spent living on the street. This naming would serve as the practical guide to reflection. I would, if I could capture a motif of life of the people I lived with, solve a number of intellectual problems, not the least of which is the writing of a book about their lives and mine together.

In the effort to name that lived quotidian, not solely from my point of view but from the fusion of their perspectives and mine, I came up with expressions like *the fictive animation of space*, or *the dramaturgy of every moment*. I understand now, though I did not then, that the world of the street was a theater of continuous fiction, where the least moment, the least gesture was a work of theatrical care and improvisation. The corner of Fourteenth and Carpenter was a twenty-four-hour performance space. Everything that happened was experienced as action having all the qualities of drama. Oddly enough there was no dichotomy between actors and audience; these were constantly reversing roles, tossed back and forth with blistering speed or languidly. There was no distinction between stage and seating, no back or front, no proscenium arch. The only connection between the street and Western theater was the urge, a fundamental ontological desire, to create fictions through dramatis personae. The street plays did not reach for a mere transcendence, as if to rise above work for a moment, as if to momentarily forget the tedium. The plays were life itself; work was shrouded in the background or was another stage for interactive performance. Life was inconceivable without the continuous flow of fictional moments between the humans for whom to create humanness was to act.

I imagine that the history of Western drama obscures rather than discloses what I am trying to convey. Greek theater, the Roman circus, Shakespeare's Globe, the theater of cruelty, performance art, experimental theater in all its manifestations, its assault on narrative sense, do not prepare one for the street. There is no theater architecture; there is no audience who gathers at a preset time; there are no notions of author or playwright or director; there is no rehearsal, no stage design, no props, no blocking, no profession called acting. These categories, though they have all been attacked or questioned, persist as the definitions of theater. Imagine black life at the corner of Fourteenth and Carpenter as belonging to a continuous stream of *performing with others* in the moments of contact, which are themselves dramaturgical and fictional: people talking or arguing, women exchanging dresses, a man watching children walk on the hood of a car, someone asking for money or pawning dry cleaning, someone dancing in front of a bar to the music inside. Imagine an even more farfetched possibility that all morality is an aesthetic morality based in the play or musical re-formation, where art criticizes or takes up a moral attitude to life in the street, where a second-order aesthetic in music takes up a relation to a first-order, performer's aesthetic; life was doubly artful.

> the dramaturgy of the contact between men and women
> the dramaturgy of speech, each utterance
> the dramaturgy of work

entirely and solely dramaturgical, deepest play and only play.

I exaggerate, you say.

Fine.

I hope that if I claim too much it will help you sustain a spirit of inquiry as you read. I want to effect a reversal of *our* everyday thinking. For example, there was no work-play dichotomy, only a world perceived through drama and stories, through emotion, through tension, through tragedy and comedy, through profane farce, through histrionics, and through confusion, disturbance, tumult, enthusiasm, laughter, and rage.

The stage, as I use it here, and as it is used in Goffman's work, is not the metaphor for public life. The world of play, which we in the West can only identify in its realization as an upper-class or Hollywood lifestyle, is, in the streets, life itself (see Hannerz 1969:105–17).

My field notes are *now* about the fictional realization of the street and of public everyday life.

• • •

I take a bird's-eye view and look down onto the street corner, its sidewalks bounded by the facades of dwellings, workplaces, consumption sites, and leisure spaces. Two spaces were represented there: the open, public arena and the enclosed, private interiors. Public and private would seem to mark off the space of performance and the space of relaxation, the dressing rooms, so to speak. The dichotomy overdraws the boundary, for within house walls performance continued unabated; performance was living. It was true that not just anyone could enter a house or even a business at will, but anyone, presumably, could walk on the street. The boundary between house and street, however, was not the boundary between performance and nonperformance.

The street was alive through sight and sound. People were aware of the street twenty-four hours a day. At night old people who could not sleep sat behind their open or closed windows and watched and listened. The street was under constant surveillance, scanned, spied upon. It was fully filled in; everything was noticed, the least gesture attended to. It was a viscous gelatin of awareness. Walking down the block was extremely intense. The facades were alive through their apertures, and all who walked on the street felt they were in the theater of total performance. People cut through the viscosity as they walked, or inhabited it as they sat on their stoops. As they moved they left indelible, communal traces; they inscribed an aesthetic nuance with their gestures, their speech, their lives.

To help capture this I will refer to *the play*, which is itself dependent on playing with words. In the *Random House College Dictionary* of 1975 there were sixty-seven numbered entries under the noun *play*. I use the word generically—in the sense it acquires in its sentenced context—in order to express that everyone I met

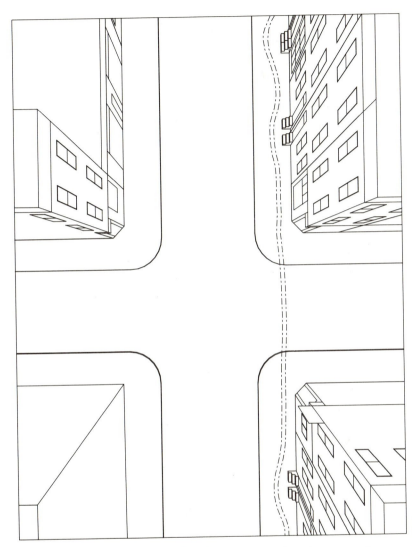

Figure 2. When a young man walked down the street alone, intent on going somewhere, he hugged the fronts of the houses, then stepped around the stoops, inscribing with his motion the pattern drawn here. Computer drawing.

played, in the moments of our being together and with others. I am mindful of the well-formulated statement by Hymes,

> Performance is not merely behavior, but neither is it the same as all of culture (or conduct or communication). It ought to be possible to compare communities as to the degree to which performance is characteristic of life, ranging from those in which it is salient and common as Abrahams has shown to be the case in parts of the West Indies, to those in which it is sub-dued and rare. (Hymes 1981:81; see also Abrahams and Szwed 1983:30ff.)

We all led fictional lives in the very moments we faced one another, even when the presence of the others who remained out of sight was only imagined.

• • •

"I am aware of a world, spread out in space endlessly, and in time becoming and become, without end" (Husserl [1913] 1962:91). Everyday life in its spatial array is the context for, the environment of, knowing-how and mundane practices. I know how to walk down the street, I know where to buy food and how to prepare it, I know where my friends live and how to get there several ways. I go to work, and at work I know how to use the machines, attend the appropriate meetings, ask advice from co-workers, work at my desk, answer the telephone, and so on.

> Things in their immediacy stand there as objects to be used, the "table" with its "books," the "glass to drink from," the "vase," the "piano," and so forth. These values and practicali-ties, they too belong to *the constitution of the "actually present" objects as such*, irrespective of my turning or not turning to consider them or indeed any other object. (Husserl [1913] 1962:93)

In America, the contexts of microscopic-sized cultural worlds are spatially spread across the continent and are highly differentiated. Life on the street in the summer in black South Philadelphia is not the same as life for a New Yorker on Fifth Avenue. From east to west, north to south, the country is divided into subcultural spaces while at the same time it is unified by certain basic artifacts: autos, malls, television, franchise food, and nationally distributed mass consumer brands of products.

• • •

Philadelphia was designed in the seventeenth century as a commercial city with a commercial rationality superimposed on a military one. It was planned on a grid by William Penn's surveyor, who was trained in the military. Every point had a numbered address and was located on or within easy access of north-south and east-west axial streets.

Just after his trip to America in 1842, Dickens wrote of his visit to Philadelphia and his impressions of the settlement pattern.

It is a handsome city, but distractingly regular. After walking about it for an hour or two, I felt that I would have given the world for a crooked street. The collar of my coat appeared to stiffen, and the brim of my hat to expand beneath its quakery influence. My hair shrunk into a sleek short crop, my hands folded themselves upon my breast of their own calm accord, and thoughts of taking lodgings in Mark Lane over against Market Place, and making a large fortune by speculations in corn, came over me involuntarily. (Dickens [1842] 1908:96)

Like other cities of the eastern seaboard, Philadelphia was a row-house city, with houses and workplaces of brick all joined to form contiguous city blocks. It was planned more with the commercially successful London and Amsterdam (which it resembles in scale, without canals) in mind, than with Paris, the most northern of the monumental cities of the Mediterranean. Philadelphia had little place for public commemorative sculpture and was never conceived to be a monument of urban form and structure.

Philadelphia has never fully modernized. Its space of everyday life in the central portion of the city and adjacent neighborhoods remain scaled much like the row-house city of two centuries earlier. The automobile, the most dominant force in the formation of twentieth-century infrastructure, imposed itself on the city; whole blocks were razed and became parking lots. Philadelphia was the last of the major American urban areas to finish its interstate highway system, the absence of which crippled commerce, manufacturing, and distribution in the city.

Everyday life, rather than the peaceful, domestic place implied in Husserl's typification of the natural standpoint, has become, with the advent of rapid personal transportation, not only a world spread out in space endlessly but a series of locii linked by trans-

portation corridors—streets, roads, highways, turnpikes, inter-
states. The natural standpoint with its coordinates of space and
time has become the field of the most massive changes in contemporary human life. Everyday life in Philadelphia and elsewhere in
this and other countries has become driven by the consumer, whose
quotidian includes the rapidly transformable sites of consumption
and use.

Despite the rapidity of change toward an economy driven by a
consuming society, Philadelphia was a city of neighborhoods with
more or less self-conscious identities. The neighborhoods, many of
whose outlines remained sociologically intact after eighty years,
were multi-ethnic: mixed Catholic; Catholic and Protestant; Jewish
and Catholic; Catholic and black; black and Jewish; Protestant and
Jewish; Irish, Italian, and Polish; black and Hispanic; or Italian
and black. There were numerous permutations. All the neighborhoods were partly accidents of history, and all were sites of everyday
life, locations crosscut by the national U.S. culture, television, automobiles, and mass movements.

The use of public space in black Philadelphia neighborhoods did
not resemble the spatiality of the late-nineteenth- and early-twen-
tieth-century ethnic neighborhoods. The latter areas were typically
composed of parishes, which were organized around churches and
parochial schools near factories. Blacks dispersed through North,
South, and West Philadelphia, displacing some of the white middle-
class neighborhoods as well as some of the white working-class ones
in the process. Black spatial order developed in two tiers in the
city, the first made up of the entire black population of Philadelphia
(served by a single newspaper), and the second of a street-by-street
local identity. Extreme localness smoothly blended in black Philadelphia. The black street gangs of the 1950s, local lords of a *turf*,
were named after street intersections like Thirteenth and South
streets, as revealed in the archaeology of graffiti and group identity
from that period.

Black Philadelphians were also aware of their location as citizens
in the public space of the country. For black America a larger
collective identity was forming in part in response to television and
its representation of American daily life. Urban space was the primary arena of the integration movement. When in 1955 Rosa Parks
took a vacant seat in the front of the Cleveland Avenue bus in
Montgomery, Alabama, then refused to relinquish it to a white man
and was arrested, the great public demonstrations by black Americans and their supporters began. The efforts of the NAACP and

notably those of Dr. Martin Luther King, Jr., transformed the entire national public space, first by mass demonstration and boycott, then by raising constitutional issues. As a result of the social and legal changes, the relations between black and white were altered toward equal access.

On the local streets there were two spatial planes: the horizontal surface of the roadway and sidewalk, and the vertical surface of the house and business facades. These surfaces defined the exterior arenas of public performance and were the macroscopic settings of everyday, public street life.

Everywhere in the rows of houses there were visual and auditory apertures. Sound passed in or out. The viewer, concealed within, established sightlines on visual surfaces—sidewalk, street, across the street—or held an auditory station, out of view inside the partially opened window.

Two uses dominated the scene: *habitation* and *passing through.* Residential streets were established by those who anchored them with the comings and goings of their daily lives, by those who perhaps worked there, and by those passing through on foot or in vehicles.

Materials of the drama-world included:

the granite cobble and asphalt roadway with a dual steel ribbon of trolley tracks

steel and glass autos parked in rows on either side

granite curbs

cement or brick sidewalks

marble stoops stepping into the wood-framed doorway

the red brick row house, windows three stories above ground

the cellar entered from the sidewalk.

On Sunday morning a man's voice echoes in the narrow canyon as he calls up to the second floor to a drinking companion.

• • •

I have worked all day, and now it is dark outside. I am on the third floor typing the day's field notes and stand up to stretch, walking to the window to look down on the street. A police cruiser is parked with its engine running, the faces of the two policemen, one black, one white, illuminated through the windshield by the streetlight. I step back from the window so they cannot see me but I keep looking at them.

The white cop looks level with the doorway, first up the street, then down the street, his eyes moving along a horizontal axis.

The black cop looks up the street, then down the street; his eyes move up and down the facades of the row houses on the right-hand side of the street, then on the left-hand side. The movements of his eyes describe a three-dimensional space unifying the horizontal and vertical planes, criss-crossing and capturing the entire visual arena.

3. Winter

Telemachus

Telemachus stood with his back against the darker opening of his repair shop, bent slightly forward from the waist. He looked up, then down the street, smoking his first Pall Mall of the day. Behind him in the garage, the old Arvin radio tuned to WDAS pulsed music onto the sidewalk.

Four boys, brothers, watched him closely as they walked toward him on their way to school. The youngest was five, the oldest ten. They were laughing, and as they drew closer and entered the ambiance of sound they began to dance.

"Hullo, Slick Willie," Telemachus called to the oldest. He gave the nickname only to Willie. Everywhere the boy went and became known, someone would give him a nickname—Slick there at the shop, another name at school, and yet another with his friends on the little street where they lived and played. He would have a different name for a different space; his various identities would be scattered through the neighborhood. Telemachus, squinting through the smoke from the cigarette in his mouth, reached into his pocket and gave a quarter to each of the boys. They danced toward school, turning once to look back.

The scene fades from my memory and is replaced by one of a hot summer day, a year later. Instead of standing in the doorway, Telemachus, in a rare moment of relaxation, is sitting just inside the garage door playing checkers with an old man. Turning toward me, Telemachus smiles instinctively as I photograph them from the side.

Now I hold the photograph in my hand. Its sharp colors, especially the bright yellows of the Philadelphia afternoon sun, have faded with time. The dark blue pants of his mechanic's uniform and the light blue cotton shirt with his name sewn in red across the left breast are also less distinct.

I put that photograph down and pick up another. It is of the four boys, posing in front of the closed door of the repair shop like a quartet of famous singers. Three of them kneel on one knee; the fourth bends forward, placing his hands on the backs of two of them. Their red and black jumpsuits are impeccable. It is Easter morning.

• • •

Telemachus, as he was disclosed to me in fragments of direct and overheard conversations, is the basis of this text, the major source of allusion, the human ground upon which the figures of anecdote and analysis are inscribed. His presence and his animation and personation of the repair shop bring together the cultural context of contact between black and white, know-how, automobiles, the organization of work, and behavior in public space. For two years he was the closest person to me other than Karen. I interrogated our moments together with the intensity of Henri Barbusse's voyeur. "All thefts are crimes of passion, even this one, which was cowardly and vulgar. . . . All offences, all crimes, are attempts carried out in the image of the immense desire to steal which is our very essence and the form of the naked soul: to have what one lacks" (Barbusse [1908] 1966:192). Through Telemachus I witnessed the production of daily life and learned how to act and with whom on what occasions. He was my unwitting tutor, and I was his partner, acting from bad faith, examining life in the shop, visiting his acquaintances, his home, his lovers, observing his daily round, his dealing with things and with customers. Through him I witnessed the ragged, ambiguous edges of black-white contact in urban settings.

I modeled my specific acts on his and mimed how he conducted himself, and I registered within myself and reenacted what I observed him do and say. Through his eyes I first witnessed life *out there on the street*.

Thus, however feebly, I learned from him and benefitted from his rare but always to-the-point advice. At the same time I learned there was a whole dimension of himself that I could not, given our historical moment together, ever learn. He had acquired stories and performances as a child in the more enclosed black subculture of rural North Carolina, and he reserved them for parties, for sociable occasions. To my disappointment, they could not be elicited in the shop, for I tried several times.

It seemed as though American culture had carved out, before he and I met, the not altogether satisfactory points of contact where we might meet. One of these points, and a basis for our relationship, was, as he mentioned in the first conversation we had, that I must treat black and white alike. The reasons he gave were from his life: he had a white girlfriend, white customers as well as black, and white friends. I promised him I would do as he asked.

In the realm between us that our daily contact formed, I felt there was room to maneuver; he suggested a business partnership, never treated me as anything but a peer, was cordial but did not repress his moods. He was easy to work for, and to work with when we were engaged in a particular task. In times that were for him or me personally difficult, he would try to shift the tensions through verbal play. He was not always successful as a businessman, and the first winter he bore a difficult situation with his youngest son, Auston, with a patience that I would not have believed possible and that on a number of occasions hardly seemed warranted. When I displeased him, particularly through mechanical ignorance or ineptitude, he sanctioned me the way he did Auston, who worked for him as I did.

Telemachus was in every respect, I suppose, an ordinary person, not brilliant or stupid, aggressive or passive. At forty-seven and self-employed for the first time, he had modest ambitions: he wanted to be known as *Telemachus*, which I took to mean he desired an essential respectability both personally and publicly, and he wanted a larger, successful business. I think his self-definition and desire for a better lifestyle was based directly on the American middle class. He held the Utopian hope that there would be a fundamental equality between black and white of the sort he mentioned to me in our first conversation. Telemachus wanted the boundary between black and white abolished; he did not share the black Muslin ideal of separation. With a black Muslim customer he argued the issue of buying shoes from whites and pointed out that even if one bought shoes from a black person they were manufactured by whites. Telemachus's point was that blacks *have* to live with whites and that separatism was an illusion. His own political sentiments lay with the National Association for the Advancement of Colored People rather than with the Black Panthers, Nation of Islam, or militant political groups of the period.

• • •

Kinston, North Carolina, is a small city servicing an outlying rural area of black and white. The landscape retains evidence of the slaveholding era and Reconstruction. The plantation house still sits on a rise. On a lower elevation, the sharecroppers' cabins are lined up on a small dirt lane between county highways.

Telemachus moved north with his family from the Kinston area.

His relatives were once distributed through the countryside and in small towns of the Piedmont like Snow Hill or Browntown. The great migration of the rural black American northward to the cities is now over; Telemachus and his wife and six children were among the last. He followed two of his brothers north and chose Philadelphia rather than New York City, where one of the two ran a successful speakeasy.

Although Telemachus and I did not have long talks together like anthropologist and key informant, and the shop was invariably busy, he disclosed on occasion his childhood and youth. He talked about his early years in terms of his mother's ghost stories and encyclopedic kin-reckoning abilities, his sharecropper father's obsequious behavior to the white landowner, his physical run-ins with his stepmother and father, his sexual awakening, and his few glimpses of black-white relations. In part his apathy for talking about the South was due to his attitude toward it. He claimed it was the worst place on earth.

My father had to bend low and flatter Mr. John just to get clabber. My father did the milking morning and evening. If he wanted any clabber he had to do all those things. I asked Mr. John why my father had to act that way, and for that reason he told me to get off the farm. I went into the woods and logged, lived on the road. In the woods we lived like dogs.

Back then I loved to cut people just to hear their skin pop. I didn't care who it was. Now I stops and thinks; I walks away and it gives me time. If I was mad, I would have hit a person no matter if he killed me.

When I was twelve I worked like a man. I came home tired one evening and my stepmother insisted I had to wash the diapers of one of her children. I said to myself, Goddam if I'll do that. She beat me then and I took one of the sweet gum ball bats I made to her and beat her. She was six or seven months pregnant and I was terrified of what I had done. I ran fifteen miles to my uncle's house, but the next day he brought me back. My father beat me with a pine tobacco cane until blood ran into my shoes. He kept calling me a tallow-faced son-of-a-bitch. I remember he called me *some kind* of a son-of-a-bitch. He only beat me once after that.

Before I knew peoples fucked I was living with my aunt and uncle. He was active in the church; he was president of the usher's association and was always going to meetings. She was doing it with men who would come over. The men would sit on the porch and talk and see who could wait all the others out until no one was left. Her husband always saw how many women he could go with.

One night I was down in the field and I saw for the first time a man and a woman doing it. The woman was on the man and I decided right there that when I grew up I'd love to have that happen to me.

My mother could always find kin relations between peoples who came over to visit my grandfather who entertained all summer long. One of the visitors was a young girl and she and I drove down to the cornpatch. I was young then; I could knock off a couple of times and still come out hard. She really loved it because no one had even done it to her like that.

When we came back we were sitting in the car all lovey-dovey and my mother came out to introduce the girl to me. She said this is your cousin so-and- so. The girl cried and cried and ran into the house after what we had done. She would not talk to me any more.

I told my mother after that, Don't introduce me to any of the girls I take out. She went ahead and did it anyway.

Right after I was married [at age eighteen] I was *tight* with a man who used to come over to my house. He would be there when I came home from work. After saying a few words to me he would leave. This went on for a while but I excused it be-cause the man and I were such good friends. At work one day I got to thinking about it. That night I said something about him to my wife. She said that he had never remarked anything out of the way to her and had never done anything.

I told him to stay away anyway. A couple of days later he was there again when I came home from work, so I threw my gun on him and beat him with a stick. I never heard from him or saw him again.

Now I regret it because we were such good friends.

Down the road a plantation owner had a white wife and two children and gave them up for a black woman who lived nearby. He had three children by her. Since they were classi-fied black, the man had a private tutor for them, two became lawyers, one a doctor. The doctor tried to go white but after seven years was discovered, and there was a terrible row.

The white wife died of grief and humiliation. Just before the old man died he called in his white lawyer and his three black sons and made out his will to them. He cut off the two white children from his estate, and there was a terrible row about that too.

In a graphic summary of Telemachus's stories, I made a diagram in the field notes:

SOCIETY

YOUTH	MATURITY
in the woods, alone	in society, family
lived like dogs	lived like men
action without thought	thought
hoodlum	respectable

• • •

After his discharge from the navy, Telemachus had some classroom training in mechanical work. No one learned anything in the classes, he said; they just sat there and daydreamed about women. Telemachus did not perceive the classroom as a place where practical knowledge could be acquired. His first job after the service was in a farm implement agency where he did unskilled work.

When he moved north he had a a succession of unskilled jobs. In Jenkintown, a Philadelphia suburb, he washed new and used cars for a Chevrolet dealer, for example. A slightly more demanding set of tasks came when he worked first in New Jersey, then in Philadelphia, pulling transmissions for TRANSCO, a national transmission replacement franchise. TRANSCO management used a contemporary factory system in which each employee performed a single task. Telemachus removed and replaced transmissions from autos on a hydraulic lift. He did not open or rebuild transmissions; other employees rebuilt subassemblies that were then put together, and the entire overhauled transmission was bench-tested before being mounted in the auto.

Telemachus had migrated north in his thirties and had found work before his family joined him. He and his wife Mae had six children. Apparently she had given birth to others before marrying Telemachus, however, and it was never clear exactly how many children she had, how many the two of them had together, and how many he had fathered. The records in the county courthouse in Kinston showed a different spelling of Telemachus's name at the birth of each of his daughters. This kind of imprecise information plagued the black records there, which were kept in separate books in a separate room. One could be led to believe that Telemachus's father was nine when he was married, depending on whether one followed the date on the birth certificate or that on the death certificate.

One morning Telemachus and I were eating breakfast together a block from the shop. I was talking about my brother, who had come to Philadelphia to visit. Telemachus, employing a series of one-liners, typified his children.

Sharon, she's the baby; she just likes the action no matter what. All she wants is a man who'll buy her clothes and let her run.

Rebie wants to have the last word. No matter what man she is with she'll have the last say.

Dolores won't marry a man who acts too boyish; she wants a man who'll tell her to do this or that.

Auston just wants to have a good time.

Danny wants to get some of the action; if there is money to be made, he wants to make some of it. Otherwise he'll split.

Jerry is different. He won't let anybody touch him when he gets dressed up. You can't go up to him and hit him on the shoulder. If you do you better look for a fight. When he's dressed, go up to him and shake his hand, then back away.

Because Telemachus lived in West Philadelphia and the garage was in South Philadelphia, he daily entered and left two nearly autonomous spatial domains. Relations with his wife, who almost never called him at the garage, were not warm, and he claimed he was sleeping on the edge of the bed. She was a churchgoer, which he was not, and she had recently undergone major surgery. These were the two reasons he gave for her indifference to him. He was buying his home with the income from his jobs. Pulling transmissions he had made about the same salary as a good secretary. He was an economic participant in, not a sole supporter of, his household.

Three daughters lived at home. Sharon was in high school and Rebie and Dolores worked and lived at home. When Auston was released from prison, he also lived at home. For four months he worked at the shop rather ineffectually because he was a drug addict, and he died the February after fieldwork ended. Telemachus called us and we attended his funeral on 18 February 1972.

• • •

Telemachus's involvement in the transportation sector was not atypical of blacks after World War II. The largest employer of unskilled men in the country was the auto industry. With the 1 January 1910 opening of the Ford Highland Park plant to produce the Model T, the Michigan assembly lines began to demand great quantities of unskilled labor.

The black ministers of Detroit, during the recession of 1921, petitioned Henry Ford to continue hiring from the Negro community. Ford agreed to employ blacks at the company according to their percentage of population in Detroit. When Ford moved toward vertical integration by building the River Rouge plant, the policy of hiring blacks was kept in force.

Telemachus was born in 1922 and would have heard of opportunities in the northern-based automotive plants as he grew up. By 1940, when Telemachus was 18, the River Rouge plant employed 11.7 percent blacks. Most worked either on the assembly lines or in the foundries, rolling mills, and blast furnaces, punishing and hazardous jobs. Despite being restricted to the work that often demanded the least skills and posed the greatest physical threats, blacks became supervisors and managed racially mixed crews. The Ford hiring policy at that time was unique in the industry (Northrup 1968).

Ethnographers Robert and Helen Lynd documented in their study of Muncie, Indiana, the transformation of everyday life that autos effected in America. Their 1937 study, *Middletown*, gave a subtle reading of technological change. The drama of the change was revealed in a footnote: "Two million horse-drawn carriages were manufactured in the United States in 1909 and 10,000 in 1923; 80,000 automobiles were manufactured in 1909 and 4,000,000 in 1923." (Lynd and Lynd 1937:25n). Within twenty years, from 1909 to 1929, America had become economically dependent on the automobile (Flink 1975).

In the South, the auto served to democratize the apartheid-like separation of the races. "A white man in Macon County [Georgia] advocated that the cars be taken from the Negroes or that the county maintain two systems of roads, one for the whites and one for the Negroes!" (Raper 1936:176). The auto affected leisure, churchgoing, morals, food consumption, clothing choices, family organization, the design and use of the house and yard, and urban design. Indeed its impact has not received adequate documentation and analysis from cultural and social historians, sociologists, or anthropologists. The meaning of the auto continues to elude our understanding.

Black Americans were incorporated most rapidly into the automotive industry during the two world wars and the period of economic growth from 1962 to 1966. In the sixties, government policy and the Detroit riot were important stimuli to industry to hire more black workers. Nonetheless, the companies were never leaders in addressing fundamental social problems or advancing the cause of black equality.

The unions, particularly the United Auto Workers, which have by no means served as civil rights organizations, have for the most part, and from the top, supported equal opportunity. An observer of the involvement of the black labor force found that "the lack of union fragmentation, and the fluidity within the plants and among the plants provided in the union agreements have been major factors in expanding employment opportunities for Negroes" (Northrup 1968:70).

Black employment among the Big Three—Chrysler, Ford, and General Motors—stood in 1966 at 129,195 or 13.6 percent of their labor force nationwide. The figures hide the uneven regional distribution of blacks within the companies. From the black point of view, there have been a host of problems with the auto industry, in the area of craft apprenticeship, particularly, and in cases in which blacks were in the minority in specific shop situations, where they suffered racist harassment—jostling—from white workers and supervisors.

The point I wish to make here is that the transportation sector of the economy, a central engine of economic growth for sixty years of this century, employed blacks and became highly visible as a source of economic opportunity. When Telemachus was discharged from the navy at the end of World War II, it was not remarkable that he sought employment in transportation-related companies.

Temporalities

During our first month in Philadelphia, Karen and I boarded a southbound trolley that took us from our own area around Clinton

Street through a strip of black South Philadelphia, then through white ethnic neighborhoods. We were on our way to buy groceries, and we felt a trolley ride would give us an idea of the social geography of the city. As we passed through a black residential belt above South Philadelphia, I noticed an auto repair shop where the first floor of a row house once had been. I remembered it, and after our conversation with Goffman, I considered looking there for work. The area seemed to be working class, mainly black in character, and the shop was on a fairly busy street with an active public life. I felt this was a site with promise for a study of everyday life; it seemed like an ordinary place—so ordinary that members of the white middle class would have deleted it from consciousness even while driving past.

I arranged to meet Telemachus by simply needing a minor repair on my blue 1962 Chevrolet Impala two-door hardtop, which had a noise of metal on metal in the clutch housing. I drove to the shop, parked the car, and then approached a man wearing a mechanic's uniform who was sitting on the stoop next to the open garage. His name was Boycie, as I found out later, and in time he became a good friend. I asked him if he were the owner; he shook his head no and directed me inside.

The open garage door was cluttered with equipment—a jack, a metal milk crate, a mechanic's creeper—among which two customers stood and talked to one another. I eased my way past them and walked the narrow path between the cars parked in the shop and the benches and bins toward the back. Telemachus looked up and I greeted him. He smiled in return and asked if he could help me. I noticed immediately his gray eyes set in a soft brown face, a greasy porkpie hat on his head, pushed slightly back. Obviously he was middle-aged. I responded immediately to his smile, his look, and his age, and I felt we could work together if he needed extra help.

Right away I was uncertain that the situation would work out for me. Another man, about eighteen, with the name *Raymond* written on his shirt, was there. I felt disappointed, for I figured that Raymond would be the reason I would not be hired. If he had a shirt with his name on it, he worked full time, and it did not seem to me that the gutted first floor of a row house made into a repair shop would absorb additional labor. The place only held three cars, and by ordinance it was illegal to work on the street. I had no intention of putting anyone out of a job, but I figured that I would at least ask if Telemachus needed part-time help. I preferred to work part-time anyway, since I wanted to do anthropology, not repair battered Pontiac LeManses.

Later, when it was not quite so busy, Telemachus ran my car into the opening of the shop, its rear end ungraciously hanging over the sidewalk, raised the front end with a compressed air jack, and, taking a tin shears, snipped a bit of offending metal from the clutch housing. The removal cleared up the noise, he charged me three dollars, and after the operation, he and I chatted for a moment. I said I was looking for part-time work and that I had no wish to put anyone else out of a job. He squinted into the street and said cryptically to come in on Monday morning about eight o'clock. I said okay, I would see him then, and drove away feeling that I had found a place where I could work unobtrusively. The area had white people on the street as well as black, though judging by his customers and Raymond, Telemachus's operation was pretty much for blacks.

The repair shop was just one of many in the area. South Philadelphia was overflowing with mechanics who believed that if they opened a garage and told their friends, they would have numerous customers and grow affluent repairing automobiles. It was by no means that easy. South Philadelphia had a lot of repair shops because the majority of automobiles there needed them; the cars were old, nearly worn out, and they migrated to the area from the affluent sections of the city via used car lots. The inherent problem of making a living from one of the operations was that the repairs might cost more than the car was worth, so the shop owner was placed in the intolerable position of working for a slim or imaginary margin of profit. If the repairman charged too much, he had an automobile on his hands that could not be resold, because he did not have title to it, and could not be given back to the owner without a complete loss of investment in time and replacement parts. This enduring dilemma confronted Telemachus daily.

I had no idea that I had invited myself into a dangerous situation, for there had been no way of knowing that Telemachus's relations with Raymond were constantly strained. Telemachus viewed Raymond as a charity case because he had been in prison on armed robbery charges and was unskilled, which made him relatively unemployable. Not known for prompt payment of wages, he also felt that the lack of a consistent payday was offset by his hiring Raymond; in other words, some money was better than no money. Raymond, however, did not share this definition of the situation. He worked when he wished to, which was when he was certain a job was big enough that he could be sure of securing a portion of the payment. This meant Raymond was often not in the shop as a regular hired hand ought to be, and also that he refused to work on jobs if he perceived that there was nothing in it for him immediately. Each man's definition of the relationship was impossible for the other to be satisfied with, and I walked unknowingly into their ongoing differences. If I had arrived as an anthropologist I would not have become directly involved in the dynamic playing out of their mutual grievances. Indeed, they might have narrated it to me. In any case, I would not have been caught in its potentially fatal web. As it was, I was to appear on Monday morning, and Raymond was not informed that I was coming to work, a fact I did not suspect.

Telemachus, I believe, saw me as a potential object of easy exploitation. He knew that if I *wanted* a job with him, I was exploitable, plus he knew, given my probable expectations about labor, that I would work as I said I would, which is how he stereotyped white men who worked with their hands. His ploy, I think, was to replace Raymond's arbitrary, unskilled, and hence undependable work with mine, which at least to his mind could be no worse. Understandably I did not perceive this matrix of definitions of the situation, and I blithely blundered into the middle of their divergent points of view. Though caught up in the plot, I had not been issued the script. As an ethnographer I would have had social license to help write the script or even to have been a principal author. Lacking the status of professional social scientist, I entered the shop without any authority except that which I could exert as would any mechanic taking a job.

Monday

Very early Monday morning I was walking to South Philadelphia from Clinton Street, down Fourteenth Street, to greet a new life, to work in the garage, to acquire a whole new, secret self. My emotions were flattened as if I were the soldier in Alain Robbe-Grillet's *In the Labyrinth* (1965). I felt nothing as I began the day alone in the early yellow light of the Philadelphia fall. As I walked, the only parts of my body I inhabited were my eyes. I couldn't feel, but I could see, as if I were watching in pedestrian time a newsreel of a city to which I was a total stranger, as if I were in the dark theater alone watching the street unwind.

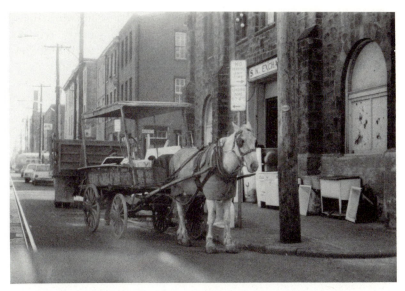

4. *Horse-drawn junk wagon. In Philadelphia in the late 1960s a number of occupations were still conducted from horse-drawn vehicles, such as knife sharpening, vegetable vending, and trash collecting. (Photograph by the author)*

5. *Men around a fire. On South Street where many buildings had been razed, people found sociable uses for the spaces. (Photograph by the author)*

The streets at ten minutes to eight were alive, people everywhere, traffic strong. Steel wheels screeched on steel rails as the trolleys rocked past me on Fourteenth Street, nosing into South Philadelphia, their overhead wires humming a high-pitched metallic note.

On my left as I walked there was a blasted space between two standing row houses, full of rubble, piss, bottles, and the jagged ends of the red brick from which the city was constructed. At Fourteenth and Bainbridge I came to a pawn shop unbelievably open at that hour, the men outside it talking loudly and joking; the biggest of them had a .38-caliber pistol stuck in his belt, the blunt handle with brown wooden grips showing. He was saying how he took the young boys with their knives, and how he had a whole trunkful of knives he had taken off *jitterbugs*. I set my face like cement and walked by them, looking straight ahead.

An ugly yellow sign above the street in front of a brick warehouse announced "ROSE AUTO" in black letters. A man standing in the doorway stared across the street at the Martin Luther King, Jr., Plaza housing project. He glanced at me as I approached, revealing one glass eye that always looked straight ahead. I remained unseen to him as he glanced away uninterested.

People were outdoors at the projects, wading through breezes made visible by the blowing scraps of paper and particles of dust that filled the gutters and that nicely offset the clear and green shattered shards of glass. At the corner of Christian and Fourteenth I stepped into a luncheonette for a cup of coffee.

In a moment of reflection I thought that there was an ordinariness in the deliberateness of peoples' movements and in the deterioration that touched each surface. I tried to capture it to gain a sense of personal equilibrium.

The luncheonette—the first floor of a row house on the corner— did not look quite complete. There was a counter that ran down the wall, with stools in front of it. A black truck driver was blowing his steaming coffee, impatient to be under way. Along the counter were racks of Tastykakes and potato chips, and boxes of fresh, unappetizing, jelly-filled pastries; toward the back there were display racks with children's toys on them—smiling pink panda bears, plastic-wrapped dolls that could cry and evacuate tap water into their diapers. And there were about six kinds of portable radios. Food and toys and radios—the place could have been Mexico or Yugoslavia: it had the half-finished look and odd combination of things I associate with other countries.

There were three black women, their hair under bandanas,

standing in a ragged queue waiting to pay for pastries. I looked at them, and they looked at me as I walked in. Joe, an Italian-American who owned the place and lived above the store with his parents, did not look at me. I later learned that he had a black girlfriend who sometimes minded the cash register and who bore children by him.

I left the luncheonette and saw a dusty real estate agency on the opposite corner; to my right there appeared to be an aging candy store. It was, in fact, a large and successful numbers bank. One night a year later, when we were living on that street, I heard the crash of plate glass and the crackle of rushing flames. I ran up to the third floor of the apartment, loaded my Bolex movie camera with black and white 400 ASA film, and shot from the window on the top floor the scene on the street below: the blaze flickering, the red lights of the fire engines flashing and lighting up the row houses on either side of the street in a regular, visual pulsing, the firemen dousing the fire. The numbers bank had been bombed. It was rebuilt right away.

Telemachus's shop was in that very block, and I stood in front of it drinking coffee until he arrived five minutes later. He drove up in a wine-colored 1963 Pontiac Catalina four-door hardtop without hubcaps, a smile wrinkling his face. We exchanged greetings, he opened the garage door and threw the power switch, and the shop began its daily electronic life. The radio and the air compressor took off simultaneously, making a competitive racket. The compressor was old and it erratically banged with an oily gurgle, stuffing air into a tank that powered tools, lifted cars, took bolts off and spun them on, and cleaned the dirt off aging transmissions with hard blasts of stale air. Telemachus noted my coffee and asked if I could use another one. I said yes. He left the shop in my charge and walked opposite the way I had come to a restaurant a block away for coffee, and, as it turned out, Tastykakes.

His rented shop had been converted from a row house by knocking out the front wall, removing the floor, filling the basement with dirt, and pouring a concrete pad over it. There were three cars parked in the shop, as there had been on Saturday. They were set extremely close to one wall. On the other wall were storage benches, which I now noticed were full of old parts. I stood in the open doorway and looked up and down the street. Raymond was not around, and I comforted myself with the speculation that maybe he did not work full time. At least he did not arrive early in the morning, whatever that meant. I did not worry about it and turned my attention to figuring out how I was going to get acquainted with Telemachus.

I could hear people moving around upstairs above the din of the radio, and through the cracks in the ceiling boards I could see light from the apartment. Surely the fumes of the garage would be intoxicating up there. The compressor full of air sighed to a stop, and the Moments were singing on WDAS, "Somebody Loves You, Baby."

> Somebody loves you, Baby, and it's me
> Somebody loves you, Baby, and it's me
> I've given you all I possess
> True love and so much happiness
> So why don't you believe me when I say
> Somebody loves you, Baby, and it's me
> Yeah, yeah
> > and it's me.

A man moving out of middle age stood close to me on the sidewalk. Ignoring me, he looked up to the apartment windows above the shop and screamed out, "I'ry, I'ry," in an attempt to rouse the woman upstairs. He wanted to ask her to go for a drink with him, though he already had a sheet or two to the wind.

Telemachus had returned with two coffees and two Tastykakes, one a French apple, the other a cherry pie. He set his lit Pall Mall cigarette on the back of the car nearest the door of the shop, and we stood facing the sidewalk, eating Tastykakes and drinking the steaming coffee. Telemachus began a long monologue about race and discrimination. He talked about people and situations and then, out of the corner of his eye, watched me for my reaction. This was not a real monologue; he was measuring me, testing. I was tested a lot that way, by everyone at first, until people came to know me. I tried to act casual, pretending that the emotionally charged issues he alluded to I merely took for granted. His disguised dialogue ended with his statements that he had a white girlfriend and that I was to treat her and black and white customers all the same.

I learned that Telemachus's white girlfriend called him there every day, usually in the slack, early-morning minutes before customers came in. The phone rang, and Telemachus told me that it was probably Angela—Angie—and he wasn't there; Would I please answer it? He instructed me to tell Angie that he had gone out to buy parts for a car. I did as he requested; it was, perhaps, another test. Angie wanted to hang on the line, but I discouraged her, telling her that Telemachus would be gone for a while, that he had to go across town. She told me to tell him to call her back, that it was an emergency. When I hung up, Telemachus was in the cloth bathroom. I yelled to him and told him what she had said. Telemachus grunted something unintelligible. When he came out, he made no effort to call Angie, and I wondered why not.

We went back to the doorway. No business had come in, and Telemachus was not making much effort to work on the three cars parked in the shop. He continued his monologue, touching on his brother's speakeasy in New York City. I did not know what a speakeasy was, but after Telemachus finished that part of the story, I had the idea that it was an illegal gaming house where cards, craps, roulette, drugs, booze, and women were to be had in any combination or singly. They were little casinos, and Harlem was as active as Vegas, in just the same way.

It might have been last on the agenda, or Telemachus might not have really cared, but he finally asked me if I had any experience repairing automobiles. I fudged on my experience with an English sports car I had owned and claimed that I had worked on my father-in-law's fleet of school buses.

Telemachus said, "Let's put these cars on the street," and we drove the two cars out and parked them, leaving only his daughter's Valiant up on stands at the very back of the shop. His timing was good, because a white man, tall and thin, about forty, wearing cheap cotton slacks and a cotton shirt, drove an old Pontiac into the doorway. The man was obviously poor and very nervous. He asked Telemachus about a transmission repair job and worried over the money, the down payment, whether he should leave the title to his car with Telemachus or not. Telemachus was gentle and tried to calm him down.

Another customer came in for a tuneup while I was under the Pontiac, trying to find the bolts that held the transmission onto the engine. I was lying on my back on a flat mechanic's creeper, using a trouble light and jointed socket wrenches. Telemachus had been under there with me, on his own creeper, patiently explaining and showing me what to do. Despite the interruptions and other things Telemachus wanted to do, we had the transmission out by midmorning and on the back bench under two fluorescent lights, ready to be washed off with kerosene and taken apart for diagnosis and repair.

About eleven I went to the door, wiping my grease-stained hands on a mechanic's rag and trying to breathe the nasty taste of scorched transmission fluid out of my mouth and nose. One leg of my jeans was soaked with transmission fluid because after I had drained it into a shallow barrel I swung my creeper around and my leg dipped into the burnt liquid. Across the street in front of the check-cashing place was a bench with advertising on it where people sat to wait for the trolley. I saw Raymond sitting there with his uniform on, his arm casually over the back of the bench. He was watching the door of the shop. I recognized him immediately, but before I had a chance to react, he called across to me, "Are you working for Telemachus now?"

"Yeah, I guess so," I said.

"You're gonna hafta take a lot of shit," Raymond answered.

I was very curious why Raymond, who had prior right to the shop, should be sitting across the street rather than coming in to work. The tiny encounter lent increased anxiety and an air of uncertainty and ambiguity to my work situation; my expectations became a little less firm. I could only wonder and remember to write it all down in my field notes at the end of the day.

•　　•　　•

It was 1:30 in the afternoon and Telemachus and I were eating lunch, leaning against the trunk of a car at the opening of the shop where we could view the street. In warm weather we always ate where we could look up and down public space. A gray-haired man with a beard walked directly in front of the doorway.

"Come in here, you old gray fox," Telemachus said. The man had a cane in one hand and a shopping bag in the other.

"Come in here, I want to fight you."

"Why do you always want to fight me?"

They bantered back and forth like this, and the old gray fox put down his cane and shopping bag and approached Telemachus.

"Come over here where you can't reach the cane," Telemachus told him, motioning where he wanted him.

The old man walked further into the shop between a car and a bench, into a slightly open space. He was now a bit behind Tele-machus. Telemachus put his plate of food down and moved quickly toward him as if to hit him. The gray fox picked up a hammer. They talked back and forth, and he threw down the hammer and picked up a larger one.

"Why do you always go for weapons when I'm about to whup you?" Telemachus asked. Then he changed the subject and asked, nodding in the direction of his brown shopping bag, "What do you have in the bag?"

"It's none of your business what I've got in the bag. You must come to my castle if you want to know what's in there," old gray fox told him. "The man who comes after me will have bronze skin and woolly hair. He'll be pure like the earth; and the Lord shall sort the pure from the mixed."

Old gray fox began to preach a kind of sermon. Telemachus said, "Shut up that ol' stuff." Then old gray fox put his head next to Telemachus's until their ears almost touched. He laughed and Telemachus said, "I can't see you."

"You can't talk to me unless you *jug* me," old gray fox replied, pulling away.

Then Telemachus called out hello to someone he knew passing by on the sidewalk. Old gray fox noted humorously, "You're trying to get rid of me."

Telemachus, looking beyond him, replied, "Don't stay around when I'm trying to get rid of you."

As the man was leaving, Telemachus asked, "What's your name?"

"Just call me Old Gray Fox."

•   •   •

Seven months later it was warm again and Old Gray Fox was standing facing the garage, showing Karen how to tie a particular knot in our dog's rope. "I can tie a knot so a man, if he were hung with it, wouldn't die," he told her.

Behind him, Stogey Joe stepped from Tony's office door, tiptoed behind the old man, and punched him lightly on the shoulder. Swinging his cane around, Old Gray Fox pretended to hit Stogey Joe.

Stogey Joe cocked his head to one side, bent his elbows, dangled his hands limply, and began to dance just beyond reach of the cane. He pranced like a formal dancer, his whole body led by the bottom half, his knees snapping to a precise rhythm that was playing on the shop radio. Both of them were laughing through the thrusting of the cane and Stogey Joe high steppin' near and then back out of reach. The game stopped and Stogey Joe put his arm around Old Gray Fox's shoulders and said, laughing, "You like to pick on me, don't you? You always like to pick on me."

•   •   •

The time was crawling toward three o'clock and WDAS was selling hair conditioner and playing the hits. The Impressions were singing theirs:

day or night
Which would you prefer to be right?

How long have you hated your white teacher
Who told you you loved your black preacher?
Do you respect your brother's woman friend
And share with the black folks not of kin?

People must move to the people
A better day is coming for you and for me
With just a little bit more education
And love for our nation will make a better society.

The song began enigmatically, but the themes, pulling at consciousness, were there in the soul of the music—themes of women and sex, blacks getting themselves together, reverse racism of hating the white teacher—and there were the moral urgings, characteristic of black popular music, for education and for inclusion of blacks as a part of the nation. The song attracted attention everywhere it was heard. Every radio in black South Philly and West Philly and North Philly had it on; it was a hit, and everyone knew the words by heart the second time through. Every black-owned car that came into the shop had its radio dial set to WDAS. I know because I checked. They sang:

Now some of us
Would rather cuss
And make a fuss
Than to bring about a little trust
But we shall overcome, I believe, someday,
If you'll only lissen to what I have to say.

And then back to the chorus, changed slightly,

If you had a choice of colors,
Which would you choose, my brothers?

I was in the shop alone now, trying to listen carefully to the unfamiliar music to catch the words, because it was not like white FM radio or the AM hit parade. As Telemachus had left the shop, he had given me an assignment. "I'm going over to the gas station on Christian Street and take that tire from my daughter's car," he had said. "I'll be back in a minute. See if you can get some bolts from that box of odds and ends and stick those Buick valve covers back on."

I had said I would do it. Bending over the cardboard box with forsaken leftovers from a hundred other jobs and searching for bolts with the proper threads that would keep the valve covers in place, I did not hear Raymond enter the shop. He was next to me when I looked up, startled. He had changed from his uniform to close-fitting black slacks, hard shoes, and a well-styled shirt. Raymond was over six feet tall and the clothes looked good on him. He would have liked to have been a model. He had the build for it, and he had never been cut, as he later said, in the face, but he was not handsome.

Where's Telemachus?" he asked.

"He's over at the gas station having a tire fixed," I replied. I did not know what to make of Raymond's appearance and did not particularly link it with Telemachus's absence. Raymond seemed jittery at the same time, agitated or something.

"I'm going to get my shit together," he told me, and with that he walked around me and moved toward the back of the shop. I figured that Raymond was pulling himself out of the job for his own reasons and that he was going to pick up whatever personal effects he had around. To me it seemed plausible that Raymond was angry at Telemachus and had decided to take his things home. I turned back to the box and kept rummaging through the greasy assortment, looking for the elusive, usable bolts.

I looked back once to see what Raymond was doing out of an idle curiousity as to what a person would leave in a garage that he might need to come back for. Raymond was squatting in front of the tool chest toward the back, holding a little cloth sack with his left hand and quickly putting gleaming metal objects into it. As I watched more closely, he reached into the bottom drawer, pulled out a short pistol, and stuck it into his waistband. I had an immediate flash of myself being between Raymond and the door and Raymond having to shoot his way out. I was suddenly afraid now that Raymond had a gun; what if he was angry at me for taking his job and would find some excuse to use the weapon where I would be the target?

It was no consolation that I had no experience dealing with those sorts of situations. I had no idea what to do next and absolutely no clue as to what the gun meant. It was the image of the gun, not Raymond's being there or his timing his presence with Telemachus's absence, that obsessed me.

Noticing that I was watching him, Raymond seemed to scoop up several things and left, pushing quickly past me. His abrupt departure exaggerated the shop, gave it an enlarged significance, as if I were seeing it for the first time. At the same time I looked at objects as if to fasten them down and bring myself back from the terrible uncertainty that Raymond had now created.

Just inside the door, to the left as one entered, was a pay phone. I would have to find a dime to call out. No, it would take too much time. Anyone standing there could be easily seen from across the street, however. For me the phone merely existed. I was not reassured by it.

Mentally walking deeper into the shop, I observed the left wall was lined with work benches. The space to the right had held the three parked cars during the night. Now there were two, the Buick I was replacing the valve covers for and Telemachus's daughter's white Valiant, up on jacks at the back of the shop.

Almost at my feet were the two jacks and two mechanic's creepers. I stared at them for a minute. To take out a transmission we used the jacks to lift a car front and rear. Then we put stands under it. The stands kept the auto high enough off the floor so that we, lying on creepers, could roll underneath, drain the transmission fluid, unbolt the transmission, place it on a special transmission dolly, wheel it from under the car, and roll it toward the back of the shop.

As we moved the transmission through the shop we passed a workbench, the small spare parts box where I was now standing, the oil drums (empty), the toilet behind a large brown cloth, another long workbench with engine and transmission parts in no order piled beneath, the toolbox, an old typesetter's desk, a waste bin; then, turning to face the back wall, we came to the main workbench, where Telemachus would tear down the transmission under two large fluorescent lights.

Just to the right of the workbench, almost touching the fender of his daughter's car, was a tall, double-doored metal wardrobe with a simulated wood-grain finish. A small black suitcase and a fireplace screen, covered with a heavy coating of oily dust, were piled on top. Two pictures of women were taped on the one door of the wardrobe. One woman was black, the other white, both nude except for bikini panties. Over the workbench was a poster of Bob Dylan. Telemachus's space, personalized by cut-out magazine nudes and the poster, revealed an iconography of intention and desire. His politics were the politics of integration and miscegination, contact between the races, and protest against racism, as in the songs of Dylan. I did not find it difficult to comprehend his point of view.

But now I was more concerned with the events that Raymond (or I) had begun. What should I do next? There was little I could do but work and wait until Telemachus returned.

Telemachus arrived back in a few minutes, as he had said he would, and I told him that the Buick was ready to go and that Raymond had come into the shop looking for him. Telemachus was surprised. He exclaimed, "Raymond! Looking for me? What'd he do?"

"Well, he told me he came to get his shit together. He went there," I pointed, "and took some stuff out of those drawers. He took out a gun, and it really scared me."

"That's my gun," Telemachus said.

"I was afraid he was going to shoot me," I added.

"He couldn't shoot you with that; it's just a starter pistol, a cap pistol."

I knew that Raymond could make a zip gun from it, and I was uncertain enough about the turn of events to imagine that he would. Telemachus seemed deflated and said, sighing with disgust, "Well, let me go back there and see what he stole this time."

Telemachus began his inventory and I stood in a pool of dread and uncertainty. Telemachus looked on his workbench with the Slim Jim disemboweled on it, opened up the wardrobe and checked the shelves, then walked back to the tall tool chest and, starting at the top, went down drawer by drawer. He walked back to where I was standing and told me that Raymond had taken chrome wrench sets, the Chrysler wheel puller, and a set of miniature wrenches, then said his children had given him the starter pistol and that all those things mounted up to maybe four hundred dollars worth. He looked pained and acted disgusted. The impact hammers, which were like drills, were expensive. They ran on compressed air and fastened and unfastened bolts; now every bolt would have to be removed or tightened by hand.

Telemachus looked me full in the face and told me, "When I leave, you're in charge, this is your shop, and nobody can come in and take anything. Do you understand?"

I replied that Raymond worked there, and that I did not know any different than to let him into the shop to get his things. I was curious as to what being in charge meant. Did it mean that if I were in charge and Raymond came in, I would have to physically stop him from taking things? I had no idea how to go about that.

Telemachus finished his short lecture by saying, "Boy, this is your place when I'm gone; you run it then; treat it like it was your own place."

Telemachus was soft with me and did not belabor the point. The lecture was also over because a man walked past the front of the shop, and Telemachus walked quickly to the door and called out, "Hey! Come here a minute."

I could overhear them talking. Telemachus asked, "You're Raymond's brother, aren't you?"

"Yeah," the man answered flatly.

"You tell Raymond to bring back the things he took or I'm going to call the police," Telemachus told him; then he repeated it. The brother was noncommittal, said he would tell Raymond, and left after that brief exchange. It was not five minutes before another person Telemachus knew stopped in and told him that Raymond was already trying to sell the items he had taken.

From that point on, Telemachus did no more work that day. He stood in the doorway the rest of the afternoon and talked to people. Everyone he knew he told of Raymond's theft, what a bad worker Raymond was, how he had tried to pick his own work on the cars—usually the easiest things—and would not pull a transmission out or learn to repair them. He said that Raymond left at noon on Friday and did not come in on Saturday until after lunch.

An old man drove an aging and scarred Ford into the shop. He talked with Telemachus, who told him the situation with Raymond. After Telemachus finished, the man turned to me and said, "You should never do that. You should never steal from a man who is trying to help you up. Telemachus was trying to teach him a trade."

I thought that he had heard the official version from Telemachus, but I wanted to clarify my own new and uncertain position by becoming involved in this role. I said to the customer, "Raymond probably stole from him because he hired me." At least I would see how this explanation flew. The man turned away with nothing further to say, so my comment clarified nothing for me.

Not for Telemachus either. He continued to stand worriedly in the doorway, looking up and down the street, his body tense. When necessary he would instruct me in something, and I worked on, aware of his growing apprehension and all too aware of my own. As if my own feelings weren't bad enough, I had to see how worried Telemachus seemed to be. After all, he, not I, knew how the system worked. Telemachus continued to look up and down the street.

He did not speak to the children on their way home from school unless they demanded his attention. At 7:30 PM we called it quits, and Telemachus said goodbye, see you in the morning. I said good night and walked over to Eleventh Street to catch the trolley up to

Clinton. I was shaken by Telemachus's depression, lack of ease, and preoccupation. On the trolley I brooded about the day's events. The question was in both our minds: What would Raymond do next? With this kind of fieldwork I knew I would be in the action.

Instead of going directly to the apartment I stopped by the 410 Bar to see if any of the people I had met were there. I did not want to give up seeing them, although I had worked a long day and needed to write down field notes. Trip was sitting at the bar wearing dark glasses, a turtleneck dickey, a knit vest, a pair of black pants, and a sport coat that seemed a little too large for him, as if he had worn it a long time and grown thinner and thinner inside it. As I walked toward him in the bar I wondered what he would say. Saturday he had agreed to go with me on Sunday to four experimental plays by black playwrights. We were to meet at the Wagon Wheel, a hotel bar that was open on Sunday, since only hotel bars were legally permitted to sell liquor on that day. To my disappointment, Trip had not shown up, and I wondered if he would say anything about it or just begin talking as if this were a completely new situation. I wanted to participate in a wider range of black culture than that on the street corner. My mistake was trying to pry Trip from his comfortable milieu. I could not meld street life with indoor cultural life, and I came to realize that the men who lived around the bars were not an active part of the larger black cultural life of the city. After that, abandoning myself to their publicly restricted world to live within its contour, I no longer attempted to bring people even halfway into my own world of interests. Rather, I drifted knowingly, but with a personal sense of diminution, into theirs.

As I sat down by Trip, he said, "Man I missed you last night, I got there too early." He told me he had arrived early because he wanted to tell me he would not be able to go. "I didn't have the clothes for it." It was an impeccable reason not to attend the theater, though one I would not have thought of, because students, especially graduate students, did not dress up for such events. Trip's definition of appropriateness and mine were obviously not the same.

After having a beer and conversation with Trip, who asked me for bus fare home, I walked to the apartment. Karen wanted to know what had happened at the shop that day. We went out for pizza and I told her what had gone on, toward the end mentioning Raymond's theft. She was immediately concerned and asked me a lot of questions. We tried to arrive at what the theft meant, although we came to no clear understanding, and we discussed whether I should continue working there. The extent to which the situation might be dangerous was unclear to us, and my own position in the proceedings at the shop remained ambiguous. I did not seriously consider quitting the garage, but I was on edge, and I could feel a wariness deep within myself, a small but growing something, which might expand to fill the interior psychic space.

Tuesday

The next morning, Tuesday, I returned, again about eight o'clock. Telemachus arrived about ten after. There was something new that morning; I noticed it in the right hip pocket of Telemachus's blue pants. It was a long hunting knife in a leather holster. The handle stuck up out of the pocket within easy reach.

Weapons tended to be kept in the right back pocket when they were not stuck in the belt, like the pistol that the pawnshop guard had. So, Telemachus's preoccupation yesterday afternoon was turning into something; he was expecting Raymond to show. Images of what the day might bring flashed in my mind. Maybe there would be a bloody, deadly scene... where would I be in it?

I figured there was a real reason for me to be worried and asked Telemachus about the situation, but he would say nothing about what Raymond might do. There was a distant look in his eyes all morning, and he seemed to be brooding. He set me to work immediately, but the white man's transmission was left lying in pieces on the back bench as Telemachus again just toyed with things, not doing much. He either stood at the door or worked just inside it, watching the street.

A black man of about sixty with a light straw hat walked slowly into the doorway of the shop, his every move consummately casual and deliberate. Everyday he walked up one side of the street and down the other, stopping at places of business, knocking on the doors of the row houses. It was Juice, the numbers runner. Everywhere he stopped someone would give him a number and some money. He was able to remember the most perverse combinations of numbers, and because he never wrote them down, he had never been busted for numbers running. Also, he was almost invisible. I looked at his sport shirt, straw hat, slacks, and shoes. The latter were of black leather, and everywhere Juice had a corn or bunion the leather was cut out in a square. The white socks underneath made his shoes look like a surrealist's melted checkerboard. Telemachus usually played a couple of dollars on the number of his street address, 339. If it came in he would receive about eight hundred dollars, he said.

As Juice was leaving, a large black man parked a red 1972 Oldsmobile four-door sedan in the space on the street in front of the door. He slowly entered the shop and told Telemachus he had a valve problem. The man's name was Moe, and he played jazz bass in an Atlantic City band. His younger brothers were bassists in Philadelphia.

Telemachus took Moe's owner's card for the car, told him what the job would cost, and asked for a twenty-five-dollar down payment. Moe gave him the money and his keys, and Telemachus told him he could come back and pick up the car at the end of the week. Then they talked casually for a while in front of the shop while Telemachus continued to look nervously up and down the street.

Moe left at noon, and Telemachus kept standing there in the cool October air, turning his head to watch the street. I had been working halfway back in the garage, close to the radio. It was frustrating not to be a part of the conversation, and I had been too far from them to hear much of it over James Brown singing "The Popcorn." I was jerked alert when I heard Telemachus yell, "Hey! Hey, Raymond! I want to talk to you for a minute!"

I had little idea of what would happen next, so I pretended to lean under a hood while keeping my eyes on the front of the garage. Maybe Raymond would keep right on going, maybe he would come in and, being angry, pull a gun. Raymond edged just inside the door of the shop and the two of them stood etched against the light. Telemachus said to him, "I want the things back you took yesterday and I won't say anything more about it."

At this Raymond leaned over a little toward Telemachus and began to talk intensely, very fast and very low. I could catch nothing of what he said. Telemachus telegraphed his intense wariness and readiness for fast action; it took no training to read it in the stiff poise of his body. I, not sorting out my growing paranoia from anyone else's definition of the situation, had the overwhelming feeling that I was deeply implicated. In a kind of final voice Telemachus asked Raymond, "You aren't bringing the things back, then?"

"No, I'm not." Raymond replied.

Telemachus, looking him in the face and with an even, unhurried voice, said, "I'm going to have to get out a warrant for your arrest.

With your record you might have a rough time. If you'll bring back the stuff, I won't call the police. Will you bring it back?"

"No," Raymond responded, turning his head so that he was looking over the street, "go ahead and get your warrant. Do whatever you want to do. I'm not bringing the stuff back."

Raymond left, and I walked with a heavy feeling to where Telemachus was standing. Telemachus just gave a forced wry grin and shook his head back and forth. I asked him what Raymond had said when he was talking low and fast. Telemachus said even he did not catch all of it. Obviously he did not want to talk to me about Raymond, and this did nothing to alleviate my sense of impending doom. Neither of us said much the rest of the day.

By 5:30 Telemachus had functionally called it a day. He and I were sitting, pulling on Pall Malls, next to the garage on the stoop where Boycie had been sitting the previous Saturday when I had driven up to ask for the job, when a round-faced black man named Russ pulled his Mercury into the doorway. He called a familiar greeting to Telemachus, came over, and sat down, filling the stoop. He began complaining about President Nixon, whom he referred to as "your president," and then looked at me.

None of the black men who mentioned politics in the shop had kind words for Nixon, and none of them felt that they had helped elect him. Nearly every black house in South Philadelphia had a calender picture or glossies of Jack and Bobby Kennedy and Martin Luther King, Jr. They were a triumvirate of heroes and had in common their death and their death-defying rhetoric.

The phone rang, and Telemachus tiredly raised himself up to answer it. Russ and I talked a bit, the conversation drifting around to the fact that I was new there. What happened to Raymond? Russ wanted to know. He had been there last week but had quit this week, I explained, and I mentioned the theft and how Telemachus had told people what Raymond had done, figuring that telling the details in the way I thought Telemachus had was culturally acceptable. I wondered if, by my talk, I was reaching out to those still hidden, very active gossip networks and news linkages that could galvanize a whole black neighborhood instantly with newsworthy events. From the press during the rioting I knew that black areas in cities could ignite almost instantaneously, and I was certain that news traveled like light on the street. There was an active search for any news: The common greeting among men who came into the shop or met at the 410 Bar was, "Hey, what's happening, man?" or, more telegraphically, "S'appenin?"

I had been persuaded by reading Goodenough and by discussions in graduate school that if I, the anthropologist, could act like a local person and elicit appropriate responses from other people, I would know I had the rules for acting appropriately in the culture. If, for instance, people laughed at me for inappropriate behavior, I had the rules wrong. The trouble with covert life was that if I did not act like the others, I might end up visiting the coroner, and, my worry was, I might even make the trip if I *did* act appropriately. But I was in it now, and I decided to play it for all it was worth.

Russ did not react to the news of Raymond's quitting or theft in any remarkable way. He asked if I knew what Raymond was going to do, and I said I had not heard and did not know. Telemachus had been on the phone, joking and laughing with Angie, and he came back and said he and his girlfriend were going on a date Thursday night. He and Russ began talking about women, and the conversation drifted from women back to the reason Russ had come over. The left rear blinker on his Mercury did not work; could Telemachus take a look at it? Telemachus told him that Danny was a good mechanic and would look at the wires first thing in the morning. They said their goodbyes and we all left.

I walked to Eleventh Street and caught the trolley north, stepping down at Pine and walking the block over to Waverly. I felt that in the shop and bar I was becoming enveloped in a life with black people, and I was satisfied that it was happening. One result of the increasing involvement was that I felt the urge to do more than write field notes; I wanted to use other, more artistic media to capture more fully the feeling in my experiences. Before leaving Wisconsin I had thought of a poetry that might embrace something of the field experience, but once in Philadelphia I quickly abandoned the idea. Trip was, I thought, willing to be photographed, and I also wanted to paint him if I could. The 410 Bar, the bar at Ninth and Rodman where I visited, and the mouth of Waverly at Tenth Street seemed like miniature stages where people played.

As I approached the 410 I noticed Trip and Al just inside Waverly with a woman I had not seen before. I walked casually toward them, and Al made some remark to me I could not hear. The woman asked Al, "Is he a soul brother or not a soul brother?" Al did not catch her question at first. They worked it out and Al replied then, "He's a soul brother." She turned back to Al and they talked, ignoring Trip and me.

Trip, who wore the same turtleneck dickey, the same shabby coat as yesterday, asked me if I wanted a taste of *salbe* (King Solomon, a sweet wine). The bottle was wrapped in a brown bag. I took a sip and handed it back.

The woman turned to me and said, "I don't know you. My name is Jazzy."

"I'm Dan," I introduced myself. I looked at her then. She was Al's age, about thirty, quite short, and she appeared to be putting on weight, or at least her miniskirt seemed too tight through the waist. A dark wig with the ends tipped almost white covered her hair, and she wore a pair of white boots. She was a little drunk.

Al had a stick and hit her in the rear. She turned on him, grabbed him, and hugged him close in a bear hug. Al pulled himself gently away and asked me, "Would you believe this girl used to rumble with us when we were younger?"

I did not answer right away and looked closely at her face. She had a scar over her right eye and other marks. The wounds of war? "I would believe it."

I sat on the step next to Trip and had more salbe. Al did not drink with him, but Jazzy picked up a glass of wine she had carried over from the bar and took a swallow. Then she came over and sat on my lap, both legs on mine, put her arm around me, and playfully said, "Don't let me fall." She adjusted herself, made as if to fall off, and I grabbed her bare knee. I sat straight, holding onto her knee antiseptically with one hand, my other arm around her waist; she had put her arm over my shoulders.

Al turned to Trip, "Look at him, he don' know what to do." Truth is, I did know what to do. I wanted to do just what I did— nothing. To be more a part of the play I should probably have put something into motion, made like I wanted her, made her feel good about being on my lap. But to have done that I would have needed to know more than I did, so I acted like an inactive robot. I was comfortable enough not doing anything more.

Jazzy stood up and Al said he was going to Ninth and Rodman to shoot pool. He turned to me, "Do you have a *quiz* (quarter)?" I didn't have one. Then he asked Jazzy for the money.

I want to listen to records, Al; come on, fuck with me.

Look me in the eye.

Come on, fuck with me.

Now look me in the eye.

No. You'll talk me out of it.

Trip interrupted and said, "Don't go shoot pool now, let's go to the 410." We all crossed the street and went into the bar.

Later I bought wax to sculpt. I intended to use the lost wax method to make a bronze sculpture of the mouth of Waverly Street. With the wax I carved a person dancing, as if through a wall, to suggest the animation of the whole place. That winter I took the wax figure dancing its way out of its wax corner over to the 410 and talked about it with Al and Trip and some of the other men who drank there. But it did not capture what I had hoped it would, and it was not among the sculptures I had cast that year.

Wednesday

Wednesday morning I again arrived before Telemachus. At ten minutes after eight he pulled up, unlocked the garage door, and told me he would be back in a minute. He walked up to the luncheonette and bought two regular coffees. In Philadelphia that meant with cream and sugar; if one wanted nonregular coffee or black coffee, one had to ask for it specially. I set my sack lunch down on the tall wooden cabinet in the back of the shop. Telemachus's mood was no better that morning, and as I looked around the shop I noticed lying here and there (by design?) tools that could become implements of aggression, of defense, and of death. There was a brass hammer on Telemachus's back bench. Halfway down one wall, on a bench near the blanketed bathroom, lay a ball peen hammer. Near the front of the shop, on another bench, was a claw hammer with one claw broken off. These were not comforting sights. The advice I had heard—never pull a gun unless you know how to use it—applied to hammers, too. If one picked up a hammer, one had better have a good reason and be prepared to use it.

Telemachus returned to the shop carrying the coffee in a brown paper bag. He opened the bag on the end of the car next to the open door, and we stood in the doorway, as we had on Monday, drinking our coffee and chatting. Again Telemachus gave a little monologue on not discriminating along racial lines. Perhaps he was obliquely referring to Raymond; I did not know. Then, since the week was wearing on, Telemachus finally decided to tackle the Slim Jim he had torn down on the back bench and launch the skinny white man's Pontiac back into running order. He had promised it by the end of the week.

He told me to come to the back bench and he would show me

how to work on transmissions but we were interrupted by the inevitable morning phone call from Angie. After joking with her, he returned to the bench and told me that he liked to joke when he was feeling bad and that he felt a lot better. This was an obvious reference to the war of nerves Raymond was waging. After mentioning that he would have to call Frankie over at TRANSCO and ask him to bring over some new clutch bands to replace the scorched ones of the transmission, he went on to explain the special tools and showed me the basic components of the interior. The only thing I knew about them, I thought to myself, was that Lee Iacocca, then president of the Ford Motor Company, had an advanced degree in engineering and had applied it to the development of the highly complex automatic transmission.

Frankie showed up complaining that Telemachus owed him money. He said he would not give him the transmission clutches for the Slim Jim unless Telemachus paid cash right then. Things were getting hot for him at TRANSCO, and it was less and less possible to sneak off and sell TRANSCO parts. If Telemachus didn't pay him right away, it wouldn't be worth it for him to bring parts over because he was taking the risk, doing it for the money, and he needed the money or he wouldn't be doing it. Telemachus made sounds of disgust with his mouth, pulled some soiled bills from his right pocket, and paid the man. Then they began talking about other things; he wanted to borrow some of Telemachus's smokers for the weekend.

Telemachus said he could, then went over and opened the wardrobe, took out the 8mm porno films, and handed them to him. Frankie set down the girlie magazines he had been leafing through and said the boss was out of the shop and he had better be going along. Telemachus walked him to the door, telling him about Raymond on the way. I was not introduced to Frankie, and we had said nothing to one another; we barely exchanged glances. After he left, Telemachus and I went back to the bench, where he showed me how to reassemble the clutches. It was painstaking work, and Telemachus's tools were worn and not up to the job, particularly on the seals and rings.

Telemachus walked from the back bench to the tall toolbox for a pair of needlenose pliers and was pawing through the drawer when Raymond came walking into the shop. Raymond edged around Telemachus, and as he was doing it, Telemachus, caught by surprise, said to him, "This isn't between you and him, this is between you and me."

Raymond responded with a curt, "I just want to talk to him. Stay out of this." Then he stood facing me.

I was caught in a cul-de-sac. The workbench was against the rear wall, my back was to the wardrobe, and Telemachus's daughter's Valiant was up close to the back bench. I had nowhere to go except through Raymond, and he was not moving. He was also too close for comfort, and I felt the implicit menace in his closeness. Telemachus had turned to watch what was happening and was right behind Raymond, but Raymond did not even turn around to check where Telemachus was. The thought of weapons crossed my mind, but none lay that close. The more critical problem—knowing when they were necessary—it seemed to me called for split-second timing. I was beginning to think that this was a situation for words, and I hoped they would not fail me.

Raymond asked, "How do you like working for Telemachus?"

I paused before answering him and thought, *How can I cool him out?* Then I reached for a familiar mode of address, figuring that might do it. "Oh, I don't know, Babe, you know, you get your hands dirty and all. I don't mind it."

Raymond just turned around, not saying anything to that, but we all knew it had only begun. Telemachus had moved back to the tool chest and Raymond walked up to him. Before Raymond could say anything, Telemachus began to complain about all the things Raymond had stolen and how much they cost. He told Raymond that he had taken even more than he had first thought.

I stood and watched them in an cold fear. Raymond reached into his shirt pocket and pulled out a pack of Pall Malls. I took a lighter from my pocket and thought it might help if I seemed willing to communicate and be amicable. Raymond had his eyes on me and said, "I didn't ask you for a light."

Telemachus motioned me back to the bench and into the corner where the pinups grinned at me from the metal wardrobe, and Raymond dropped into that low, rapid mode of talk of which I could not pick out one word. As they talked back and forth, Raymond reached for a linoleum knife that had the hook removed and the end sharpened into a point. It was one of those tools lying around that seemed menacing by its mere presence. Then he asked Telemachus for *his* knife.

Telemachus, in a completely flat voice, asked, "What do you want to see my knife for?"

"Just let me see your knife," Raymond said, "I'm not going to do anything with it."

Telemachus pushed his hand into his right pocket and slowly withdrew his small pocketknife. He handed it to Raymond. I did not know what had happened to the hunting knife. Thank God he did not hand that to Raymond. But I thought, *Now why did he do that?* I felt like my life had just been thrown off a tall bridge and was already winging the shortest route to the hereafter. Raymond opened the knife and held it loosely in the palm of one hand. In the other he held the modified linoleum knife. Both palms were up with the knives nestled in them, a thumb holding each securely in place.

I noticed this in the infinite slow motion that seems to accompany fateful situations. With his hands poised in front of him, he walked to the corner where I was standing weaponless. Telemachus drifted in quietly behind Raymond and casually placed his hand next to the handle of the brass hammer. I did one of those rapid calculations always done in one's last agonizing moments and figured if Raymond wanted to use the knives that Telemachus, with all the speed in the world, would not have time to bash Raymond's head in with the hammer before I fell to the floor.

Raymond, who had his hands poised, the knives lying dormant but ready to burst into weapons of death, asked me, "Why did you have to answer me smart like that, using words like, 'Baby,' when all that I asked you was how you like working here?"

I replied that I did not know I was answering smart when I answered the question. "I didn't know why you asked me how I liked working here in the first place because I've only been here two days and I really don't know yet," I went on. "I didn't know what kind of answer you expected. I'm confused by this whole business."

I thought I was beyond registering shock but was not prepared for Raymond's next move. Raymond placed both knives next to me on the workbench in no particular fashion. It was not like he was suddenly going to pick them up again. "Maybe you won't be so nervous now, and you will feel more free to talk," he continued. "I'm talking to you now; I'm being honest with you."

"I'm being honest with you, too," I replied.

But Raymond was not through; he was about to pull the rug out from under the assertions of honesty I had made. "Why did you tell a man last night that they were looking all over for me?"

Even with the knives temporarily down on the bench, the terror I felt now was greater than when he had held them, and my mind went blank. I felt in that split second that I had only one option. I had to explain—no—deny I had said anything last night to Russ.

"I never said anything to a man about you," I replied, lying as smoothly as I could. I was astounded that what I had told Russ last night had come back to me already this morning. *This is what I get for acting like I belong here*, I thought. I continued, "I haven't said anything to anyone. Besides, what would I say?"

"Then the man must have lied," he replied.

I hurried on, savoring the moment of dishonesty: "Since we're being honest with each other, I want to ask you something."

Nice bit of irony.

"Okay," Raymond replied.

"I figured that you think I asked Telemachus for your job and he gave it to me." For me, this was the crux of the matter.

Raymond explained, "I told my mother that's probably what you thought. But that's not it. I like to see a man work. I can go out there and get me jobs. I have nothing against you working here."

He turned away then, leaving me to recover in the alcove made of car, workbench, and wardrobe. Raymond picked up his conversation with Telemachus, and again they discussed returning the tools and taking out a warrant on Raymond. Raymond pulled another cigarette from his rumpled pack and turned back to me.

"Do you have a light?" he asked neutrally, without rancor, or even much thought, it seemed. I was still extremely angry inside and did not understand how he could now accept the situation and request something from me when I felt like I wanted to kill him.

I brought out my lighter and lit his cigarette. Raymond turned away without a further word and started for the door with Telemachus trailing despondently after him. They talked for ten more minutes in the doorway. I decided to eat my lunch and so picked it up and walked to the front of the shop, past them and across the street to Tony's Transmissions where there was a Coke machine. I figured I might as well die on a full stomach as an empty one, but really the incident was all over. If I had known more, I would have understood the meaning of Raymond's request for a light. Little gestures made with lighting a cigarette were profound, but it was not until I witnessed a public argument that Boycie began that I would understand some of their import.

• • •

After eating, I was in the shop alone while Telemachus went around the corner to Tartacks for his lunch. A black woman there cooked platters. I could not stand the complete uncertainty about what Raymond was going to do next, and so when Telemachus returned, I asked him what had just happened. He knew I was asking for more explanation. Raymond wanted to start a fight with anyone to get rid of his own hostility, he said, and with Raymond's record he would be up for a long time if he called the police. Raymond had two brothers in jail right then. "Raymond doesn't have any sense," he told me, "and he doesn't have any friends." Then Telemachus revealed that Raymond had stolen other things from him but he had not said anything about it to him.

I was not particularly relieved to hear the details of Raymond's life. He seemed to have nothing to lose in any situation that might come up between us again. I believed Telemachus felt the same way, because he then asked me where he could buy a gun. So it was going to escalate again; I remained anxious and did not know what to think.

I told Telemachus I knew some people at a bar where I drank, and maybe they would sell me a gun. I also thought, *if I find a gun, I'm going to buy it for my own damn self*, but I did not really intend to ask Al or Trip or any of the others for a gun. I just wanted an excuse to leave the shop early and get myself together. We worked through the afternoon mostly in silence. The shop was busy. I worked in front, and Telemachus was busy at the back bench.

When I started for the trolley to go, as I had implied, to the 410 to see about buying a pistol, Telemachus said he would give me a ride. As we rode up the one-way street I could tell that he was still worried about Raymond and the effect of the incident that morning. As if to offer the good times with the bad, Telemachus asked me if I liked to dance. "I love to," I lied. Then he asked if Karen and I would go with him and Angie to a club in Jersey Saturday night. He went on to assure me that he respected the wives of his friends and thought that we would have a terrific time going out. I agreed.

I could not let Telemachus take me to Clinton Street, where I needed to go to change clothes, for that would have precipitated another kind of crisis. I would have had to explain why we lived on an elegant street, and then at some point why we wanted to live in a ghetto. Neither Telemachus nor anyone else would have bought any kind of line about my *wanting* to work as a mechanic. When I asked him to let me out on Lombard Street, he said he could take me all the way home. I said no, that I lived just around the corner, and thanked him for the ride.

Telemachus had concluded that the scene with Raymond and the knives was enough to scare me off, that I was too inexperienced to go up against someone so consummately streetwise. As I opened the door of the car, he asked, "Do you need any money?"

"No thanks," I replied, "as long as I have a dollar in my pocket I'm okay."

Telemachus figured he owed me something for the three days, and he also thought he would never see me again. He said good night, and I said, "See you in the morning."

•   •   •

On the second landing I smelled naphtha fumes. Karen and I had just bought a nineteenth-century meetinghouse bench that had once served in an auto garage located near the Delaware River waterfront. Greasy objects had apparently been stored on it, and Karen had learned that naphtha was used to remove grease from wood. As I walked into the apartment she was washing the bench over and over with the naphtha. The grease was slowly leeching out to reveal the red finish of a century earlier concealed beneath the industrial waste of this century. Yellow and green accent lines were now faintly visible.

Karen's face seemed unusually white to me, for I had looked into black faces for three days. The shock of her whiteness seemed a reversal of the more usual one—for us—of encountering black in a predominantly white context. Seeing her long, slightly reddish hair in a single braid falling over her shoulder was a jolt of familiarity but was not sufficient to break the depression I felt after the encounter with Raymond.

Karen passionately wanted the field situation to succeed and had, in the two previous evenings of the week, listened to me tell of the days in the shop, days that were dominated by the anxiety over Raymond and what he might decide to do. There was nowhere she or I could turn for reassurance, for a word from someone familiar with the situation, who could explain and place in cultural perspective what was happening. Karen had the additional weight of not knowing firsthand what it was like in the shop, and she had not met Telemachus. She worked days over the bench in an attempt to use physical activity to dispel her own mounting anxiety. In what seemed the endless job of washing half a century of grease buildup from the delicate, handmade pew, she found something to do while she thought and waited.

I did not clean the grease from myself right away, but instead turned on the tape recorder and told Karen what had happened during the day. After I was through she said she worried every time she heard a siren, wondering if it were me. I told her that I did not know if I should return or not, but as I answered her questions and we talked, I decided that perhaps Raymond had made his point and the worst was over. I did not understand the significance of his moves, the meaning of what he did. I needed more cultural context. The wariness I felt at the beginning of the week fully inhabited my psyche, mixed as it was with a continuous anxiety for Karen as well as myself.

Telemachus asked me if I liked to dance," I told her.

"What did you say? she wanted to know.

"I told him, 'I love to.' "

"What a damn lie!" she laughed. I laughed too, because I had never been allowed to dance while I had lived with my parents, and I never felt the urge to learn once I left home. It was one of those lies fieldworkers tell in order to become more involved with their informants. I told Karen we had been invited out to do the clubs in Jersey with Telemachus and Angie Saturday night, and I asked if she would go, since she had no more "done the clubs" than I had. Although she was uncomfortable with the thought, as I was, she agreed to go.

When I went to clean up, I noticed that the pores on the back of my hands had distended and filled with burnt transmission fluid, grease, and dirt. I could not scrub them clean.

• • •

Months later, in January, I overheard Telemachus and Raymond talking. Perhaps I was meant to.

Would you really have hit me with that hammer when I had those knives on him?"

"Believe it."

• • •

As I think back over the week with Telemachus and Raymond, two elements of life in the shop and locality stand out. I learned how rapidly and fatefully words traveled from person to person and returned to the utterer. I was also alerted, because of my interest in social relationships, to the nature of briefly formed local ties, if not exactly to the kind of ties between Telemachus and Raymond and myself. The three of us were locked for the better part of a week into a dramatic series of minor episodes. I began, almost unconsciously, to look for what people gave to and received from one another. Increasingly I concentrated on what went on between Telemachus and his customers, and between him and the men he hired, his friends, and his family. I became compulsive about observing the practices of social contact, for I found them far different than those I had experienced in the Midwest and not wholly like those I had read about in the anthropological literature. More to the point, I paid attention to what people were doing to one another because my own emotional and intellectual, if not physical, survival were tied to them.

At no time was it more obvious to me that ethnographers have traded on an identity made sacred by whatever means were available—a rifle across the knees during interviews, a letter from the president of the republic, or the visible, verbal, or written authority of the local gendarmes—an identity I was not privy to, though being an anthropologist meant more to me than any other self-description I could have called upon. I could not, when Raymond had me backed into the corner, say, "Excuse me, Ray, I'm really an anthropologist here to study your way of life in the ghetto, so please back off." Covert research gave me no transcendent locus from which to observe everyday life. The incessant self-privileging of the academy did not attend the identity of auto mechanic, and its absence produced in me a profound shock, not only to my assumptions about ethnography, but about the way of life entailed in such research. I began then and have continued until now to question what it is that ethnography claims to be doing and its moral impact, not only on the observer and the observed, but on the reader and the society in which the reading is done (Rose 1982, 1983, 1984, 1986).

Saturday

Raymond did not reappear either Thursday, Friday or Saturday, and Telemachus, if not relieved, began to work productively again in the shop. Saturday was by far his biggest day, for customers had received their weekly paychecks and were in the shop to have their autos repaired, if possible, in order to use them for the remainder of the weekend. It was on Saturday that Telemachus hoped to make the wages to pay his help on Saturday evening.

By seven o'clock Telemachus drove the third car into the shop and shut the overhead door. He paid me a third of what we had agreed at the beginning of the week I would be paid, which had been a dollar an hour, tax free. I had twenty dollars from him to show for a week's work. He told me to come down Sunday afternoon and he would have the rest of my wages for me. I did not consciously realize that by asking me to do so he had put into play a rather elaborate con, of which I was the mark.

Telemachus drove me to the corner of Tenth and Lombard and promised he would meet Karen and me there for our date with him and Angie at eight o'clock. Karen's notes record the events of that evening:

> Dan did not arrive at the apartment until seven o'clock and we were to meet Telemachus at Tenth and Lombard by eight o'clock. Rushed to say the least. While we were getting dressed I realized that actually this would be the first time Telemachus would see Dan "dressed up." That is, in something besides Levis and a blue work shirt. Dan's first meeting with Telemachus was in the same outfit. Now he wore this costume to work. Dan put on a corduroy jacket, blue wash-and-wear pants, shoes with a buckle, and a blue shirt. The usual college outfit (conservative) except for a mod tie. My outfit was not important as girls from all classes dressed like I did. We met Telemachus at eight o'clock. He was late and seemed to be rushed. We sat in the front seat and exchanged pleasantries of introduction. He smelled very fragrant. One of the first things Telemachus said was, "Dan brought me luck," I didn't know how to take it and said, inappropriately, "Everyone who knows Dan likes him." Eventually, we found, however, the "luck" happened to be that he won at numbers. His number 339 had come up that day and he was going to win money because of it.
>
> Dan expressed his ignorance of how the numbers operated, and I expressed my curiosity to find out. It would have probably been difficult to avoid some kind of an answer, but he did not seem to mind telling us, now that we had asked how it worked. He did warn us good naturedly not to tell anyone. Two things stand out about his explanation. One, the Senators make the decision as to the winner in some established manner and Telemachus did not ever want to find out who his Senator was. He related an incident of how a girl who was on the level of knowing and working as a secretary for the Senators wanted to quit the numbers racket. Six months after she quit, she was discovered floating in the Schuylkill River. "No, man, I don't wanna know."
>
> Two, the manner in which he chose his number: He said,

"You choose some number you 'like.' " He had been playing his house number 339 for either one or two years and finally he won today.

For some reason he did not mention the amount he won. Maybe he did not know exactly; perhaps he did not want us to know. He had not been able to pay Dan but twenty dollars for his week's work. But he was not going to brag about the amount. We did not ask either. Actually he did not have the cash in his hand.

He told of his son who left Philadelphia with sixty dollars in his pocket, went to New York, and played the horses. He came back with two thousand dollars. He seemed proud of his son for being successful at the horses.

We drove to the north side of Market Street and parked the car. That is where we met Angie. I walked in first to the little diner and saw one booth with only one person in it. I took it that it was Angie and waited by the booth. She did not look at me. Dan and Telemachus came in and we sat down. Dan had already met Angie and he introduced me. Angie, it seemed to me, avoided an eye confrontation with me. The one thing she was occupied with was that Telemachus was late. In the several conversations that went on she kept returning to the subject that she was "through waiting." Telemachus tried to suppress her whinings with, "Baby, let's forget about it now and have a good time."

"Don't ruin our evening." He was not severe with her in front of us and said it smiling, sort of appeasing her with a good-natured smile. He was ready to forget and have a good time during the evening.

Telemachus had planned on getting a little lunch at the diner. But since Dan and I had just eaten we told him that we would get a cup of coffee while he ate. Angie noticed that we were relatively dressed up and remarked how she "didn't dress tonight." We all individually assured her that she looked quite all right. I said I only had a skirt and blouse on and so did she.

"Yeah, but this is nothing," she answered.

"All you have to be is yourself; be who you are. It doesn't matter what anybody else thinks," Telemachus said. She did not really seem to dig what he said nor could she feel comfortable with what she had on no matter what we told her. Angie repeated two or three times that she was not going anyplace tonight. It seemed that she did not know we were actually going "out" tonight. He just ignored her when she said that, although he heard well what she said. He said to her a couple of times, "Let's not spoil a nice evening."

Telemachus did not order a lunch. We all only had coffee. Then out of the clear blue Telemachus said, "I thought we would all go out for lobster." That was music to my ears and I jumped to second the motion.

Angie then asked me to go to the bathroom with her. When we got there she invited me into the toilet part. She proceeded to clue me in. I said very little, but here are relics of hers:

I don't know what he wants with me tonight; he knows I'm bleedin'. . . .

I'm not waitin' anymore. For two or three months I've sat in here and waited for two or three hours. He'd say eight o'clock and not show up until ten or even midnight. But no more, buddy. It's too late. If he really cared for me he'd be here on time. And this is only the second time he's dressed for me. Usually he comes in his clothes from the garage. Now it's not because he's a Negro or because he's married, but if he really cared . . .

I'm not really dressed to go out. You should see me when I really dress. Don't tell him, but this guy I met at the mountains, I'm writing to. Last year when I met this guy I told him I was going steady and couldn't write to him. This year I'm writing. Just got a letter two weeks ago from him and he really cares. It's just too late.

Don't say anything to Telemachus. I've been going with Telemachus fifteen months and he's only dressed twice. He doesn't mean anything to me.

After returning to the table we decided to leave.

The ride over to Jersey was more of Angie telling him she was through waiting. One phrase of Telemachus's was memorable. "Once I've found what I want, Baby, I knows it." Dan and I had no idea where we were going. Telemachus said he did. Angie did not seem to care.

We drove into a typical middle-class, vacation-type restaurant. As we drove in Angie said, "We can't go in there, my nephew works there."

"You're kidding!" Telemachus replied.

"No, really, he works in there." It turned out she was faking; we all went in.

It was obviously a white-dominated restaurant. In fact, Telemachus was the only black in the whole place. We were quite

visible in our entrance but the waitress was extremely nice.
That surprised me. Perhaps her desire for tips was more important. She carried on conversation with all of us and especially Telemachus, for he talked with her quite a bit.

Telemachus did not bother to look at the menu but the rest
of us did and Dan and I noticed the prices. I immediately figured out what it would cost the two of us to eat there. We all
ordered lobster. Angie asked me to go into the bathroom with
her again; she said she wanted to wash her hands. It was more
of the same. When we came out she remarked how she had
forgotten to wash her hands. Telemachus remarked to Dan
while we were in the bathroom that he was happy to see Angie
and myself getting along so well. Angie, he said, did not have
many people to talk to.

The meal was delicious and we talked constantly. Our conversation centered for quite a while on being black: black music, how Tom Jones was made popular through the Harlem
Negroes, Negro communication networks, Telemachus's solu-
tion to the generation gap: "I takes time to talk to my children. We communicates." I was curious as to how he was hip
to so many youth-centered problems. How he knew all the
things he was telling us, about Tom Jones, etc. Although he
was fuzzy on the answer, it seemed that he had relatives in
Harlem and he talked with his children.

Telemachus was saying how some people refer in a slander-
ous way to Negroes by speaking of "them." He was sensitive to
discrimination in that form. In other words, talk that is
shrouded by vague reference to Negroes, ambiguous terms
used which everybody knows the meaning of. It is evidently
easier to say "them" than to say "Negroes." We laughed at his
telling of a call-in radio show host who made callers come out
and say who they meant by "them."

Angie obviously unaware of what we were saying mentioned,
"Well, its true since THEY got their freedom some of THEM
take advantage of it." Telemachus said, "You don't say, *them.*"
Angie is dumb. She wasn't sensitive enough to Telemachus to
catch what he was saying.

When the waitress brought us the check, Telemachus looked
at it, handed it to Dan, and asked Dan if he were seeing right.
Dan said, "Yes." The rest of us had known what it would cost
because we had read the menu and prices. Telemachus ordered lobster because that was what he had come for. He did

not look at the menu seriously. I do believe he opened it up but obviously did not focus his eyes on what it said. He already knew what he wanted. The bill was twenty-six dollars. Telemachus asked Dan for his money. Dan gave him the twenty dollars that Telemachus had paid Dan for the week's work. Telemachus paid the bill. Dan's part of the bill would have been around thirteen dollars. But when Telemachus gave Dan his change from the twenty Dan had given him, Telemachus only gave Dan four dollars in return. The conclusion was that Telemachus had to use some of Dan's money as he did not have enough. Nothing was mentioned to Dan that he did not have enough money, however, at the time of receiving the check at the table or paying the cashier. It was all carried off very smoothly. Not until we got in the car did Telemachus mention that he had eaten there before and thought it was much cheaper. But still he had not said anything to Angie or myself about being short of money. I did not know what had happened until we were home and Dan told me about Telemachus coming up short.

On the way out Angie and I again went to the bathroom. Nothing significant happened. But Dan and Telemachus confronted white glares. People, at least one couple, tried to discipline the black-white date by obvious stares of disapproval. Dan deliberately turned and talked to Telemachus directly and ignored what had happened. As we left the door to go outside, Telemachus asked if we had noticed what happened. Telemachus was gentle about the whole event but was sensitive, very much so, that it had happened.

Dan and I did not know what to expect for the rest of the evening. Telemachus suggested that tonight we would drive by the clubs that we were going to go to but couldn't go to because we were broke. He would show them to us tonight and we would go to them some other night. It was a rather long drive but he showed us several clubs all located almost across the street from one another, Cotton Club, etc. I don't remember the other names. As Telemachus drove, Angie played the radio. She commented over and over how she liked the hit tunes. She mentioned how Telemachus got a kick out of her when she moved and danced to the records. She also mentioned how much she liked to hear her name said. She liked the sound of *Angie*. She liked Telemachus to say it and she liked the boss at work to have to call her more than once so she could hear the sound of her name.

It was eleven thirty. Telemachus asked Dan if he wanted to go home. Dan said he was tired. We pulled up beside Angie's car. She asked Telemachus, "What do you have in mind?" I wondered what it was all about. Telemachus said, "I thought we'd go up and get married." (I think if I were in her boat I'd jump at the chance. She seemed a mess.) Dan knew what was going on. I knew nothing. (I think: Did Telemachus get a divorce and no one knew about it? Can you just get married in Pennsylvania without any blood tests? Would Dan and I be the witnesses?) Angie asked, "What would they do while we got married? Telemachus said something like. "I could take them home." Angie said she did not want to get married tonight.

Finally we decided to go home. And Angie almost insisted that she take us home. Telemachus agreed to go along with her decision. She gave Dan her car key and we went and sat in her car while she stayed and talked for five minutes. Angie took us home. Some of the conversation:

"Telemachus owes me a lot of money. You wouldn't believe how much. I only gave the money to him because I felt sorry for him and his family."

She had told me that before in the bathroom, only the amount Telemachus now owed her had skyrocketed.

"Telemachus means nothing to me...."

A "colored" woman came into the garage when Angie was also there. The colored lady, Mrs. Jackson, told her to stay away from Telemachus. She told the woman that he "didn't mean anything" to her, she could have him. The colored woman had some kind of weapon. She threatened Angie with it. I don't know whether the woman actually pretended she would use it on Angie or not. But Angie said she didn't act scared. She said her father had always told her, "Never show fear to a nigger." Never let them know you're scared.

Angie said I should come over and play records with her someday.

Monday

Sunday afternoon I went down to the shop for my back pay. Telemachus looked up from a car he was working on and we chatted for a few minutes. Then he told me that he could not collect

6. *Telemachus, Angie, Karen, and Dan at a cotton club in New Jersey. At these clubs it was common for a person with a Polaroid camera to come to the table and take a photograph to sell to the customers as a souvenir of the evening. (Photograph by the club photographer)*

his winnings from hitting his number. They told him he would have to wait until Monday.

When I went to work on Monday he said, "I'm mad." He told me that he did not win at the numbers after all, even though his number had come in Saturday. "They told me I only played it three ways and that the winner had to play it six ways." Telemachus contended that he had played the number six ways for months. Later in the afternoon he complained how it churned his stomach that he had been cheated at his win. He had never let people who cheated him get away when he was younger, he told me, adding some fearful stories about his revenge on people who had done him wrong.

I had been hustled. Not only had Telemachus hustled me by not paying me my wages, but I had been hustled for much of our dinner on Saturday night. I had four dollars to show for a sixty-hour work week. And, deeply submerged in a play I did not understand, *I did not know that I had been hustled.*

What I had experienced that week but had not comprehended was what can happen after a long series of unsuccessful exchanges, like those between Raymond and Telemachus. A kind of negotiation of grievances went on. I had also experienced, but not at the conscious level, a most mundane feature of the local everyday economy, what I am calling the hustle, because that is how it was referred to.

A hustle occurred when a person who had promised to pay failed to deliver as promised. The lack of payoff was usually obscured, as it had been on Saturday night, by words or by some other situation, as if either words or situation might satisfy the person who had come up short. The hustler might create a triumphant theft or a personal vulnerability or both. With Telemachus, the hustle of my wages, the con about his hitting the numbers, was the making of a vulnerability, for he placed himself in my debt. He created a line of credit with me; he owed me. I could, if I knew how to play the game, acquire what I needed from him. And indeed I did. I did not realize that *my* hustle, the bald if reluctant manipulation of my identity, had been met precisely with his own. And I also did not realize that my voracious demand for information just to get along on a day-to-day basis was part of an exchange system. In a sense, what I demanded in terms of verbal advice, I lost or payed for in terms of money. I never received full pay at any one time in the nearly two years that I worked either steadily or intermittently for Telemachus. But at the same time he would help me do things I needed done and would ask nothing immediately in return, as when I needed the engine of my car rebuilt.

If I did not request my wages from him or force or hustle him into repaying or partially paying for a social occasion, I made a thief of him. At first I easily made a thief of him by not claiming what was rightfully mine. Raymond, from this perspective, might well *not* have been a thief in that, if he figured Telemachus owed him, he had to *take* what he was due. If he had not done so, *Telemachus would have stolen from him*, because Telemachus owed him back wages, just as he did me. I can argue the point this way because Telemachus *did not call the police, though on the surface he was justified in doing so.*

In a metaphysic of local morals, I could claim that all contact between men, at the 410 or at the garage, was based on the hustle. Each party to a transaction promised more than he gave, each party felt wronged, each then had a justifiable, continuing claim against the other. Each had been issued a line of credit against which he felt justified in demanding from the other some redress. If I were to extend this local metaphysic to the entire country, to black-white relations, then I would have to argue that blacks felt that they were owed, for the long duration of slavery, for the essential and nurturant services they had rendered for whites, and for the failed promise of the American Dream. They knew they were owed, and the way in which they made political claims reflected the underlying metaphysic of America having placed itself in their debt. Through the 1960s they required a payback.

Sexual Economy

Angie, forty years old, still lived at home with her adoptive mother in a two-story house, two rooms deep, in the Italian-American section of South Philadelphia; her step-father was dead. She worked as a clerk at a large discount store, Atlantic Thrift, in southwest Philadelphia. When Angie's green 1957 Chevrolet Biscayne four-door developed transmission problems, she took the car to TRANSCO, where she met Telemachus. TRANSCO was located on the edge of black and white neighborhoods and employed both black and white workers. It was two blocks from the Italian Market, an open-air produce and meat market that stretched north and south along eight blocks of Ninth Street and pierced a band of black residential space stretching between the Schuylkill and Delaware Rivers. With its old-world air, the market was by far the most picturesque and, to the non-Philadelphian, interesting feature of South Philadelphia. The last time I drove through the market a black bear, quite dead, lay stretched over a wooden box behind one of the vegetable stalls.

At TRANSCO Telemachus engaged Angie in prolonged conversation. He told her about his family, how his wife refused to support his ambition to open his own transmission ship. Apparently Angie borrowed sixteen hundred dollars, or two thousand, or twenty-four hundred—the figure varied in the telling—and helped Telemachus capitalize the garage. To launch the business, he needed first of all an enclosed space off the street in which to pull and repair transmissions, and he needed oils, fluids, greases, specialized equipment, jacks, and all-purpose tools.

It was critical to find an appropriate location for the shop. Apparently he had been what was called a *jackleg mechanic*, one who worked on the street, doing pickup work for friends and neighbors in his spare time. In Telemachus's current residential area in West Philadelphia, however, and on his street in particular, doing mechanical work in front of his house was not possible. He lived on a quiet street, solidly middle-class in appearance. The neighbors were very active in making sure there were no crippled autos on the street, no debris out front, nothing stored on the porches, no loud music playing (according to the complaint of one of his daughters), and they constantly attempted to have the local, street-corner bar closed because it threatened the restrained collective image of the immediate area. If Telemachus wanted to be an entrepreneur, he could not be one on his property, as is common in small-town or rural America. Spaces owned by the urban working-class in Eastern cities, because they are small and restricted as to use by ordinance, militate against a number of semi-skilled and skilled, home-based economic activities.

Telemachus chose wisely in finding a location for his shop two blocks from TRANSCO. He knew the area and some of the local people, and it was close enough to Angie's residence and racially integrated enough visually (at least to a casual observer) to enable him to maintain easy contact with her. Fourteenth Street was a street of both black and white: a white business area during the day, a black residential area after working hours. The intersection of Fourteenth and Carpenter contained a bar, a boy's suit factory, an auto glass replacement shop, and a check-cashing establishment. Black people lived upstairs over each of the businesses, but not over the factory, which had no residential quarters.

The black businesses of the immediate area, unlike the white, were largely hidden from view. Those visible included hotels, bars, barbershops, churches, and one Model Cities office, which ran neighborhood social programs. Hidden from view were black numbers banks, speakeasies, single-room rentals, boarding houses, cooks who sold food from their home kitchens, handymen, jackleg mechanics, and hustlers of all sorts.

On the horizon, surrounded by black residences and contrasting in symbolic standing with the Italian Market, stood the Martin Luther King, Jr., Plaza. Even my adventurous friends told me that it was too dangerous to go inside it, and they would not accompany me when I wanted to look it over. I believed them and so never went in. The patrolmen walked in groups of five. The plaza was a monument to national and urban public housing policy; the Italian Market, physically less monumental, was a transformed remnant of southern European social organization devoted to the pursuit of wholesale and retail trade.

Eleventh and Twelfth streets formed a boundary between worlds: the latter was black, the former white. Walking from one to the other was like crossing the Mediterranean, for Twelfth Street had its history in West Africa, Eleventh Street its history in southern Europe. The differences were inscribed in the urban form. The distinctive ways of life there were not marked merely by dark skin and light skin. In the black section there were almost no retail or wholesale businesses, nor were there any black manufacturing firms. On white Eleventh there were publicly visible small and large businesses—a beer distributor, food and housewares stores, night-clubs, a ravioli factory in an old bank building, a meat packing and distribution plant, restaurants, gas stations, suit factories, a cheese and milk processing plant, a coal yard and heating oil distributor, and an awning factory. During the period of fieldwork, the contrast between immigrant business successes and a notable absence of comparable Negro success became, in Eugene P. Foley's review of black enterprises in Philadelphia (1966), part of a national discussion (see also Drake and Cayton 1962: 109; Glazer 1969; Rein 1969).

If the first contrast in the area was between black and white and the second was between few incorporated businesses and many businesses, the third was between outdoor public life and indoor corporate life, a bifurcation of everyday life. Black everyday life was consummately public and verbal, as could be seen in the way Raymond confronted me with what he had heard I had said. White cultural life was conducted more in private, behind closed doors, and local business was an integral part of the whole corporate economy of the capitalist national system. The people of European descent lived wholly within a capitalist economy; those of African descent around Telemachus's garage tended to employ a pre-cap-italist, face-to-face mode of exchange.

Telemachus found a place to rent from Tony Antonini, an en-trepreneur who had started up a series of businesses on Fourteenth Street. He tried to create a tiny mafia within which to launch his enterprises. I say *mafia*, not because Tony was necessarily connected to a ruling South Philadelphia mafia family, but because he used the principle of organization recognizable as a mafia: In addition to money payments he used fleshly rewards—women and other favors of many kinds—to bind the men he hired to him, and he coupled this with the threat of systematic and violent reprisal if someone failed him. He had opened a transmission repair shop managed by a black man, Jess; an auto glass replacement shop managed by an Irish-American, Tommy; and a property rental firm and whorehouse managed by himself. Since the businesses were not at that time very profitable, he also worked nights as a forklift operator in a warehouse on the waterfront. In the morning he drove his dark blue Cadillac to his office and made sure everything was in order for the day. Telemachus rented the space next to Tony's office, right across the street from Tony's transmission shop.

In keeping with my covert inquiry of black life, I was polite to Tony but otherwise avoided him. He did not seem inquisitive when I began working for Telemachus in October. Karen and I had a few white friends but did not want to jeopardize our involvement with black people by identifying and associating with too many whites, including local ones. Our white friends and acquaintances were all from outside the area. Before we moved east Karen had known a man who lived on Philadelphia's Main Line; we became friendly with him and his family. In the apartment next to ours on Clinton we were friendly with a young couple from Baltimore; he was a student of optometry. Our colleagues at the University of Pennsylvania remained distant, for Goffman wanted us in the field and did not want the fieldwork diluted by our associating with the university community. When he was conducting covert inquiry on the Shetland Islands, posing as an agricultural expert, he wrote his advisors at the University of Chicago to request that he be permitted to travel to Edinburgh to meet A. R. Radcliffe-Brown. He obliquely noted the fact that he did not secure their approval in the dedication to his book *Relations in Public*. Whether his own history of fieldwork motivated him to help isolate us, I do not know, but it seemed that he did so.

John Szwed, as director of the Center for Urban Ethnography, sponsored several conferences we attended during fieldwork which stimulated thought. With the readings he suggested, I interrogated black life, insofar as possible, for elements of historical continuity. Karen and I spent most of two years living and associating on the street in black residential space. We hosted some friends, mostly white, and relatives; one black couple visited us, as did my brother, a poet friend and his wife and daughter, and a few others.

After our conversation with Goffman, Karen and I began looking for housing in a black neighborhood. White real estate agents did not want to show us their black rentals, most of which were abysmal. The tiny rooms that the men from the 410 rented on a week-by-week basis on Pine Street had peeling, ugly green or yellow paint, vermin, the cheapest furniture available in English-speaking North America, and filthy toilets that were shared with other renters. White slumlords would not let us see these sorts of places. As I

Figure 3. This perspective looks north on Fourteenth Street toward Center City Philadelphia. To the right, beyond the bar, is a block of houses owned by Tony. The east-west street intersecting Fourteenth Street is Carpenter. The building on the immediate left without windows is a boy's suit factory. Across on the northwest corner is a check cashing establishment. Tony also owned the shop and buildings just beyond. The tallest building on the horizon is located in Center City, while the large building with the fire tower on the roof to the left, just a block away, is the Martin Luther King, Jr., Plaza. Computer drawing.

worked for Telemachus over the winter, I began to understand how involved Tony was in the real estate of the area of Fourteenth and Carpenter streets. Karen and I had not had much luck in October finding housing, so I mentioned to Tony that when he had an apartment available we would like to rent it. His first response was positive: he would rent to us. His second response was vaguely threatening: if I had anything going he wanted a piece of it, he said. To this I simply said I had nothing going. I am not sure that he believed me because he took me around to impress me with how well connected to the police he was—which rumor on the street, in a sense, verified—and what a good time he could have: he took me to a tiny nightclub where an old comedian told ethnic and sexual jokes while we had a drink.

In February an apartment above Tony's office became available, and Karen and I visited Tony's office together. It was a small room with a desk, a file cabinet, and an overstuffed couch. A door opposite where we came in, as we later learned, was the entrance to his sporting parlor. Tony gave us a tour of the upstairs apartment. A dark stair ended on the second story in a narrow hallway, off of which a back room, a kitchen and bath connected, a front room, and another stair to the third floor. There were five rooms plus the bathroom, all unfurnished.

I was very pleased we would be living next to the shop because I liked the compactness and proximity of living and working space. Our furniture was in Madison and we were not inclined, for reasons of time and cost, to drive out and get it. Besides, like ethnographers in some foreign country, we both perceived our location as temporary. We bought some used furniture at Fortieth and Market streets in an old bank building. A three-hundred-pound white man was seated, it seemed permanently, with a cigar in his mouth and a pistol stuck in his belt, dealing with customers and directing young black men where to move things and what to carry. I felt as if I were on some wild, uncharted frontier.

When Tony put his sporting parlor in full swing on weekends, our second-floor back room was unusable because the highly amplified music in the space below penetrated the room as if there were no floor in between. I used it to store art supplies and other items. The front room became a bedroom-sitting room, and the third floor remained undeveloped except for its front room, in which I put the typewriter, fieldnotes, and several books.

My field notes, upon which I now rely as memory, as supportive text underlying and, importantly, making possible this writing,

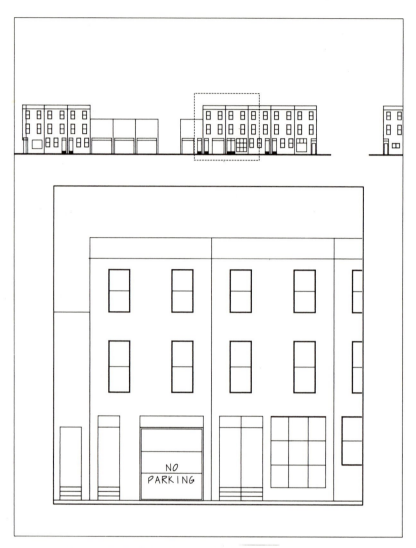

Figure 4. The NO PARKING sign is printed on the door to Telemachus's shop. A woman and her children lived just above the shop. The first doorway to the right of the garage door is the entrance to our second- and third-floor apartment. The second doorway to the right of the shop is the entrance to Tony's office and sporting parlor. Computer drawing.

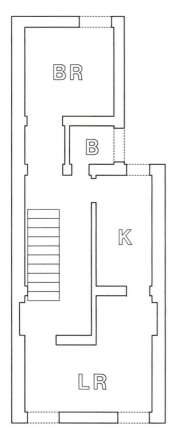

Figure 5. This is the floor plan of the second floor and was the space we used, particularly the living room and the kitchen. Computer drawing.

were not a docile genre. There were at least three parts to them, in a sense, three subgenres. The first was documentation, a descriptive narrative like that I imagined other ethnographers had done, for I had never seen another's field notes. Perhaps the field documentation was a logical extension of note taking in seminars in graduate school: get down the main points and as much detail as possible. On my five-by-eight-inch cards I recorded mainly conversations I was in, conversations I overheard, and economic exchanges and encounters I could witness in the shop. I also wrote down new words and phrases, as well as greetings and partings between others, and I constructed logs of life in the shop and on the street. The logs were bare-bones temporal frames, not quite stories. The cards documented talks I had with Afro-Americanists, conferences attended while in the field, television shows by and about blacks, talks with advisors, and newsworthy events in both the nation and in Philadelphia. I drew pictures of the floor plans of bars and diagrams of social spaces; sketched, photographed, sculpted, and documented my own reactions to people and social situations; and described public behavior and clothing. I also kept a card on each person and family in an effort to build an understanding of who was connected to whom and in what ways.

The second subtext, unselfconsciously entered like documentation, ran parallel to the first. It contained the language of the textually informed domination of experience, the language of expertise, the ethnographer's terms of art, the academic register, the lexicon of the academy, the nouns we believed connected directly to thought and to our notions of culture and society.

To *write* about October (working in the shop, the encounter with Raymond), I must reread my field notes and Karen's account of our date with Telemachus and Angie. To write now I must *read* October as I wrote it then. On the cards I mentioned the names of authors I was drawing upon in my effort to make sense of the way I was thinking about how people lived their lives. I now use the literature I read in graduate school to query the field notes, even as I had on the evenings I had written them. For example, I wrote on the first of February, "I noticed that the concept of sincerity is lacking in interpersonal relationships. Lies and honesties seem to come out the same way. However there is so much going on besides the lie that I wonder if it's right to talk this way. See David Riesman's concept of sincerity in *The Lonely Crowd*."

The third subtext contained my practical speculation and efforts to explain. "I wonder what black children and adults conceive as their spatial domains in the city," I questioned on a notecard the first day I worked for Telemachus. I reflected on the temporal fabric of everyday life, the local social organization, the local idea of what it meant to be human, how to translate from their experience of life to academic language, what the economic transaction schemes were, and what the models of the actor or course-of-action types were (Schutz 1962). I set agendas for what I ought to do and look for, tried to establish patterns, and speculated about peoples' social lives—in other words what we in the academy call *hypothesis formation*. Later, while writing the dissertation, I developed two more boxes of notecards. One contained analyses of the field notes in the original box, and the other contained notes I took on books and articles I read. I intended to outline the dissertation and then mix and match the cards as needed in order to write.

The field text, doubling as *documentation* and as *inquiry* informed by the academic literature, shaped what as an ethnographer I was to observe, act like, write down, and think, *for the profession*. My writings reveal contact between the culture of ethnographers and the culture of Fourteenth and Carpenter. The one internalized the other through prose. As a direct result of the concealed nature of the work, I could not overcome the anxiety that my field notes were not usable as subtext for the standardized genres of scholarly articles, the dissertation, or a book. Nothing fit together adequately. I felt alienated from ethnographic practice even while attempting to master it. My larger concern, one that seemed to logically follow the other anxieties, was the course my career might then take, for careers in the academy are literature-dependent.

• • •

After Angie loaned the money to Telemachus, whether she knew it or not, she entered his economic system, temporal order, and mode of substantive and always theatrical exchange. She now had to manage the credit line she had extended, and he had to manage the payback. Their definitions of *economy* were, I believe, vastly different and yet touchingly compatible.

The sexual economy, in opposition to a capitalist economy, tended always to obscure indebtedness by generalizing it. Apparently operating entirely outside a strict pricing system, it prevented the placement of an exact value on who owed what. A capitalist exchange is usually reducible to a money value placed on goods, services, communications, labor, and other media. Between Telemachus and Angie, however, the firm values associated with double-entry ledger accounting became muddled.

Angie, by entering into an exchange relationship with Telemachus, now had to collect on her debt. Several notable features of her situation emerged. She could not collect in kind, that is, money, because Telemachus converted the medium of exchange from money to other things, and he continuously redefined the terms of his payback. She also had to manage his return. There was no explicit or implicit payback *schedule* he had to meet, so she was forced to show up at the shop and request a return if she expected to receive one. Angie either requested or received what Telemachus had to offer: repairs on her auto; sexual favors; sociable occasions, such as the date with Karen and me; and money. The money, however, was never paid in large increments; the payments were never in the hundreds of dollars, but rather were a fourth of that at most. Frustrated at having received no substantial monetary payback, more than a year after the initial loan, Angie apparently threatened to collect the money by alerting a gang of men related to the women from whom she originally borrowed the money. They, she claimed, would cause bodily harm to Telemachus if he did not return the loan in money payments. The threatened mayhem never materialized.

Telemachus as debtor managed the loan repayment through the conversion of money to other forms that he considered a return. His major strategy was simply to string out the payback as long as possible through stalling and media conversion. When Angie appeared on Thursday evenings, he invariably had little money: it was a bad day, some expense had come up, a customer did not show up with a payment, and so on. He used an array of convincing but fictional reasons why he could only pay a little at a given time, if anything at all. In the hustle, the hustler always attempted to shift the burden of the repayment to the lender, usually through fictive means. It was invariably up to the lender to collect as best he or she could. This necessary strategy led to hard feelings. Note that this system of exchange created instant credit, bad feelings, long-term contact, and a lack of trust. The street exchanges were not the good-faith contracts of the ideal capitalist mode; instead they depended on one's ability to acquire what one was owed, though the process was frustrating, difficult, and even personally expensive in terms of time spent.

If one remained unsatisfied with the course of return by one's debtor, one could sue through an argument in public or, in cases of extreme dissatisfaction, engage in secret reprisal by damaging the other's property in some material way but remaining unseen in doing so. Some types of theft were themselves legitimated, as was Raymond's, in this way.

•   •   •

Telemachus had, at this same time, a black woman friend, Mary Jackson, from whom he had also borrowed money. On our first double date Angie had told Karen she had been warned by her father never to show fear to a nigger. She was referring to the confrontation she had had with Mary Jackson on Wednesday, the same day that Raymond had confronted me with the knives. While it is convenient to analyze economic and social relationships, as well as speech acts, in dyads, life is far more complex, and the economy of the street, the hustle, was indeed a complicated form of exchange involving many people simultaneously; one could imagine the entire neighborhood so connected. What Angie came to realize was that Telemachus had indebted himself to Mary Jackson in exactly the same way (though for a lesser amount) he had to her. Both Mary and Angie suddenly discovered they were competing for *the same scarce resources*. Mary used their face-off, in which she at least implicitly threatened Angie by means of a weapon, to secure the advantage for herself. If indeed she could scare Angie away, there would be, potentially, better paybacks for her.

The larger point is that Telemachus had a number of demands on his scarce resources: he owed Tony weekly rent on the shop; he owed wages to his help; he had to pay utilities, expenses for parts and supplies, and support for his household; and he owed his creditors, Angie and Mary Jackson. His strategy to manage his payout was in keeping with the form of the hustle: pay a portion, promise the remainder. He was, as a result, always in arrears to everyone. He owed Tony back rent for the space, thus effectively hustling Tony; he never paid his help the full weekly wages at one time; and he never scheduled repayment of Angie or Mary in money. I do not know how he managed the flow of money from the shop to his household; that remained strictly private and I could not acquire a firm idea of its magnitude or frequency. My feeling is that he did not have much to take home.

Multiple obligations meant multiple indebtedness. The hustle that provided temporary advantage also brought with it the re-payment tactics played out over relatively long periods of time. These obligations also meant there could be no savings; the possibility of saving money seemed remote if not, in this system, far-fetched.

Auto Culture

"I think," wrote Roland Barthes of the new Citroen DS, "that cars of today are almost the exact equivalent of the great Gothic cathe-drals: I mean the supreme creation of an era, conceived with pas-sion by unknown artists, and consumed in image if not in usage by a whole population which appropriates them as a purely magical object" (1972:88).

From its inception the automobile has been an object of desire. This supreme creation of an era is indeed gothic, rather than clas-sical or arabesque; the cultural geography of its origin lies in the American interior, the Upper Midwest (see Davenport's comments on the contrastive geographical sources of the American imagi-nation, 1981). From the same region as the farmlands, the auto drew on an agrarian people's love of machinery and experience with it. The auto was not born of the city but was delivered to it. At first, Americans associated the auto with speed. Opposed to it, representing slowness, was the horse. By 1987 the auto, no longer appreciated in terms of speed, was contrasted with the airplane.

If the automobile is the supreme creation of a mechanical age and a purely magical object, it is also a part of the system of signs that makes up contemporary culture (Barthes 1967:28–29). Autos, ranked by price and ordered by make, exist in a large, coded domain. Between the exoticar, such as a Lamborghini Countach, and the most basic Nissan Sentra Standard, are numerous levels that for the consumer identify social values.

The importance of the automobile in contemporary culture is due to the fusion of necessity and cultural values (Sahlins 1976:chap. 5). The auto is a quintessential feature of everyday life; indeed it typifies the quotidian of capitalism by making large physical and cultural ambiance readily available, by being a necessity for travel to work and leisure, by being marketed by sophisticated agencies, by being an object like food, of nature and culture simultaneously, by changing rapidly so that change itself informs one's sense of the object, and by being meaningful and expressive of one's identity. It is connected to oneself while linked to the all-encompassing cultural system of signs.

Art, speed, personalization, and democratization coalesce in the use of the automobile, but the very characteristics that imbue the object with significance ensure a continual transformation of everyday life (Silk 1984). Part of that transformation results from the uses of the auto, uses that themselves continuously organize and reorganize social relationships.

• • •

The significance of and preferences in automobiles among the black customers of Telemachus's garage and the men and woman on the street who owned cars, were not reflected precisely among middle-class Americans or white lower-class cohorts. There is an interesting story told of the indirect but powerful influence black preferences exerted in keeping alive the General Motors line of Cadillac automobiles. During the Great Depression

> Cadillac could not sell its high-priced cars at all and was about to be liquidated. The only question was whether it would be abandoned altogether or whether the nameplate should be kept alive, with the majority of the GM executive committee,

including Alfred Sloan and Donaldson Brown, in favor of giving it up. It was then that Nick Dreystadt—whom none of the members had ever met—gate-crashed the meeting of the executive committee, pleaded to be given ten minutes, and presented a plan for making Cadillac profitable again within eighteen months. And he did so by marketing it as a "status symbol." In charge of Cadillac service throughout the country, Dreystadt had come to realize that the Cadillac was the most popular car in the very small community of wealthy Negroes. An amazing number of big new Cadillacs brought in for service were owned by black entertainers, black boxers, black doctors, black realtors. It was company policy not to sell Cadillacs to Negroes—the Cadillac salesman aimed at the white "prestige" market. But the wealthy Negro wanted a Cadillac so badly that he paid a substantial premium to a white man to front for him in buying one. Dreystadt had investigated the unexpected phenomena and found that a Cadillac was the only success symbol the affluent black could buy; he had no access to good housing, to luxury resorts, or to any other of the outward signs of worldly success. And so Dreystadt, in the depths of the Depression, set out to save Cadillac by developing the Negro market—and sold enough cars to make the Cadillac division break even by 1934. (Drucker 1979:268–69)

Although white people used to joke about blacks' preference for Cadillacs, by 1969 the joke was obsolete. There were several Cadillacs around Fourteenth Street, but customers and neighbors preferred the Buick Electra 225, which was given the name *Deuce and a Quarter*. There was also a preference for Oldsmobiles and Pontiacs. A few men had Chrysler Imperials, and there were almost no Ford products to be seen. The General Motors lines dominated in the cars we worked on.

Change in preferences came with each model year. The pony cars and muscle cars with their exaggerated cubic inches and horsepower were available, and young men who could afford them dragraced illegally near the waterfront on weekends. If one owned a Volkswagen Beetle, it tended to mark one as a student. While the Italian men of South Philadelphia still bought Cadillacs, the discriminating black was in 1973 trading in his Deuce and a Quarter for a Volvo.

The folk term for auto was *short*, and long conversations revolved around one's shorts. Although the pimp and hustler had been dramatically documented in urban black life, their characteristic automobile, the Pimpmobile, was not much in evidence in Philadelphia (Milner and Milner 1973).

In the black aesthetic, motion was the metaphysic of beauty; that which moved received the most aesthetic enhancement. People and automobiles, even bicycles, were *dressed*, whereas unmoving objects such as houses tended to receive less artistic attention. This was true of the Fourteenth Street area, though not of all of black Philadelphia, and was as well very much a function of relative affluence. When people talked of their cars, the major aesthetic judgment was based on how a car made them *feel*. The auto was an object of desire, but the desire was to feel good, to experience an aesthetic completion, on entering and driving it.

There were a number of driving styles, but one especially was widespread and so deserves comment. Men drivers styled their driving position while sitting behind the steering wheel. They sat low in the seat, leaning away from the window toward the center of the car, as if to make it symmetrical. And in the car there was always music on, sometimes but not necessarily loud. The auto enabled one to establish either a cool motion as one drove or a furiously intense one. It varied according to how one felt.

Telemachus, rather than spending his time driving, serviced those who did. The shop, rather than being devoted to the stylish use of the car, helped make using it possible. Through the winter months, I found that mechanical work, and the conditions in the shop, were not easy. The seemingly carefree presentation of self that an auto afforded was itself often based on costs that were not obvious.

Winter

Telemachus asked Angie for money again in the first week of December, even though he had not repaid the first large loan. He told her how much he needed help. The successful hustler could do that, could talk the person who gave into giving more. At that time Telemachus's wife was putting strong pressure on him to pay for their youngest son's release from prison. Auston was a drug addict, and Telemachus explained to Angie how relentlessly his wife was urging him to arrange Auston's release. Angie lent him the money, and Auston then joined us as third man in the shop.

With the door closed to fend off the cold dampness of the Philadelphia winter, the shop became a tiny, inward-looking social system, an intense stage for dramatic action, a small submarine of relative warmth submerged in the bitter cold. Three or four men were confined in the shop each day for up to twelve hours, at work on cars, listening to the radio, talking to one another and to customers who came in. Auston entered the tight little scene with the biological compulsion of addiction, and to the other anxieties of the shop he added endless disappointments, feelings of futility, and the impotent anger that seethes within those who must deal closely with drug users.

Auston was dark and small-boned like his mother but overweight from the physically undemanding prison existence. He seemed soft, in contrast with the tough arrogance of Trip's brother Tex, back at the 410, who also lived as an addict and drug pusher. November had not been a month of dramatic and unnerving newness for me as October had been. Raymond did not appear at the shop but twice. In summarizing the month in the field notes, I wrote down that by using a systems model I could account for all the major activities in the shop. I felt certain I had the outlines of the business operation, but I knew I did not have a secure sense of the business transactions and how they were conducted. I did not like in the least working sixty-hour weeks and desperately wanted some sort of leverage that would let me work less, though I then had no wish to stop altogether.

When Auston arrived I seized the chance to tell Telemachus that I would work fewer hours, that I had something else going, and that now that his own son was there, he would not have to put up with Raymond's self-defining work habits. Telemachus did not like the idea of me reducing my hours, and he constantly pressured me to work more with gifts of food and a stream of expressions of disgust when I would "leave early." Often I relented, but I made the effort to stick to my own time scheme by working mornings, for I had not become an anthropologist to lie under wounded autos sixty hours a week. It was necessary, I believed, to broaden my contacts and pursue the networks of the friends I had made at the 410, for I was still trying to salvage the field situation and make it resemble, if on fewer hours a day, what I imagined ethnographers usually did. I wanted to talk with people, not wash down valve covers with kerosene.

Auston was, in a different way, no more reliable than Raymond, and he was as completely unskilled as both Raymond and I. He often missed whole days, even a week, but, worse, when he was there, he was scheming how he could get high while obscuring the fact from Telemachus. He had his hustles, and part of the strategy was getting over on Telemachus. Telemachus doled out money to him—not, I think, like a wage—bought him food, and subsidized him in other ways. Given his condition, Auston could not, as I learned, render decent mechanical work.

Telemachus complained that Auston was holding him back. In retrospect, I find it incredible that Telemachus took Auston into the shop and tried to do something for him at all. The man caused frustration and heartbreak. Telemachus, who counted heavily on luck—for playing the numbers, for repairing transmissions, for understanding unexplained events, whether good or bad—felt deeply that Auston had brought him ill fortune.

Just as Auston came to work, Raymond began to appear at the shop more frequently, perhaps to escape the cold, perhaps to stay away from the house, where he had twelve brothers and sisters. Auston's hustles and addictions and Raymond's presence, the meanings of which I by no means had solved or well understood, kept me uncertain and at times despairing.

The last week of January I made mistakes reinstalling a transmission. I forgot to tighten the rear universal joint where the drive shaft connects to the differential. Telemachus started the car for the customer, put it in reverse to back it out, and bolts went flying everywhere, the drive shaft clattering madly on the floor. Fortunately no further damage had been done, but the car, of course, just sat there.

Telemachus was justifiably frustrated and angry. He had enough problems with Auston and Raymond, and now I was working part time and not getting it right. When he told me how he felt about my lack of competence, I began to talk back to him for the first time about his. Until then, I had said nothing to him about how angry and frustrated I became when I had to pull each transmission three to eight times so he could tear it down and rebuild it. He was illiterate and could not use a mechanic's manual. In fact, there was no automatic transmission manual in the shop. He tore one down, looked for what he could see was wrong, replaced it, and put the transmission back together again. Then Auston, Raymond, or I, or any two of us, would reinstall it in the car. Transmissions were complex and often could not be repaired based on a visual inspection, but worse, Telemachus did not systematically make the essential replacements before reinstallation of gaskets and relevant parts that were functional necessities. He had no algorithm for each job he did, no minimum set of necessary steps. His only systematic strategy was to get by with as little capital investment in the machine as possible. Unfortunately the tactics invariably failed, and I was thoroughly frustrated by the situation. The reasons for his problems with machinery may well be explained by the history of education in the South.

> The southern refugees of the 1950s were among the least-skilled and worst-educated of all Americans. The skills that they had were largely agricultural; the little education that they had was obtained in rural southern schools of poor quality. Their few skills and talents were not widely demanded by urban employers." (Fusfeld and Bates 1984:116)

I went home that day after airing our differences and told Karen I was quitting fieldwork. I said I was calling Goffman; I did not come out here to replace the same transmission a thousand times...

When I told Telemachus my side of the story, I felt that the air was cleared somewhat and I relaxed a little, though not enough. I wanted desperately to quit, to be rid of the whole situation. Karen and I talked, I cooled off, and since I really do not know how to walk away from something, I did not. Perhaps I should have at that time adventured further and found another kind of involvement in the community, for working in the shop was a kind of imprisonment. With the door down, with the endless string of cars we had to do over and over again, and with Raymond's presence constantly preventing me from keeping an emotional equilibrium and Auston always high or cutting out or selling old metal parts he found under the benches for money at the junk shop next door, I felt trapped and claustrophobic. I experienced the involuted, internal-looking craziness that comes when people are too close together for too long and things are not going well. What I could not then define, but can in retrospect name, was that the hustles of Telemachus and the threatened extinction by Raymond were rough theater, a bawdy, self-contained source of excitement, provocation, and thespian turmoil.

•   •   •

Karen and I, with much uncertainty and a suspicious wariness, had moved into the apartment above Tony's office in February, the dead of winter. Now, in March, she was in Minnesota visiting her sister. That week Telemachus asked me to work extra hours

Figure 6. When Telemachus and I were discussing my working in the repair shop more hours, he doodled these drawings as he talked.

in the garage because he wanted me to help him *stir* (strip) a new, stolen yellow Buick convertible for parts. This was not Telemachus's scam. Someone, a white person, had contacted him and asked him if he would do it. There was no money up front for stripping the car, but Telemachus said yes because he figured he could sell the radio, the engine, the transmission, and miscellaneous other pieces. After he tore it apart he was to leave it on the street where the cops would find it. From what I overheard I figured out that a man had borrowed money from a savings and loan association to buy the car. He had fallen in arrears, and a repo man from the association was looking for it. Every night the man had to park the car in a different part of the city to keep it from being repossessed. He grew tired of the chase and decided to call the police and say it had been stolen. Such a claim would relieve him of further responsibility for the vehicle because his auto insurance would pay what he owed the savings and loan association if the car were found damaged. That was where Telemachus came in. After we dismantled the car, Telemachus detaching what he thought he could use, under the cover of darkness we pushed it a couple of blocks away and parked it in front of a row of abandoned houses. Then the "owner" called the police and reported it stolen.

Earlier that day when I returned from lunch I walked into the shop to find Auston and Raymond's brother Clarence kneeling on the floor. Clarence was holding a pistol while Auston aimed Telemachus's electric drill into its barrel. I was sure it was the starter's pistol that Raymond had taken from Telemachus in October. I casually walked over to where they were working, hiding my fear completely; they paid no attention to me. I stood and watched what they were doing. They figured they could make a zip gun, something that would fire a live bullet rather than a blank. Since the barrel of the starter's pistol was solid metal, they first wanted to drill it out so a bullet could pass through. I noticed that if they succeeded in drilling the barrel, they would still have a big problem, because the chamber that held the bullet did not line up with the barrel. I went back to work on the yellow Buick and thought to myself that whoever fired the pistol would be in as much mortal danger as the person threatened with it. If the gun were fired with a live bullet in the chamber, lead would fly everywhere but down the barrel; I was sure the gun would explode.

That they decided they needed a gun encouraged my sense of dread. Both Auston and Clarence were *junkies*, but it seemed to me that they were upping the stakes Auston had played for, which until now had been selling the scrap metal lying around the shop in order to support his habit. Every time I saw a pistol I worried that it might be used against me. I took the presence of weapons *very* seriously.

I was vulnerable to Auston, Clarence, or Raymond because they knew Telemachus had given me the key to the shop the second week of October. Even when I worked less than eight or ten hours a day, I opened the shop at eight in the morning and had everything running when Telemachus arrived. I worried that at some time they might try to muscle me into getting what they wanted from the garage.

Raymond came into the shop and stood next to me and commented on what they were doing. I noticed that he still had a shirt with his name on it. Telemachus told us to get to work on the Buick, and he continued to mumble or curse under his breath at Auston and Clarence.

•　　　•　　　•

The next day Raymond, I thought, would get one of us killed. He introduced street plays into the shop that involved everyone and were deep, dramatic, potentially fateful, recursive, and turned inward. His plays were theft games, a genre of play I had often heard about when I drank at the 410 Bar. The theft game was in a sense a play on, and a subversion of, legitimized exchanges, even of the street hustle, for it omitted the first face-to-face encounter where one either offered or requested some necessary medium. Above all the theft game was a form of profanity, the roughest of rough theater.

On the morning of 6 March I was lying under a car thinking about my sister's twenty-seventh birthday, which was that day, and feeling anxious about Raymond, who was at Telemachus's direction working with me. Raymond's threat to me of five months ago was too vivid for me to feel comfortable with him. I watched my back, never trusting him, and Telemachus showed his distaste every time Raymond came through the door. We pulled a transmission from one car and set it on the back bench, then installed a repaired transmission in another car. Telemachus left for lunch and I finished a brake job on a Chevrolet.

When Telemachus returned I said I was going over to Tartacks to buy a hamburger platter. Raymond said he would come along. The weather was warming, the sun was bright; Raymond joked with a woman who was walking that way. A nondescript, small dog followed Raymond and he drove it off. The woman laughed and Raymond said, "I don't want no dog following me."

At lunch Raymond told me that he got mad just thinking about Telemachus:

He doesn't even have to do anything. . . .
There's a lot going on in the garage. This morning I saw Auston take a small box of threading tools. I'm telling you just to see if Telemachus will blame me for it. . . .
I wouldn't take anything from Telemachus. I don't exactly respect him, but I like him.

After finishing his platter and telling me about the threading tools, Raymond left, leaving me to eat a piece of lemon meringue pie and wonder why he told me the story about Auston.

When I returned to the shop, Raymond and Telemachus were there but Auston had left for the day. Telemachus motioned me to the back of the shop and Raymond came with us. Telemachus looked at me and asked, "Do you have any tools up in your house?"

"No," I answered. Here it comes, I thought.

"Some are missing," he went on, "and only three people could have done it—you, Auston, or Raymond. I'm not accusing anyone you understand, but only saying who could be suspected. Any of the three of you could have done it; I'm not here all the time."

He nodded to me and said, "You could have done it because you have the key." Looking into neutral space, he went on, "Raymond and Auston could have done it because they both work here."

Raymond responded, "I didn't do it because if I did I would have the money."

"Whoever did it wouldn't make very much money because you can't get a lot for that stuff," Telemachus replied. "Why would anyone steal from me, I don't have anything worth taking?

"Whoever stole that little stuff would have to turn right around and do it again because he wouldn't be getting ahead with non-valuables like that.

"I knew it was stolen when I was in Tony's this morning and saw the box of threaders on his work table."

I held my head down while Telemachus was talking, as I had seen Auston do, but I raised it up and asked, "Did you ask Tony who sold him the threaders?"

"No, I didn't ask, but I think I know who did it," he answered.

Raymond repeated himself, "I didn't do it, but I expect I'll get blamed for it because I get blamed for everything that happens around here. I'll be right back."

Raymond turned and walked quickly from the shop, calling over his shoulder to me, "You can tell Telemachus what I told you at Tartacks."

I turned to Telemachus and told him what Raymond had said at lunch. Then I added that it was implausible that Auston stole them because he left walking in the opposite direction that morning. "Perhaps he doubled back," I added.

"I doubt it." Then he revealed that Dave had told him that Raymond sold them to him.

Raymond returned with the box of threaders and said that he had traded two Cadillac tires for it. The transaction must have been the most rapid on record, and I doubted what Raymond claimed.

As Raymond walked in, Telemachus asked, "Why didn't you tell me this morning, when you saw Auston take the box, that he took it?"

Raymond answered, "I just wanted to wait and see if you'd blame me for it."

The two of them discussed other thefts, things missing, and the accusations that Raymond had taken things in the past. It came out that Telemachus had once unjustly accused Raymond of taking tires when in fact a customer had put them in the trunk of his car himself. But Telemachus claimed that he had not accused Raymond of taking the tires but had merely asked where they were. Raymond fell silent then. He hung his head in what seemed to me to be an unselfconscious and deep depression.

Telemachus left, and Raymond and I discussed the issues again. Then Telemachus returned and Raymond left. Telemachus said he'd like to go upside Raymond's head with a hammer.

The next day Auston told me he heard about Raymond's accusation. Then he told Telemachus that he would leave if he were accused of stealing and that if Raymond continued to work he would not.

Later Auston told me that Raymond denied to Telemachus that he had told me he had seen Auston take the threaders. It was as if Raymond had removed himself from the entire play that his theft had created by denying even the verbal account of it. It was a radical form of moral detachment (Rose 1974).

Telemachus had once told me something that Raymond's theft game then made me remember. When he lived down south on the

farm, he recalled, the old people always had some shit going. Someone had to be the boss on this job or in that field, and someone
else had to be the boss in the next field, and there were endless
arguments over who should direct people's labor. Usually someone
was running home for his shotgun or others were running home
for theirs. His grandmother or someone would have to come into
the field to cool out everyone.

Every day during the summer someone was accusing someone
else, "So and so did this, so and so did that." The air was full of
sexual accusations and innuendo. He told me he couldn't take all
that "she said—he said."

"They were always raising hell," he had finished; he did not like
it, could not stand it: "That's why I left."

That day was Raymond's last in the shop. The next morning
when he came in, Telemachus asked him to return the uniform.
It was the end of the relationship. Much to my relief, Raymond
ceased to frequent the shop. Now I had to worry about Auston
and Clarence and the implications of the starter's pistol, and so did
Telemachus.

•　　•　　•

People owed Telemachus money the way he owed Angie and
Mary Jackson. He had to collect from customers, just as Mary had
to appear at the shop to specify what she needed from him. A man
who lived two blocks down Montrose Street brought his Comet
convertible in for repair. He made the cash down payment that
Telemachus requested of all his customers; with this money Telemachus bought parts and supplies. As with all hustles there was
danger in the repairman-customer relationship, and the situation
as it developed proved troublesome. Telemachus did the job and
the man came for the Comet, bringing not money but some bonds,
which he said he would redeem when he had more cash. Telemachus did not like the arrangement but let him have the car. The
week had proved to be costly: he had paid Raymond for the last
time Friday and let him go; he had stripped the yellow Buick but
had received no money yet for the parts he had torn out; he had
not worked on paying customers' cars; and he had given Auston
extra money earlier in the week when he had asked for some. Now
it was Saturday, and Telemachus needed more cash, in part to pay
me and in part to take money home, for they were behind in the
house payment. Auston, who had been told where the bonds came
from and the circumstances of the deal, discovered that Telemachus wanted to negotiate the bonds but was unable to. He offered

to fence them, and Telemachus, for whatever compulsion, told him to try. Auston took the bonds and left work at noon on Saturday.

At the end of the day Auston had not returned. Telemachus paid me only a third of what he owed me, which did not surprise me; nevertheless I kept the pressure on. I then went upstairs to clean up. Karen was still in Minnesota, so before my shower I decided to take the young dog we had bought, a black and white border collie named Jennie, for a walk. She was a herding animal and wandered now in front, now in back of me, and I had her on a long piece of clothesline rope to give her a little space to exercise back and forth.

I walked north to Montrose, a block from where the man with the Comet convertible lived, and walked Jennie toward the house of the young boys who stopped by Telemachus's shop every morning on their way to school. As I turned the corner I saw Auston walking toward me in the fading light of late afternoon.

He had not been able to fence the bonds and wanted me to open the door to the shop and let him use one of the cars, a local customer's 1961 Pontiac with a badly defective transmission. I knew the Pontiac could barely be driven, and I mentioned to him that Telemachus had instructed me never to open the door for anyone.

Auston replied, as if unconcerned because he was Telemachus's son, that when we got to the shop he would call his father and clear it with him. I reluctantly agreed to that, opened the door, and Auston dialed a number on the pay phone.

Hello, Telemachus....

I'm at the shop and need to use the man's Pontiac....

I know it doesn't shift right....

As the call progressed I was impressed with how well he simulated a dialogue, for I was more and more certain that there was a dial tone in his ear. My problem now was whether or not I could stop him from taking the car or, more to the point, whether or not I wanted to try. He was the one who had just finished drilling the barrel of a starter's pistol for a zip gun; he might even have bought a gun that worked. I feared the consequences of a physical confrontation. If he were high he might shoot just to hear the gun go off.

Before he hung up, Auston told the phone, "I'll be back in an hour." Then he drove the car away.

I shut the shop door and went upstairs to try to call Telemachus at home. His daughter answered and told me he was not there. Though not surprised, I was more upset than ever. I hung up, went in and turned on the television for fifteen minutes, then called back. By that time he had arrived, and I explained to him what happened. "Auston was too slick for me; I'm going to give you back the key to the shop," I finally told him.

Telemachus said he was going to dress and come down to look for Auston. Since the transmission did not shift correctly the car could easily overheat and destroy the engine. Telemachus had no desire to repair a transmission and replace an engine at his own expense.

I showered to wash Saturday's dirt and grease off. The doorbell rang and I went to the window and looked down; Auston had returned with the keys. I called out, "Leave the keys."

"I need a jump," he responded; "the car stalled."

I said I would be down in a minute, then called Telemachus, who had not yet left his house. "Make him wait," he instructed me; "I'll be right there."

It was now pitch dark out, except for the feeble illumination from a few streetlights. I went into the shop, took two electrical cables, put them and a battery into an Acme supermarket shopping cart, and wheeled it over to Eleventh and Montrose streets where the Pontiac sat. When I opened the door and turned the key, I could see that the electrical system was fine but the car was out of gas. Auston, I was convinced, was too stoned to know if it was an electrical or a fuel problem.

At that time of night we had few options, since no gas stations were open, so Auston and I began to push the Pontiac the several blocks back to the shop. A tall man came up to us as we were struggling slowly along and asked me where we were going with the car. I did not like the question. "To Telemachus's shop," I replied. Then he turned to Auston and asked if Telemachus had sold the car. Auston told him no. I was relieved that he was talking to Auston, not to me. Then he helped us push the car the rest of the way. The man asked what was wrong with it. I offered no information and the two of them discussed it as we continued.

When we arrived at the shop Telemachus was there waiting. He did not try to hide his disgust. In my anxiety I believed it would be clear to Auston that I had called Telemachus. While I preferred to remove myself from incriminating situations, I felt that the circumstantial evidence that I had brought Telemachus in on this was undeniable, and I wondered what, if anything, Auston would do about it. My first thought was that he would somehow try to intimidate me for pulling his father in. The face-off with Raymond was never far from the surface of my memory.

Telemachus cursed Auston audibly under his breath. "I wanted the car to stay where I put it; it wouldn't run and I told you that this afternoon," he told Auston, just as I had heard him say earlier.

The man who had pushed the Pontiac with us apprehensively asked Telemachus about it—it turned out to be his—and he reassured Telemachus that he would have the money soon. They discussed the problems with the car. Auston drifted into the shop and stood at the back bench. When Telemachus and the man were through talking, Auston motioned Telemachus to the back. I overheard Auston tell him that he had just talked to the lady whose husband had brought in the Comet convertible and left the bonds as a security deposit.

Auston explained that the woman, while he was standing there, went to look for the bonds and found them missing. Only then did she discover the theft by her *old man* (common-law husband). He had simultaneously hustled both her and Telemachus to keep his Comet running. She told Auston that she had bought them for her children's education. Auston suggested to her that she could recover the bonds if she brought money over every week and received a bond in return each time. "Oh, would he really do that?" she asked. Auston told her they could work it out like adults.

I was moving back toward Auston and Telemachus because I desperately wanted to be a part of what I heard developing. Auston suggested that he and Telemachus return to her house; he explained that she and Telemachus could confirm what was said earlier and work out the details. He wanted the money very badly, I was certain. Telemachus asked him if he really wanted to go over there. From the way Telemachus asked the question it seemed that he was letting Auston say no in case he were lying, thus preserving his son's autonomy. Auston asserted he did want to return, and I asked to ride along.

Telemachus stopped the car in an unlit corner of Montrose at the mouth of alleyway. There seemed to be no street lights at all. The only illumination was from the yellow paths of light cast by the windows of the narrow houses. After Telemachus got out of the car, he put his head in the car window and asked us to go with him to show how serious he was.

Auston went up the narrow marble steps and knocked on the woman's door. It opened inward and Auston's body blocked my view. I stood almost on tiptoes, wanting very badly to look in, for I was sure the people were extremely poor, and I was curious about the interior. It was difficult to see past the woman , who was very large, but I could make out behind her a mirror above a sink. In the mirror there were parts of a teen-age girl, several small children, and the moving blue image of a fraction of a television screen.

"I expect him about ten o'clock," she told us.

We left and Telemachus said to Auston, "Why don't you sit up here in front with me."

I opened the back door of the car to enter just as Auston walked past me to the front. "Are you afraid I'll bash your head in?"

"No," I said, as casually as I could.

Telemachus drove me to the 410 Bar where I had a couple bottles of Schlitz with a hustler I knew named Smitty. After the beers I began to realize how angry I was with Auston, and with Clarence as well. In back of Auston's use of me was the unspoken force of a gun. I wanted a pistol to carry. My logic was impeccable. In a democratic society where all are armed, I needed to be as well in order to participate with the same unspoken firepower, with the same equality, as the others. I had an overpowering urge to buy a pistol, if only to include myself in a democratic situation, and felt I needed something small that I could get to fast. Unfortunately, in Pennsylvania one had to register a pistol, which I was unwilling to do.

I went home, called my brother, and asked him to buy me a gun. Since he was underage he could not do it, but to my surprise my father said he would send me one. We had never had a gun in the house. A week and a half later, a twenty-five caliber automatic pistol arrived in the mail. I put five bullets in the clip, one in the chamber, kept the safety off, and slid it into my right front pocket. I was angry.

In an effort to keep myself calm I began to take scopolamine.

Telemachus, Auston, and I had collected no money that night from the woman, and she did not come over to the shop with money each week to redeem the bonds. It was not until nearly five months later, when once more Telemachus was perilously short of cash, that he decided to try to collect from her again. At that time a junkie had appeared in the shop a few times, several weeks apart, selling hot auto repair equipment. Telemachus bought most of what he offered. On 31 July, Telemachus called him into the shop and talked so low with him that they could barely be overheard. He gave the *hoodlum*, as he called him, money to go over and throw a brick through the windshield of the Comet convertible. The day after he instructed the hoodlum to work his vengeance secretly, indirectly, and powerfully, the man with the Comet came to the shop, paid Telemachus, and took the bonds home.

With the door down, the shop was a microcosm of the street and its jagged theater of theft games, games that in our case were complicated by Auston's addiction and his equally addicted friends. But there is another way to think of the shop. It was *itself* a staged social space, a front, a simulation; it *was* theater in which the major drama was the daily life of the shop itself and the endlessly futile attempts to repair transmissions. The garage—as a longer-lasting dramatic production—enclosed the smaller scenes of the theft games. It was as if Telemachus wanted to turn the street hustle, which wrapped within itself a whole mode of local exchange, into a capitalist enterprise but with none of the market rationalities of ownership, legitimacy, licensing, or access to wholesale parts and supplies. My reaction to the whole situation, which I could not then grasp, blinded as I was by inexperience and ignorance of the street, was one of despair. I wanted out.

I wrote in a field note on 25 March, "I feel incredibly nervous when Auston is around." I went on to type, "Tonight after work Auston was dressed in street clothes, perhaps waiting for a ride home with Telemachus. He did not acknowledge my presence and seemed to define the situation in such a way that no interaction at all was expected. There is no apparent reason that one can point to for why Auston should ignore me this way. He has a very pained look on his face, perhaps because he is so high." Then, on another card dated the same day, I wrote, "Lately I have been feeling suicidal, terribly depressed and very hostile."

My frustration, before the weather broke, was hair-trigger. The work in the shop masqueraded as repair, drug addicts constantly threatened the most mundane moments, I failed to establish a sense that I was conducting competent ethnographic research, I was unable to understand fluently the speech of everyone I met because of dialect differences, and I lacked the knowledge of how I ought to perform as an actor among actors. All these things contributed to a deepening disorientation. At times I felt I was close to understanding, and then the moment would bleed away, die, it seemed, in my hands.

Six days before writing the field note quoted above, I worked for Telemachus. In the evening, after the news at eleven, I fell asleep on the bed. The doorbell woke me up, and I went to the window and pulled the shade back slightly to see who it was. Boycie was standing just below me on the stoop with his back to the door, waiting for me to answer it.

As I write this I think of Boycie with affection and amusement. He was the man who had been sitting on the stoop the first day I had driven to the shop to have my Chevy repaired. He was, I remember with a touch of sentimentality, the first person I had really spoken to in that locale. Over the winter he had added to the theatrical tensions of the garage, leaving a profound impression on Auston and me.

Telemachus told me on more than one occasion that he thought the most critical aspect of running the shop was the quality of his help. He needed good, consistent labor but never found it. The initial contract between him and workers was usually a more or less tacit understanding that wages were to be paid for labor by the week. In a sense the contract was fleshed out when Telemachus stopped for lunch near midafternoon and bought food for himself and whoever was working for him at the time. The food offerings, effected without fanfare, were an attempt to add an increment of indebtedness to the worker to offset the cash Telemachus owed. He tried, when I worked mornings, to buy me food so I would feel indebted enough to stay and work through the afternoons. If I said no, he acted disgusted, and I responded with silence but became angry inside.

In addition to the food and the promise of wages, Telemachus directed his help in their tasks, threatening them with bawdy humor when they did the work improperly—"I'm going to cut off your nuts"—promising them more money if they would work more, and displaying disgust at slip-ups or misunderstandings. The sign of disgust, a sound made with the mouth, a turning away, was very personalistic and very directed. It was an antiaesthetic, gustatory sign, used as if to say that someone's course of action was unpalatable and needed to be spit out. Disgust was a metaphoric sanction within intimate relations when the disgusted person could not enjoy consuming the unsavory behavior of another nearby.

When especially busy, Telemachus would ask Boycie or someone who was on the street between jobs to come in and help. One cold February day, Telemachus needed to switch an engine and transmission between two Chevrolets, and because he had a lot of work he asked Boycie to assist. Boycie did most of the job; the good engine was in the correct Chevy, and the transmission needed to be bolted up. When I asked Boycie how to do it, he became angry, or acted as if he were, saying "I ain' no teacher." Telemachus had to stop his work and show me what to do.

When the parts were fastened together, one of the cooling lines leaked transmission fluid and Boycie repaired them. Then Telemachus tested the car on the street and it overheated. Boycie started a *whole lot of shit* behind that, screaming that the car would freeze up in that weather. The shop was in an uproar, with Telemachus, Auston, a customer, and me all talking and arguing simultaneously. After the customer left with the car, Boycie loudly demanded his *dust* (pay) from Telemachus. During that performance, Tony, wearing a mechanic's uniform, which was rare for him, lifted the door looking for Boycie; he interrupted abruptly to say to him, "Don't step foot in my shop again," and accused him of stealing. It must have been patched up quickly, for I do not think Boycie stole things as a matter of course, and Boycie was back working for Tony off and on by the following day.

Telemachus paid Boycie and told him to get out. Auston turned to his father and, in a rare display of disgust himself, asked if he were ever going to use Boycie again. Telemachus said no and Auston replied, "Bullshit." Telemachus said that Boycie could be useful at times, to which Auston responded, "I can do without all that crying. You have to go through too many changes behind Boycie."

All the labor Telemachus hired was unskilled or, especially like Boycie and Raymond, organized the world around themselves rather than around the repair shop. Several months was the longest anyone stayed. Our lack of skills was revealed in our mechanical work but was even more apparent in our troubles with electrical wiring problems.

A man came into the shop with a red 1961 Mercury Monterey hardtop coupe. Its rear brake lights did not come on properly. Telemachus told the man I could repair them, that I was "good with wires." That was news to me. Since the left rear taillight was broken, I went in the accepted way to the junkyard, found a decent one, and replaced the broken one. The replacement did not repair the lighting problem and the auto was returned. Telemachus told me to buy a new brake switch, which I did. The Mercury still did not have a set of working brake lights.

Telemachus built transmissions and conducted repair in general around a replacement strategy: Keep patching things until the problem is solved. This was the way he addressed the brake-light problem as well.

On another cold February morning, I came into the shop to find that the Mercury was back. Under the dashboard, all the electrical wires to and from the fuse box were disconnected like so many dead ganglia. Telemachus had apparently figured that the fuse box was at fault. None of the wires had been keyed to the box, and there was no electrical wiring manual or diagram available for the '61 Mercury. He had torn the spaghetti of wires out and last night had instructed Boycie to rewire it. Boycie obviously had not done it, and when I came in Telemachus said to me, "Wire up the car any old way, just put it together." He then left to buy parts for another job he was working on.

I was put off by the unreasonableness of the request and sat in the back of the car wondering what to do, feeling the situation was more than a little bizarre. Boycie came in and saw me there. He gave off a sound of disgust and he stepped around the car I was in on his way to the back of the shop, mumbled something like "everyone looking at or working on this stuff has it all messed up."

I replied, "I've done nothing at all to it. I found it this way this morning."

When Telemachus returned I was standing at the back of the garage. I mentioned that Boycie had come in, to which he said, "I put you on the job, don't quit when someone comes in."

"I quit because it's such a mess, not because Boycie came in," I told him.

It was Telemachus's turn to act disgusted. He had to leave again. Boycie returned and discussed with Auston what was wrong with the car. We talked over the behavior and history of the brake-light problem. Auston asked Boycie, "Why don't you get together with Telemachus? You're both mechanics."

Auston's idea was to go to the junkyard, cut out a fuse box with its wires, and match them to the mess of wires under the dashboard. When Telemachus returned later, he agreed with Auston and left with Boycie for the junkyard. I also left and visited one of the 410 Gang in Holmesburg Prison.

That was partly how I knew Boycie, a man who was known on the street as a good mechanic when he was sober, which was not always, and who could litigate—*pitch a bitch* or *kick up sand*—when he had to collect on what was owed him. Now I opened the window a little and told him I would be right down. When I walked out of the door he said nothing but motioned for me to follow him. As I caught up to him I noticed he had on a French beret, something resembling a Navy peacoat, Army fatigues, and low-cut black shoes. We walked south toward Carpenter at the end of the block. The building at the corner was Tony's, and the first floor was like an office and storeroom for his glass repair shop. A large window faced the Fourteenth Street trolley stop but was masked by a full curtain. Boycie stopped at the entrance and fumbled in his pocket for a key. Inside there was no light and he did not turn one on; the only illumination came from the streetlight through the curtain.

Boycie motioned for me to sit on an old couch. "I want to talk to someone," he announced. I could see as I looked around that he was living there. His familiarity with the place had a domestic air, and there were some clothes, a clock radio, and a blanket for the couch where he must have slept. He turned on the radio and music from WDAS began to play.

Open your heart to what I mean,
In the whole world you know
There's a million boys and girls

Boycie reached over and turned it up slightly.

Who are young, gifted, and black
And that's a fact...

(Nina Simone)

Boycie opened a quart of beer and we took turns sipping from it. Speaking below the music, which made it difficult to hear him, he asked me questions: What is your nationality? Are you married? What is your wife's nationality? What nationality am I? Why do you work for Telemachus?

"I need a job."

"Telemachus," he explained seriously, "will always be under you because you're white. Do you understand what I'm saying to you?"

I said nothing, but took another sip of beer.

"Can you paint letters?" he asked me.

"Sure," I told him.

"Can you paint the way I move or feel?" he asked.

I liked the way the conversation was going, but I had to admit that I could not paint the way he moved or felt. "Music," I said, "would describe that better."

"I'll show you the *blackest* black," he said, emphasizing strongly the word *blackest*, all the while moving his body in place to the rhythms from the radio. He made motions with his hands. He raised his right arm and clenched his fist. He pulled his arm down slowly in time to the music, his head bowed, his eyes squeezed shut in concentration or communion with the music. He slowly moved his arm, describing a line back and forth across his chest. I felt a kind of anthropological elation and thought to myself, *this is why I am here, this is the essence of it.*

Just then I heard footsteps outside the window walking toward the way we had come a few minutes before. I was worried about Karen in the apartment alone and got up to look out through the curtain.

"Aw man, you blew it," Boycie announced, and the magic moment was over.

We talked more. He called his mother, and when he got up to go to the bathroom he handed the phone to me and asked me to talk with her. I went home about one o'clock, a little drunk, and wrote down what had happened with no comment about it, just a flat narrative in the field notes.

• • •

For a long time blacks were unwelcome at the Broad Street Diner at Broad and Ellsworth in South Philadelphia. By Sunday morning, 14 June 1970, blacks were being served reluctantly, though waitresses and white clients made it clear that "they" were not the preferred customers.

That morning Telemachus said he wanted to buy me breakfast. He was feeling good because he had just made some money. He and I had driven over to low-rent garden apartments in a white section of South Philadelphia to deliver a blue Cadillac convertible that he had sold. Wearing clean uniform shirts, each with our name on it, we now sat at the counter of the diner. Telemachus eased onto a stool next to a man, and I sat on the other side of Telemachus. The man was white, about fifty, and did not look away as we sat down.

The Broad Street Diner was historically patronized by men in somber suits with white shirts and ties, who wore black fedoras and talked with a kind of hoarse whisper. They were intimidating to black people, but their dominance of the diner was waning. We examined the menu, discovering that all pastries were baked on the premises and that the water was filtered. After we ordered breakfast, Telemachus began to tell the man next to him that he was in business for himself and that I worked for him. It was a minor theatrical event richly embellished with material that, though fictional, nevertheless portrayed Telemachus's self-conception. He told the man how he owned and operated his own garage that specialized in transmission repair. The most important part of the business, he asserted, was the customers. He claimed he was good with them. I was listening along and smiling, enjoying the performance, which at that point I took for granted.

All customers thinks all mechanics is crooks and they don't want to pay for what is done.

When they come to me they have problems. Their problems hurt them more than what is wrong with their car.

I listen to what they say is wrong with their car and then I try to figure out what to do.

I make up some lie about something that happened to me and try to make them forget what their problems are.

When Telemachus said that, I was reminded of a customer who came in several times, always in a foul mood, cursing and saying he was going to blow his car up because it did not run, or he was going to blow up Telemachus because he could not make the car run. Was he serious? Telemachus commented to me that when that man came in, "I always have to bullshit him, talk rough to him, so he'll calm down."

I broke off my reminiscence. Telemachus was making up a fictive story, telling the man sitting next to him how one of his mechanics interrupted him while he talked to customers and how that drove them off. For Telemachus the repair encounter was more encompassing than any single event within it, or even the technical repairs on the job.

The man listened with interest, nodding and commenting, smoking a filter cigarette. I wonder what he thought. He was civil, which was a minor achievement. We finished our breakfast and left. Telemachus stayed in a good mood. We drove back to Fourteenth Street and he spent part of the day there helping a man from a block and a half away repair his car on the street, just being sociable.

•   •   •

Mr. Johnson did not share Telemachus's view of himself, which he had expressed while sitting at the counter of the Broad Street Diner. He stood for a few minutes in front of the shop, his white Cadillac parked inside, then growled in a low voice to me, "Your man isn't very with it."

Mr. Johnson criticized rather completely Telemachus's general lack of mechanical ability, his poor use of time, his hurry to get through a job, his lack of thoroughness. Telemachus had built his transmission four times and was over his head with it, he said. Telemachus was imagining how important it was to manage people while he would have benefited from adding to his repertoire the skillful manipulation of complex machines. Finally our conversation shifted away from Telemachus.

Mr. Johnson told me that he was a member of the musicians' union, a drummer. He used the old jazz terminology such as *fey cats, cool,* and *blow,* and he named performers and their credits. "When the Duke's boys are in town I go there and blow." He was culturally far wiser than Telemachus. We discussed the Philadelphia jazz scene and the devastating effect of rock on it. He told me where the good clubs were and who was performing, and invited me and the Madam (Karen) to join him sometime.

The conversation ended with him saying, "Monday I'm going to take my car to another transmission shop and find out what's really wrong with it." I believe he did, for I never saw him again. I assume, though, that Mr. Johnson was performing for me, with the talk about the Duke, as a sociable fiction of the self, just as Telemachus did with the man sitting next to him at the Broad Street Diner. It was an entertaining way to pass the time.

• • •

Caesar had difficulty with Telemachus's technical failures, just as Mr. Johnson and the others had. Caesar was tall and drove a green Cadillac Coupe de Ville. He split his time between a place around the corner on Montrose Street where he lived with his common-law wife and their two children, and another residence in North Philadelphia. A good performer at parties, he might take a baby, as I saw him do one Saturday night, set the child up in front of him at the table, and proceed to use her as a miniature straight man to a continuous and humorous patter. Caesar had named a men's singing group the Coupe de Villes, after his auto, and they with others sponsored a cabaret each winter. When the transmission of his hardtop went bad, he brought it in for Telemachus to repair. The busy Fourth of July weekend was coming up, and Caesar wanted his car in a hurry. Telemachus promised it right away, wanting the money the job would bring, but the job, hence the transaction, did not progress smoothly enough to satisfy Caesar.

At nine o'clock in the evening two days after the Fourth, Caesar, his sister, and a friend of his were standing by the trolley power line pole that was right in front of our apartment door. The light from the shop illuminated their faces, and the three of them looked coldly upset. Telemachus had kept Caesar's car in the shop for the entire week and had rebuilt the transmission at least twice. Caesar's emotional state was linked directly to his dissatisfaction with the time taken: he was angry and abstracted. On the other side of the garage on a doorstep, a couple of Telemachus's friends—Reverend Forrest, his brother, and Ed Maddox—were sitting.

I walked onto the scene closer to Caesar than to Telemachus's friends and I asked him how it was going. I probably should have said nothing. He did not look at me and replied, "Not so good. There's a knock in my car that it didn't have before I brought it to your buddy here."

"Oh yeah," I asked, "where's your car?"

"Telemachus is testing it," he answered, still not looking at me.

"It's rough getting around without a car."

He said, "I'm tired of walking; I've been walking for five days."

"I'll bet it cramped your Fourth."

"It cramped everything."

He did not want to talk with me, so I walked across the lit shop doorway and stood by Reverend Forrest and the others. Their polite greeting was followed by a silence I felt compelled to join.

Telemachus roared by in Caesar's car. He circled the block again and parked the car in the mouth of the garage. Since he parked in the doorway it meant there was more to be done. Otherwise he would have stuck it into a parking spot on the street.

Caesar walked to the front of the car where Telemachus was standing. They talked at first in private tones. Then we heard Telemachus say, "Give me the rest of the money and you can take the car."

Caesar replied, just as loudly, "You kept the car for five days, and you were supposed to fix it in two days."

They argued this point back and forth loudly for a time. Then Caesar cut around Telemachus and jumped into the driver's seat.

"Where are you going?" Telemachus asked.

I'm going to test it out," Caesar said.

Telemachus quickly moved around the fender and entered the passenger's side. Caesar backed the car into the street and they drove off. In a minute they returned. Caesar also parked the car in the doorway. Things did not look good. They both went to the front of the car again. Caesar's anger continued to build. I heard Telemachus say that he would fix whatever it was that kept the transmission from performing properly.

"Forget it," Caesar said. "You've had the car for five days. If you can't do it in that time, you'll never do it."

Telemachus was almost pleading, "You'll have it tonight, I'll stay here until I fix it."

"I want the car tonight," Caesar insisted. "I need to use it."

"Give me the rest of the money," Telemachus told him, "and you can go."

Caesar escalated the event by quickly starting the car in an attempt to back out and leave without paying. Telemachus shoved a large hydraulic jack under the rear wheels, yelling "I got your goddam governor back on the bench."

Caesar almost leaped from the car. "I don't even have all the pieces," he yelled; "now I am mad. I'm bringing this car back tomorrow, and you can fix it right."

Telemachus begged him not to take the car out, repeatedly saying that he could fix it that evening. Caesar was not in a conciliatory mood, however, and repeated that he would use the car that night and bring it back the next day. There was not much Telemachus could do. He pulled the jack away from the rear wheels and Caesar backed straight into the middle of the one-way street. He then tried to shift into a forward gear, but transmission fluid evacuated all over the street beneath the car.

"Now I'm going to get my fifty dollars back," Caesar yelled to Telemachus as he quickly left the car.

Telemachus walked calmly over to the driver's side and attempted to find a gear that would engage enough to pull the car forward off the street. The Cadillac did not move. Telemachus got out, walked to his shop door and pulled it down, effectively blocking the Cadillac, still crossways in the street, from being moved. A car coming down Fourteenth Street could not maneuver around it; two black men got out, sat on the hood, and kept up a loud commentary addressed to each other and to onlookers on the sidewalk. They called down to men standing in front of the corner bar who were obviously watching the unfolding drama and enjoying the dealings between Caesar and Telemachus. When a trolley pulled in behind their car, they shouted to the driver that they would explain it all to his supervisor.

A mother stuck her head out of her second-story window and called down to her young daughter on the street, "Come on up here, Dum-Dum." The men on the hood of their car echoed, "Go on Dum-Dum."

All the elements of high street drama were in place. While the potentially momentous, dangerous, or fateful event was unfolding, everyone could perform or watch as the mood and opportunity stuck them.

After a minute or two of very high-pitched discussion, Telemachus walked from the garage and pulled Reverend Forrest aside. They talked out of earshot of everyone in very low voices. He evidently borrowed fifty dollars to give to Caesar.

After Telemachus returned Caesar's money, the men jumped off their car and motioned with burlesque gestures to the trolley driver. The trolley and the line of cars backed up half a car length, making room to jockey Caesar's car around until it faced south on the street.

Telemachus sat heavily on the step with Reverend Forrest and the rest of us, watching Caesar and the two men pushing the Cadillac. He said, "While we were testing the car, Caesar put the car into reverse gear by mistake. That's what tore up the transmission like that."

Caesar and the others turned the ignition of the Cadillac after it was squared away. Evidently there was enough fluid to engage some of the forward gears, because Caesar drove the car around the corner and traffic began to move again. His sister left the sidewalk, crossed the street, and entered the car. The rest of us dispersed. I wrote in the field notes that night, "Telemachus acted like a beaten man."

The next day Telemachus asked me to help him, but I intended to look for a construction job on Montrose Street; he seemed shocked I was unable to work for him that day. Referring to Caesar's public suit against his failed workmanship, he told me that he was going to quit the show and get himself a gas station. "White people don't act that way," he complained. The rough theater of the street, from which the shop was in no way immune, was taxing on everyone involved. Caesar read the failure to repair his transmission as a hustle and met it exactly as a hustle had to be met by a strong person (one with the *heart* for it)—with a fully produced public scene. Despite the fact that Telemachus understood from the inside how to litigate like that, he could not respond in an offhand manner. For both participants, the performance demanded the whole self and carried with it the constant possibility of loss and death. It was fateful in that sense.

The construction crew in which I sought a job was headed by a black man who had a company that was constructing turn-key housing with Federal grants. I was not hired that day and gained the impression that there was nothing for me there.

There was a formal relationship between the syntax of strategic exchange between persons and the syntax of redress for grievances induced during exchanges. A street argument such as Caesar produced with Telemachus was not so much a script or a set piece as a complex of tacit understandings on how to manage the public performance of such situations. A successful hustler was wonderfully skilled at avoiding confrontation or at confronting more vigorously than his suing opponent. A major method for dealing with a grievance arising from a successfully begun hustle was to claim all sorts of contingencies outside the hustler's control, for example, hard luck stories, or *crying*, the claim that the hustler was influenced by exogenous forces, either powerful or evil, and so on. Telemachus's pitch that he could repair the transmission that evening was weak. He had, in Caesar's view, run out of time.

On the street it was believed that the world was constructed along the lines of the hustle. The hustle was a fundamental feature of human social relationships; everyone was attempting to hustle everyone else (Milner and Milner 1973). There existed a counterideology too, and it was expressed in the only medium that reached across the range of urban black consciousness, popular music. The locus for collective consciousness, at least in South Philadelphia, was dynamically present in music, especially popular music and dance in their various and continually changing forms.

For example, in an immensely popular record Stevie Wonder criticized the hustle, thereby making a moral and aesthetic bid to re-form everyday life, to exhort a fundamental change. Employing a blend of Jamaican reggae rhythmic structure and a muted, black gospel phrasing, he recapitulated the hustle format in order to critically evaluate it.

He's a man
With a plan
Got a counterfeit dollar in his hand
He's Misstra Know-It-All

Playin' hard
Talkin' fast
Makin' sure that he won't be the last
He's Misstra Know-It-All

Makes a deal
With a smile
Knowin' all the time his lie's a mile
He's Misstra Know-It-All

Must be seen
There's no doubt
He's the coolest one with the biggest mouth
He's Misstra Know-It-All

If you tell him he's living fast
He will say what do you know
If you had my kind of cash
You'd have more than one place to go oh

. . . .

Any place
He will play
His only concern is how much you'll pay
He's Misstra Know-It-All

If he shakes
On a bet
He's the kind of dude that won't pay his debt
. . . .

Give a hand to the man
You know damn well he's got the super plan
He's Misstra Know-It-All

If we had less of him
Don't you know we'd have a better land
He's Misstra Know-It-All

What is missing from the song, entitled "He's Misstra Know-It-All," and tends to be missing generally from symbolic forms such as the folksong and traditional story, is the replaying of the sanctioning process on cultural modes of exchange. The details of litigation, such as Caesar's, tend not to be represented in lore. Although daily life is formally richer than its representations, representations reshape continuously the flow of daily life. The two cannot be separated artificially and contrasted, however. It is analytically necessary to understand together the form of exchange, which sustains nothing less than the form of life, and the form of litigations appropriate to it and the elliptical modeling and sanctioning in symbolic modes.

Black popular music represents, among the other work it does, the aesthetic morality mentioned above. Aesthetic morality occurs when a symbolic form remodels and comments on some aspect of daily behavior.

In Stevie Wonder's song, the hustler, Misstra Know-It-All, is characterized ironically and gently ridiculed; we are told that if he did not practice hustling, the country would be better off. This moral story-song is aimed directly at the black listener and adds to the beat a powerful meaning. From the aesthetic position of the symbolic re-formation, the phenomenal level can be critiqued or ridiculed. Stevie Wonder attempted to re-form the thought and practice of hustling at the most intimate levels of black life. Telemachus, I am certain, would have agreed with the song, but he was unable to convert the shop from a street hustle into a capitalist business.

•   •   •

Our lives were about to be transformed again, this time by the coming theater of the street. Caesar's strong legal action against Telemachus is the reader's preview of the drama on the summer street. The long winter was over. The involuted thefts of the shop fell away by the end of March, and the summer season with its thousands of public events was about to begin in the arena in front of the shop. People began to strut their stuff, tread the boards, and make their productions. The miniature theater of operations, the battleground of the shop, at once a military sphere and microscopic histrionic economy, was now to be writ large as the actors took up their places on stoops, on chairs, walking by, visiting, watching, and assuming their posts on street corners or behind open windows.

Levi-Strauss, reaching for a scientific metaphor, wrote that the

> customs of a community, taken as a whole, always have a particular style and are reducible to systems. I am of the opinion that the number of such systems is not unlimited and that—in their games, dreams or wild imaginings—human societies, like individuals, never create absolutely, but merely choose certain combinations from an ideal repertoire that it should be possible to define. By making an inventory of all recorded customs, of all those imagined in myths or suggested in children's games or adult games, or in the dreams of healthy or sick individuals or in psycho-pathological behavior, one could arrive

at a sort of table, like that of the chemical elements, in which all actual or hypothetical customs would be grouped in families, so that one could see at a glance which customs a particular society had in fact adopted. (1974:178)

We can no longer follow his theoretical reverie, the idea that a community has accumulated from the human storehouse an integrated, autochthonously designed system for itself. At the same time, Levi-Strauss touches a most responsive chord in the ethnographer. For the corner of Fourteenth and Carpenter, the customs taken as whole, or rather, the everyday life grasped as a quasi-totality, formed a continuous, democratized, improvisatory play. Telemachus hustled me for my first week's pay in a minor theatrical piece played out over a weekend. It involved a welcome, if raggedly orchestrated, sociable occasion at a New Jersey diner, which to Angie appeared a rather paltry repayment for his monetary indebtedness to her. Telemachus, his women friends, and his household were held together in a web of exchanges that were continually reshaped by enacted and storied need or desire, by claims in dramatic moments of great need or too few resources. Boycie developed an exaggerated act to collect money; Auston fended off Raymond's theft games by oratorical flourishes; and Caesar realized with Telemachus a whole street full of dramatic space born for the moment to witness and authenticate their differences, all within (in a sense) the larger dramaturgical production of the shop itself, the supreme fiction for Telemachus in those years, and, in that winter certainly, for me.

We cannot in America agree with Levi-Strauss's idea of a community whose psychological aberrations, aesthetics, dreams, and living arrangements represent a coherent selection from a chemical table of cultural life, because here life is too culturally interpenetrated. Here there has been, up to the present time, a continuous flow of numerous cultural streams, now accommodating one another, now resisting. An overarching fusion of cultural wholes, if such a thing exists, results from sometimes violent collisions, and yet the boundaries between cultures surge back re-formed and reformulated to resist annihilation.

Edges

Levi-Strauss's reflection raises the issue of heterophony and the polyglot cultures and identities of Americans. The ragged edges where black and white come in contact tend to be avoided in the ethnographies of members of a specific race. It is as if the borders represent change or even disintegration, while the interiors are imagined to preserve purity of either black or white. For Telemachus, who was in no way *typical* of black life, the boundaries were everywhere. Telemachus did not move easily in most white space; he was constrained from outside himself and from within from going where he, under then current law, might go.

The two main categories of Telemachus's everyday life, home and work, were each crosscut by his engagement of both black and white worlds. Permuted, these characteristics of black and white, home and work, constitute a four-box grid.

	BLACK	WHITE
home		
work		

Figure 7. Four-box grid.

By using the familiar categories that socially oppose black and white, I here wittingly but reluctantly reify the social categories, stable since slavery, used by such agencies as the United States Bureau of the Census. Once the categories of opposing color have been set up, whether in the bureaucratic folklife of the country or in the social sciences, we then ask, as if the boundaries were real, what the transactions across them were, are, or can be. By filling the boxes we can gain a mechanically generated picture of Telemachus's culturally shaped black-white relations.

For Telemachus, money was always moving across the borderline from black to white; money for food and auto parts, rental on his shop, mortgage on his house, and wages to some of his employees were all paid to whites. In return he received goods and services. These empty accountings do not capture his feelings—his relations, for example, with Angie—or his sense of himself and others that he drew from his retail transactions with auto parts dealers or his dealings with me and the other white man who worked briefly for him.

White people, by contrast, did not for the most part know how to verbally play with Telemachus, or even how to sustain joking for long. Even joking that he initiated was demanding, for it was culturally based and required that both parties fund the byplay with equal amounts of humor and cleverness. His relations with many whites—Frankie, who stole parts from TRANSCO, or Dave, who worked with Tony, for example—were cold and unfeeling. Telemachus was all business. Telemachus used a form of hustle on Frankie, and Frankie appeared at the shop with his stolen parts, full of complaints. There was no humor, no warmth between them.

If I were to summarize the entire black-white borderland between Telemachus and others as I witnessed it and later formalized it through analysis, I would say that there appeared to be a lack of penetration either way across the boundary. Peoples' intimate lives were not intertwined with one another; destinies did not cross and recross until the polarities of racial color were broken down. The white people, a few of whom might exchange brief pleasantries or banter on the street, were not involved in black work or home life. The blacks, even those who worked for whites or, like Telemachus, rented from them and employed them, did not penetrate deeply into white everyday life.

Telemachus was not invited to Angie's house, which was in an all-white Italian-American neighborhood. He went over once only, so far as I know, and took a gift of food to Angie's stepmother. The zone of contact was more like an invisible but structural surface film meant to sustain distance; it certainly did not encourage intimate involvement, business partnerships, intermarriages, or deep friendships. There seemed little possibility for reversal where black employed white, or black life caught up and ordered white life, though in all too rare instances it does happen throughout the country.

Although I have focused on what I observed and overheard, in the rare moments when Telemachus would talk about life in the South, he retold several times the story of a black man who while traveling had to use white bathroom facilities. Invariably in the story, white men forced him to wash his hands in lye as punishment for breaking through the zone of racial exclusion.

4. Spring

In Late March Karen walked out of the apartment to exercise the dog. The weather was not particularly warm yet, but the street was beginning its slow awakening to the theater of summer. Within a few minutes she was involved in a comedy, largely at her expense, one that embarrassed and confused her, and from which we learned more on the theater of publicness.

Karen went downstairs from the apartment to walk Jennie. [Karen often started her field notes in the third person and then in the second sentence switched to first person.] I walked up the street toward Lombardo's junk shop. There was a van unloading junk near the sidewalk. I was walking leisurely, stopping to let Jennie do mostly what she felt like. There was one black man unloading a few things from the van and talking to the owner on the sidewalk. Another Negro who looked as if he were working with the unloading came walking down the sidewalk. He had been talking with Lombardo and the other man unloading, so apparently they knew each other at least. I stopped not too far from the van and watched Jennie. The man came to where I was and asked me if I were Irish. I turned away and said I was a bit of everything. Pressing the question he said, "No, just tell me, Irish?" I said, "Yes, a little Irish, a little Norwegian."

I tried to make my exit by looking away and walking a step or two. I did not want to offend him but I tried not to talk to him any further. He, however, was obviously in control of the situation. I had moved closer to Lombardo and the other man.

The man talking to me said, "It was those blue eyes." I replied, "No, greenish-blue." He responded by asking, "Are you Italian?" I answered, "No." I was still trying to discontinue the conversation and look away. He then said to me, "Let me shake your hand."

What could I do? In my repertoire I offered him my hand before I knew what was happening.

He shook it and then bent and kissed it and said, "You take care of me and I take care of you." I was by then embarrassed and absolutely puzzled. He walked off, but not before Lombardo said, "Sonny, I didn't know you had such a way," and laughed. The black man standing next to him laughed with him.

I said, "I haven't seen such gallantry for a long time." The black man said, "He was just trying to force you into talking to him." I could not keep track of the exact words. He and Lombardo both knew I was puzzled by the whole thing. I said to the black man, "I guess I shouldn't have answered his questions, huh?" He said, "Maybe not."

Lombardo, still enjoying my predicament, said, "No, he's alright."

I went downstairs a few minutes later and related the incident to Telemachus and Dan. Telly said, "You cannot talk to people on the street. Carolyn [which is what he called her], you have a lot to learn about people in Philadelphia. When a man talks to another man, pretty soon they want to go with you, and when a man talks to a woman, the same thing. I don't talk to people around here. I'm scared of them. You don't just talk to people on the street."

[Two days later, Karen wrote] The man who had earlier made a fool out of me in front of Lombardo's came by. It was the first time I had seen him since the incident. I looked away. He came up to Eve [an eight-year-old girl from Montrose Street], shook her hand, and asked her something. Eve let him shake her hand. He bent over and was in quite close proximity. He then looked at me and I was still looking away. He said nothing to me and walked on. Eve told me she knew him, where he lived, and what his name was.

He also came back while Eve was sitting there. I was talking with Eve (making sure I was quite involved with her), and also playing with the dog who was barking. This time he aimed for me. I looked straight past him, and continued talking to Eve. As he asked me if I were Italian, I shook my head no, continued talking with Eve and looked away. He left without any further pursuing the interaction. I imagine he was confused as to my first incident with him as compared to my last two. I was proud.

Four months later, Sonny was a topic of ordinary conversation between Mrs. Stokes, who lived around the corner on Carpenter

Street, and Telemachus. I overheard the discussion at first, then joined it to interject something about him. Mrs. Stokes knew that the police had been called on him the other day; the caller, she said, was the man with whom he was supposed to be staying in order to collect his welfare check. Sonny had been sleeping on the step in front of his rooming house, across the street from our apartment, and the little man he was living with had called the police. Sonny was back the next day.

Mrs. Stokes told Telemachus that Sonny used to be a fine-looking man; his clothes were pressed, he had a good job, and even worked nights. Then his wife accused him of something, in one week sued for divorce, and fixed it so he would not even be able to see the children. After that, she said, he just let himself go. The theme, and the evidence I found on the street of men destroyed by women, was not unusual.

I mentioned I had heard earlier that Sonny was Raymond's brother and had once been married to a German woman. Mrs. Stokes did not seem to know that, and that fact or my other comments or my presence destroyed the interaction.

Sonny appeared to be a derelict; he had a feral, hairy look about him, but he was also a person whom tragedy had befallen, the victim of a dramatic domestic withdrawal, not a locally unknown or strange occurrence. At the same time everyone on the street *knew* him. If they knew him in no other way, people knew that he did errands for Lombardo, such as walking to the luncheonette, for tips. To *see* a person in public, on the street, was to *know* that person and to be able to talk about that person. Everyone, even those passing through, was memorized and held for a time in consciousness, the style of dress and manner of passage noted. The street was the most radically empirical place, where the least gesture was interrogated for clues to personhood. Every movement was interpreted as belonging to character, to the actor, and was a part of the continuous performance of biography.

The street was consummately a theater of contact between men and women, usually conducted by humor. Men spoke to and about women abstractly and directly in their presence. Women had two general options for response: maintaining a cold and eloquent silence with eye avoidance, or joking back and shaping the talk with their own humorous speech.

The corner of Carpenter and Fourteenth streets was not a middle-class public space, composed of urban and suburban middle-class people whose lives had been increasingly shaped by the use of the automobile and an avoidance of nonrecreational walking. A local, public life made up of adults, gathered in public with no other purpose than sociability, is either foreign or hostile to most Americans. In my adolescence, the people I saw in public were seemingly indigent men *sitting and spitting* around the county courthouse in Jessamine County, Kentucky. Faulkner characterized similar characters, both black and white, in his novels.

Sonny's performance with Karen, before an appreciative audience, was not out of place, out of character, or designed in any way to humiliate her, although it did. She was supposed to enter the play and shape it as her interests warranted, or refuse it altogether by the appropriate avoidance. She did not play partly because she did not know how, but even if she had known how, I do not think she would have done so with Sonny, at least not in March. There was a difference in expectations between them. Karen, from a small, midwestern town, had a white, middle-class sense of the public. But to reduce her response or mine to our particular biographies would miss the larger, more significant picture.

In northern Europe, and by extension in the United States, there has developed a pronounced hostility to public space—Pieter Bruegel notwithstanding—one that I can neither date nor explain. I want to address the hostility, for it interferes with understanding the street in front of the apartment. Even in the fourteenth century, William Langland, in *Piers the Plowman*, showed that shrines and other public places were scenes where "you could tell by the way they talked that their tongues were more tuned to lying than telling the truth, no matter what tale they told" ([1367–70]1966:26). The image coupling public space and lying, a perhaps unbroken theme continuously moralized, can be found from Langland to Faulkner. In one of his essays, Montaigne wanted to learn, "if I can, at what time the custom began of weighing and measuring words so exactly, and attending our honor to them" (1960:375). Words in the street were not so much weighed as performed, flung sometimes between persons.

The hostility to life in public space (not public life, which means quite another thing) can be easily witnessed in the north European philosophers because they attempt to get to the heart of the matter, a heart that tends to be unconscious of its cultural determinants. In making the effort, they reveal some of the deepest cultural assumptions that we in the West unconsciously hold. Heidegger, for example, used public transportation and reading newspapers as illustrations of publicness. Publicness was made up of the "they" in his thought, where Being *dispersed* itself through averageness, leveling down, and distantiation. To characterize the public he used terms such as *dictatorship, manipulation, alienation, tranquilizing,* and *glossed over.* Despite the overwhelmingly negative tone of each of these and other words, he ironically asserted that they were meant to be neutral.

Sartre, less ingenuous, was nevertheless as resistant, in a different way, to life as performance in public space. In the section of *Being and Nothingness* on "The Look," he continued to argue against solipsism by a philosophical analysis of the existence of others. His examples were drawn from public arenas—the urban park, the apartment hallway. I am interested not in his philosophical point here but in his rhetoric of publicness.

I am standing in the park; I see another man. "Thus suddenly an object has appeared which has stolen the world from me. Everything is in place; everything still exists for me; but everything is traversed by an invisible flight and fixed in the direction of a new object" (Sartre 1963:343). He evokes the presence of the other man in the park as forcing a hemorrhage, escape, disintegration, and flight. "It appears that the world has a kind of drain hole in the middle of its being and that it is perpetually flowing off through this hole." The emotions accompanying the public gaze of the other are fear, pride, shame, slavery, and the feeling of alienation from my possibilities. In these writings room seems nowhere to be found for the spontaneous and continuous performance between oneself, other, and an impromptu audience as the most authentic mode of being.

In the work of Erving Goffman, neither European nor philosopher, there was both continuity and appreciable discontinuity from the Sartrian *situation.* Placing himself as an observer self-consciously in middle-class American life, Goffman defined public places as regions freely accessible to members of the community, a definition that in a racially bifurcated society was partial at best. His sociological discourse on public behavior was far more varied than the philosophical ones. In *Behavior in Public Places* (1963), using the notion of involvement, he divided public spaces into those having focused and unfocused interactions. People's involvements were based on their presentations of themselves before one another. His most central concern, in a word, was order, whether public and large-scale or more private and small-scale. His fundamental question was, How do we *order* our social lives?

Goffman's emphasis was remote from Heidegger or Sartre, and far more affectively neutral. It shifted attention to the way we conduct ourselves in middle-class America and was not hostile to the idea or realization of public gatherings. At the same time it held out little place for spontaneous play or the improvisatory encounter on the street. Indeed, it would not be amiss to imagine that Goffman's American middle-class public would react, as Karen did, to humorous, male-to-female performances in public as threatening the very foundations of its culturally sedate order.

• • •

A woman was sweeping the sidewalk in front of the shop. Telemachus stood in his doorway and did not speak to her or look at her. I took a break and joined him there. First she swept her front steps, then the sidewalk in front of them to the curb of the street. As we stood in the door, she swept briefly in front of the shop, though Telemachus kept it immaculate. She said nothing to either of us and when she was through returned to her apartment just above the garage.

When I asked Telemachus why he did not say hello to her, he asked if I had seen the man sitting on her steps the other day. I said I had. Telemachus told me that the man was her boyfriend and was extremely jealous. If Telemachus talked to the woman upstairs and the man found out about it, he would have to kill the man.

That conversation took place in the fall when I first started to work in the shop. The woman was Ivery Sims, thirty-five years old and the mother of several children that I could sometimes hear running and playing on the upstairs floor as I worked in the shop below. I was curious about their living arrangements, in part because I did not know how many children lived upstairs and in part because I could not even speak to this woman, who was to become a very close neighbor.

When Karen and I moved into the apartment next door, my curiosity got the better of me. I fell further, if reluctantly into the role of voyeur. The row houses on Fourteenth Street were three stories tall, and the top floor was two rooms deep while the second floor was three deep. This meant that I could stand in the back room of the third floor and look over the roof of the second-floor bedroom. One day I was on the third floor and heard voices of two of Ivery's young children through the window. The urge came over me to crawl out the window onto the roof, across to the third-floor window of her apartment, which was right next to ours, in order to catch a glimpse of what it was like in there. I knew the children spent most of their time in the house over the winter because they were not in the street and had not gone to school very much. What did they do there all day? I found it difficult to imagine, because Telemachus and I did not hear them fighting although we heard them playing vigorously at times.

On hands and knees I crept across our second-floor roof and onto theirs, moved quietly beside the window, and peeked in the rear, third-floor bedroom. The tan paint on the walls was peeling, and a ruined mattress, gray with urine and countless years of use, lay on the floor. Two boys, ages six and seven, sat on the springs of a single bed, the only furniture in the room. The boys balanced on their knees a tray with two glasses of juice and a bag of cookies. Just then their *sooner* (a "no-breed" dog), named Pal, trotted in. Pat, the oldest boy, exclaimed, "Oh, Pal, I didn't see you there, come in and have a cookie and some tea."

The boys were pretending to have a high tea in some of the poorest physical conditions in the country. The apartment had no furniture to speak of; what was there was not much more than bedding, such as it was. I once figured that the children did not eat more than several meals a week. Despite the shock of seeing their material conditions, for this was the first time I had looked into a neighbor's house, I was more staggered by the boy's playful dignity and simulation of a higher social occasion.

The apartment Karen and I rented was in the middle of the base of a triangle of households (from our standpoint). Each of the other three households was anchored by a woman, and while we lived there, each was in motion, owing to births, deaths, new people moving in, old people moving out, and changing relationships between adult men and women.

Surprisingly, Karen and I came to know *households*, the members of households, our immediate neighbors, through public life on the street, itself a function of warmer weather. From the field notes I counted the people I met; there were eighty-one adults that I knew more than casually; seven single women and their children, twenty-six single men, and twenty-four couples. Of the seven single mothers, five did not live with their mothers, while two did. If I had been single the ratios would have been far different; if I had not conducted covert research, the numbers and my knowledge would also have been far different. If we had had children the knowledge Karen and I accumulated would also have been fuller; as it was, Karen knew more children than I did. She spent a lot of time during the summer talking with the younger girls who played on the sidewalk at the base of the triangle.

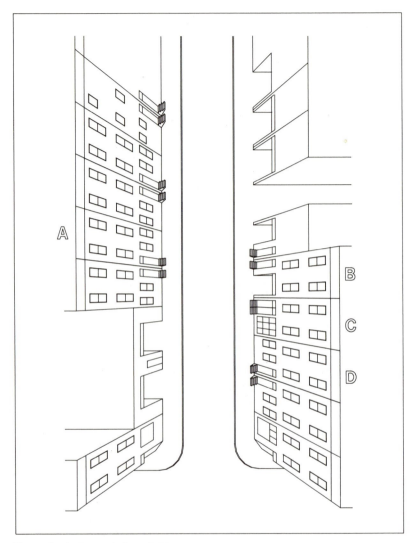

Figure 8. A. *Franny's household.* B. *Ivery's household.* C. *Rose's household.* D. *Maryjane's household.* Computer *drawing.*

The men I counted were not casual bar acquaintances or customers I saw only once or twice at the shop. I had to know some biographical details and have some daily or weekly contact on the street with a man or I did not include him among those I *knew.* Of the twenty-six men who lived alone, three had children who lived elsewhere, one I knew did not, and three were deformed or had speech impediments; of the rest, I was unsure of their earlier relations with women.

Of all the men I knew, both those living alone and those living with women, three were over sixty-five, four were alcoholics, one, not counting Auston, was a drug addict, one was on disability, five were unemployed, six did pickup work, two were custodians, two worked in warehouses, two were longshoremen, two were retail clerks, several lived entirely from hustling off the street, three were bartenders, and six were, respectively, a mechanic, a delivery person, a truck driver, a sailor, a bootlegger, and a construction worker. One of the custodians had two full-time jobs, both custodial. I did not know the occupations of nine.

Of the twenty-four couples, I was able to verify that one was legally married. Five were childless insofar as I knew because they were past childbearing years (though each could have had grown children living elsewhere). Five couples were unmarried, living together, and had children together. Five more couples, not married to the person currently lived with, had children with them belonging to the woman; the men had children by women living elsewhere. I did not know whether or not six of the couples were legally married, and two of the couples we were acquainted with may or may not have had children.

The numbers I have just given are completely subjective and are organized around what Karen and I could learn, given our limited ability to gather information overtly. The quantities only represent a situated count that in no way reflects an arbitrarily objectified reality. All of the people enumerated lived within a two-block radius of our residence. I omitted counting the children because I did not know as many as Karen, and I do not know now who she knew then.

• • •

By some criteria hidden from me, Telemachus graded women he met at the shop and on the street. At one extreme he showed them great deference and respect, and at the other he engaged them in licentious joking. The most deferential I saw him was with a very religious woman, older than he, who brought her car in for repairs. But his attitude could not be attributed just to religion, because his wife was becoming a churchgoer and that upset him. Other religious women who brought their cars to the shop were given little respect; one he called "Miz Poom Poom," which invariably made me laugh.

In April Telemachus was forced to deal with Ivery because the hookups to the utilities in her apartment were in the shop. When she did not pay some bills, a city employee came and turned off her water. She entered the shop and asked Telemachus to turn it back on, which he did, because the spigot was there and because he felt the children were victimized by the cutoff. Ivery also lost the gas for her kitchen stove and the electricity. Every month she received a welfare check for herself and her children, but much, if not most, of the money went for alcohol, not for utilities or for food and clothes for the children. It was several months before her services were restored.

Ivery *pitched a bitch* to Tony, who was also our landlord, to fix up her place, called city inspectors who wrote out citations on him, and generally did battle with him. It was not a bad strategy since he charged her, and us, about twice what white people were paying for comparable apartments a block away. Telemachus was in the middle of the fray since some of the arguments between inspectors, Tony, and Ivery were held at the various utility cutoff sites in the front of the repair shop.

At this same time, the jealous lover Telemachus felt he would have to kill if he spoke with Ivery was supplanted by a new lover, a fifty-year-old Irish-American named Moon Mullins. She called Moon her ghost, and he acted like one, only coming out of her apartment at night to go somewhere. Until late spring he was virtually never seen in daylight on the street. He too was an alcoholic, the youngest child of a family of twelve. Moon tended to prepare food for the children more than she did, I believe.

On 5 April Ivery was sweeping her steps and leaned on the broom for a moment at the front of the shop. Telemachus walked to the door, wiping his hands clean on an oiled mechanic's cloth. I raised my head from under the hood of an old Buick I was working on and watched as Telemachus began to perform in front of me.

"I'm going to rape you," he told Ivery, joking.

"No need to do that," she answered him, and gave a list of hotels they could go to.

"We could climb in the back seat of this old Buick." He pointed to the car I was working on.

Ivery turned from Telemachus, thereby cutting off the game, and, like Boycie had in February, asked what nationality Karen and I were. I told her Karen was Irish.

"My old man's Irish too. We ought to get together." She then invited herself up for drinks to our apartment the coming weekend. Right in the middle of her sentence Telemachus said, "No." She

7. *Ivery. Ivery leaned from her window for a conversation with a person on the street. (Photograph by the author)*

wanted to know why not, and I sensed that Telemachus objected to her offer to get acquainted *at our place.* I therefore changed the situation and suggested that we have a picnic, but Ivery replied that she would be ill at ease being the only colored person with Karen, Moon, and me. After she had gone, Telemachus warned me, "You can't let these peoples up to your apartment. They'll see what you have, and then later, when you're gone, they'll come up and take everything."

Piecing together numerous conversations and overheard remarks, I can sketch Ivery's biography and document the changes

8. *Moon and friends. On Easter Sunday morning not everyone dressed up, but those who did not watched and commented on those who did. Notice the Martin Luther King, Jr. Plaza, the tall, windowed building at the left of the picture. (Photograph by the author)*

in her household. Apparently she was reared by a maternal aunt outside Norfolk, Virginia. In her teens she bore two children, a boy and a girl. She met a man named Sims who, on receiving his discharge from the navy, brought her to Philadelphia where she bore one or two children by him. Her first two children remained in Virginia, where her mother cared for them. Ivery adopted Sims's name, and some on the street argued that she had had her name legally changed to his, while others argued that she had not. Her relationship with Sims did not last, and she made her living as a whore, turning tricks at a hotel four blocks from Fourteenth Street, at least until the advent of the federal program Aid to Families with Dependent Children (called ADC). She lived in the hotel and gave birth to four more children.

Ivery's boyfriend, Babe, the one Telemachus claimed he would have to kill, helped her move from the hotel to Montrose Street, where she and her six Philadelphia children lived on the third floor of small, three-story row house. Mamie Tinsley, a tall, very light-skinned, big-boned woman, rented the top floor to her. Miz Mamie's mother we heard, had been raped in a Mississippi farm field by a white man; Miz Mamie was the issue of that union. Three of her four children lived with her; three—Juanita, Pig, and Bubu—were adults, and one—Eve—was a child of about ten.

The Sims children did not enjoy the living arrangements at Miz Mamie's; the house, they said, was haunted. Ghosts floated up and down the creaking stairs at night. There would be a knock on the door, and when it was opened the devil would be standing there. Miz Mamie also had her utilities disconnected, and water had to be carried from neighbors' houses for drinking, cooking, washing, and flushing the toilet. I thought Miz Mamie lacked charm. She was loud and profane in public, and I figured she would just as soon cut you as look at you. Ivery and her children moved from Miz Mamie's on Montrose to the apartment above Telemachus's shop the summer before I went to work for him.

At the end of May, Karen and Ivery were talking on the front step, so I walked over to them from the garage. We talked and Ivery, somewhat embarrassed, revealed that she had children by five fathers. Pat, the seven-year-old, she said, came out ass-back-wards and was a *phone-booth baby*—one whose paternity was uncertain.

Both Pat and Poof, the two youngest, and less often Godfrey, the next oldest boy, hung around the doorway of the shop as Telemachus and I worked. Sometimes Pat would sit next to me on the creeper as I did a brake job. By watching me take the parts off he could tell me where and in what order each went back on. I used mnemonic devices to do that and was impressed with his recall. On 10 May I invited Pat up to the apartment in the evening; he watched television with us. At eleven, hinting that it was time to go home, I said, "It's time for me to go to bed."

"Don't worry about me," he replied, starting to play.

"I'm worried about you," I said, going along with him.

"If you're worried about me, don't say anything."

"OK," I answered, "I won't say anything, but I'll still worry."

He had the last word, "Don't say anything, and don't worry, just think."

I had the distinct impression, one that grew stronger over the spring and summer, that Ivery's young boys would have moved in with us in an instant. As I look back I think that perhaps they should have.

In order of age, after Poof and Pat, was Godfrey, who was then ten. Born with cataracts, he did not see at all well and had been, he told Karen, "left back" a grade. In June Karen took Godfrey to our optometrist friend for tests; later she took him to the doctors at Will's Eye Hospital. At her insistence Godfrey underwent a series of surgical procedures that cleared his vision somewhat, and in the fall, she worked with him on his reading.

In the early summer Godfrey announced that we were his godparents. When Karen asked him how one became a godparent, he told her that if a man walked up to him and gave him five dollars, he would say, "You my godfather!"

On days that Ivery received her ADC check, her oldest boy living in Philadelphia would show up and wait. Everyone called him Sims, and he lived with a boy his own age named Ike, also fourteen, and Ike's mother, near the Leo Hotel where the family used to live. Sims waited inside the window on the second floor overlooking the street. Ivery cashed her check and gave him money, which he then gave to Ike's mother for fostering him.

Ivery's two girls, Judy and Contessa, were twelve and eleven. Contessa was quiet, content it seemed to live in her sister's shadow. Judy was a pleasant person, outgoing and alive to the happenings of the street. She carried gossip well and, in her unassuming way, made it a point to know as much as possible. She connected through her talk several households and the street because she knew much of what went on locally. On 24 May Karen recorded a conversation between the two of them, a conversation that echoed, through Judy's voice, other people in her and her mother's networks.

On Friday evening while I was sitting on the step Judy came over to where I was, sat down next to me, and asked me, "Is Dan a hippie; now you're a lady, but Dan?" I asked her what a

Figure 9. Pat's drawing of the author.

Figure 10. Poof's drawing of his mother.

hippie was, how you could tell a hippie, and why she thought Dan was one. She then proceeded to give me five basic reasons for thinking Dan was a hippie.

(1) When Dan comes walking down the street after working he's dirty.

(2) Dan wears a big mustache and used to wear a beard.

Figure 11. Poof's drawing of a house. Note that he did not draw an image of a row house, the only form of house in which he had lived, but rather drew the American ideal house, which is detached from its neighbors. As in the American Dream, an automobile is associated with a free-standing house.

(3) He says some of the strangest things to us.

(4) He's white. Most young people that are white and have the rest of the above qualifications are hippies. There are some colored hippies.

(5) He wouldn't give you this kind of a wedding ring unless he was a hippie. [I had designed the ring, and it was crafted by a goldsmith.]

Judy seemed very intent on finishing this conversation, which was interrupted by smaller events at least three times. She would come back and pointedly continue trying to decide and have me assist in her decision as to whether Dan was a hippie or not. She cannot put Dan in any other category. It is interesting that she didn't even mention that he works as a mechanic, which is the identity that we have tried to establish mainly, or that he is an artist which she had heard (I know) that he does in the afternoons.

Formal role is not as important as presentation of self.

She made me promise that I would not tell Dan what we had talked about. I solemnly swore to secrecy.

After that talk, Judy, usually with Contessa a step or two behind, gave small presents such as flowers to Karen, and later art supplies taken from school to me, binding in thoughtful gifts our two house-holds. With my brother's half-frame camera, I took pictures of the Sims children on the streets, then invited them over to see them.

By the end of May we were with the children a great deal; we took them for rides in the car, brought them up to the apartment, and talked with them on the street. In a sense we did not listen to Telemachus's warning not to let "those peoples" up to the apart-ment. The Sims children were often in our place and were beau-tifully mannered. My own vision expanded, beyond my reliance on Telemachus, to include in part the world of Ivery's children and the world that the summer street became. Although we did not, like most enthnographers, say who we were by citing a cor-porate-derived identity, people like Judy made up their own minds. Mr. Jimmy, a short bachelor who lived alone up the street and worked at a furniture warehouse, shared a drink with me toward the end of the summer.

"Let me tell you something, Jim," he began. I still did not know how to react to being addressed by a generic name; it was like being called John Doe, except that this was an aesthetic verbal form, both concrete and abstract. He poked his finger hard into my chest a

9. *Judy. Graduation from junior high school. (Photograph by the author)*

couple of times, as if to keep my attention, and thus the interaction, from wandering off the topic. He listened to public radio, he said, and he knew why I was living there. I began to counter him immediately, because I could hear where the monologue was going, but he shut me off. "I know you're here to study poor people; you should go on the Merv Griffin Show and tell how it is." He would not let me respond. "But you're okay. You're *in deep* with me." He added that he saw us with the children. "And that," he added finally, "is beautiful." After that he shut me off completely by turning away and walking down the street.

Pop, an Italian immigrant and retired hospital worker who spoke English poorly, watched Karen closely in public space; several times when she parked the car, he tried to recruit her, and through her me, to live on a white block, "where we could talk with white people," he explained. We were identifying wholly with black people, and no other whites lived on our street. White residences began on Carpenter, which was racially mixed, and increased in number as one walked east toward the all-white area surrounding the Italian

Market. Pop offered to find us lower rents, by nearly 50 percent per month. It was an attractive proposal, but Karen declined.

At the same time that we came to know Ivery's children, in far less direct ways, people other than Judy and Contessa were contacting us, playing it an occasion at a time to see how things might go but involving us more in their daily lives. I was in the shop working with Telemachus on 26 May when Franny, a woman from directly across the street (at the apex of the household location diagram), entered through the open door. She wanted to know if we had anything in the shop that would strip the varnish off furniture because she was refinishing a chair. I told her that Karen had paint remover and I rang the apartment bell. Karen came down and went over to Franny's.

Franny's household was changing rapidly. She lived with an older sister and her widowed father. Her mother had been killed seven years before by a trolley. Only nineteen when we first knew her, Franny forced her sister and her father out and her old man, Herb, moved in. Herb had fathered children by another woman, but his ex-wife and children now lived in the Martin Luther King, Jr., Plaza. Franny's father, Mr. Joe, was a longshoreman of Portuguese descent who had married a black woman from Alabama; together they had had five children, of whom Franny was the youngest. Herb, a truck driver, hauled limestone for a large trucking firm and kept very much to himself; he did not socialize on the street at all and never went to the corner bar. Both he and Franny had been (and perhaps still were) members of a motorcycle club, which was where they had met. A principal network of their friends routinely partied together at the club.

Franny had lived in the neighborhood, although not in that house, most of her life, and she knew nearly everyone she saw on the sidewalk on a day-to-day basis. Through her, Karen and I heard several accounts of businesses, such as a pharmacy and a grocery, that had been on the street corners but now were gone. She and Herb had a child later that year, which consolidated her claim to the spaces in the house.

The people of the third household that described the third angle of the triangle were far more difficult for us to get to know. For one thing, their dialect was more difficult for Karen and me to understand; Boycie said they were *Geechie*, which was a derogatory term that bundled in its connotations both back-country dialect and the Gullah dialect of the Sea Islands off the coast of South Carolina and Georgia. Maryjane, a woman of forty, anchored its member-

ship, but her kinsmen—a mother, two brothers, perhaps others—
and their families were found throughout the area. When we first
moved in, Maryjane had just evicted her boyfriend from her bedroom to the third-floor front. Telemachus remarked that she kept
him *drunk up* so that she would not have to have sex with him.
After that occurred, another lover—a man named Paul—began to
stay more and more. Telemachus commented, "Another *nigger's*
moved in."

Spatially the house was arranged so that the first floor, on entering, was made up of a living room, a dining room, and a kitchen.
From the hallway entrance, stairs led upward. Under the stairs
there was an entrance and stairway from the kitchen to the basement. On the second floor there were two large bedrooms split by
a bathroom, as well as a small bedroom and the stairway to the
third floor. Maryjane and Paul slept in the back bedroom on the
second floor, and her daughter Joyceann, who was nineteen, and
Joyceann's two-year-old son, Little James, slept in front. Maryjane's
ex-lover, Richard, inhabited the third-floor front, while a man who
had rented our apartment before us now rented her third-floor
rear bedroom.

Richard traveled south during the summer and we never saw
him again. Word seemed to float up from down there that he could
not get the money together to return. After Richard left, Maryjane's
brother's daughter, Diane, who was thirteen, came to stay and took
the third-floor front bedroom that Richard had vacated.

Joyceann was pregnant that spring. She would lean back against
her added weight and slowly walk down the street holding corn-
starch in one hand and eating it with the other. Her neck where
it could be seen above her blouse was splashed with white bath
powder. When her mother's lover, Paul, moved in, Joyceann moved
out briefly. Maryjane and Joyceann had a terrible fight in their
kitchen, which I could not help but overhear through our apartment kitchen window. Joyceann complained that she got sick *behind*
(because of) Paul. After that she stayed up the street at her grandmother's house for a few weeks before delivering a baby daughter
she named Chavonne Davette. The Davette was a feminization of
David, the baby's father. It seemed that many young mothers while
we lived on Fourteenth Street named their children for the fathers,
as if to remind the world of their role in the production. One
woman, for example, named two of her daughters Kenyatta, after
their father, Kenny.

Maryjane's household, then, was in relatively rapid motion: Rich-

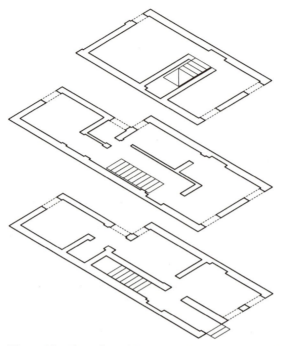

Figure 12. Floor plan of Maryjane's house. Computer drawing.

ard went down south; Paul moved in; Diane came to stay; Joyceann, after she delivered her second child, Chavonne Davette, moved back into the front bedroom with James, the two-year-old, and the baby. Maryjane had wanted Diane to help Joyceann with the new baby, but Diane was too immature.

If I were to generalize, I would say that all the households on the street were noticeably in motion, adding members, changing members. I had a sense of continual and rather rapid change, relative, that is, to the middle-class families of my childhood; there was a fundamental, ongoing expectation of changes, realignments, and domestic movement. One left the street for a day and returned knowing that someone had moved out or moved in, often accompanied by some excitement or a minor dramatic episode.

Three years later in 1972, John Szwed, in his capacity as director of the Center for Urban Ethnography, was invited by the Bureau of the Census to consult on the failures of the 1970 decennial count. The bureau had seriously undercounted minorities, including blacks, and was inviting experts to share their perceptions with bureau personnel. Szwed asked me to accompany him and offer a

10. Joyceann. On Easter Sunday people tended to dress up, but not all, necessarily, went to church. Hot pants, modeled here, were in style in 1971. (Photograph by the author)

case study based on my field experience to illustrate counting problems. I used Diane as an example of a counting difficulty, since she had moved into Maryjane's household during the spring of 1970, when the census was conducted. Diane's mother and father were separated, her grandmother lived nearby, and she had just left her grandmother's house for her aunt's. How was she counted that spring? Was she counted at all? She could have been counted by all, some, or none of the four households to which she belonged: her mother's, her father's, her grandmother's, and Maryjane's.

The different division heads sitting around the table at the bu-

Diane's mother's household	Diane's father's houseshold	Diane's and grandmother's household	Diane's and (aunt) Maryjane's household
X	X	X	X
X	X	X	—
X	X	—	—
X	—	—	—
—	—	—	—

X Possibly counted
— Possibly not counted
This chart provides an example of some possible counts of Diane "for census purposes," though it does not exhaust the possible combinations of count and miscount.

reau dismissed the possibility with the argument that *for census purposes the various heads of households knew how to include Diane on the forms.* My question was, What census purposes? Do people in neighborhoods read the minds of the designers of census forms?

The 1970 forms were sent out by mail and followed up, at Fourteenth and Carpenter at least, by census takers who helped people who had problems. The process was, I knew first-hand, hit or miss on Fourteenth Street, for we and others had not been counted. While it is not germane to my point to address all the issues raised by a single, simple case study, a question from one of the heads of a research division proved how difficult census taking was in a population that was not particularly middle-class in its social organization. He asked, Who picks up the mail? Good question. By that query he meant to say that whoever picked up the mail made out the census response.

My answer was a question: Who received mail? Not one person I met during fieldwork used a checkbook or a credit card. My impression was that people did not write letters to one another. Only utility bills would arrive by mail, unless the utilities were paid by the landlord. If Maryjane was easing Richard out of and Paul into the domestic arrangements, did Paul pick up the mail? Did she receive mail at the house or at the postal station? Would Paul fill out a census form for what was to him a new household? Would he have taken Maryjane's form and filled it out for the family—a woman and children—he was no longer living with? Would he have thrown the form away? Would Maryjane have picked up the form and filled it out and included both Paul and Richard on the response? And what of Diane and the renter?

My impression based on my years there was that households were always reforming themselves and that changes were closely monitored by people living nearby. Changes in a household were something that everyone talked about and frankly moralized on whenever they occurred. The street, a public and communal place held together by sight and by gossip in the form of picturesque stories, was a communication medium in which households were monitored routinely as a part of local theatrics.

The census undercount may well have missed not only the Dianes, who had a number of options in living arrangements, but also the Pauls and Richards, who were in transition between houses or who were resident lovers but not anchors for a household's membership. My belief now is that the heads of the census operations did not much care for the implications of the case study, although I think these implications were far-reaching for counting people in this country, particularly because the makers of census forms seemed to have a solidly white, middle-class image of a household and its organization and behavior.

•　　•　　•

From my file box of field notes I have pulled a selection of cards from seven different days in May in order to illustrate the effects of advancing warm weather on the cultural uses of street space. Always forced into looking backward from this moment in time to those moments, I rethink what evidence I have for what I did and thought then. Karen, in taking notes and in talking with me, compared explicitly and implicitly what she experienced in terms of how she and I grew up. We juxtaposed our traditions—white, midwestern, educated—against those of the people we were living near. In the notes I also attempted to fit what went on during the day with what I had read in the anthropological literature. Layered over my childhood traditions was my resocialization within the academy with its literature of intellectual interpretation.

In this section I want to illustrate the growing life of the street set against my life. I want to take the everyday life of the street and frame it, implicitly contrast it, reinscribe it self-consciously, as a way of life *adjacent to my way of life*. I do not mean, however, that I want to compare Fourteenth and Carpenter public space with my childhood space of small-town America, although my early experiences obviously unconsciously inform any observations and interpretations I make. I also do not mean that I want to take my personal reactions written in the field notes as a reconstituted text to accompany the development of street life. Rather, I want to juxtapose, for purposes of understanding, life on the street as everyday life with academic life as everyday life. Two modes of being in the world, two variations of everyday life, were slammed together, purposefully, and I want to take a definite stance on the artifice of that union.

The academic life, especially for those who practice ethnography, has made information gathering and thought about it central features of its subculture. The culture of ethnographers as members of a profession, in this case anthropology, housed within a larger corporate structure, the university, represents a series of subcultures of the everyday, the departments and their associated disciplines. I address life in the street as being penetrated and appropriated by the ethnographer's culture of knowing. The street was to be written about and then inscribed for another realm of everyday life in America.

By drawing on Heidegger and Sartre for contrastive purposes, I imply that the attitudes fixed within the larger culture are already hostile to outdoor street life. The quotidian of the academy is no less so. The ways of life of people in the street and of the ethnographer cannot be merely juxtaposed. The relation between them is based on tacit if not open conflict.

Drama depends for its life on fiction; and the street, for children and adults alike, was an arena of fiction-encounters. People engaged one another with what appeared to be complete personal autonomy, fictional selves, and masterful inventions of intentions and activities. Diane was one of a number of people who attempted to play with Karen, but she did so in such a way that Karen and I were baffled, partly because neither of us understood how to fictionalize ourselves in the discourse of imaginative play. It was a speech genre we both found difficult to understand, much less master. On 2 May Karen wrote:

> I was sitting on the steps watching our dog, Jennie. I was facing to the right of the steps, Diane was facing the street. We were sitting close but not facing each other. Diane said she was going to see the Jackson Five, a rock group. I had read about them in the *Philadelphia Tribune* so knew about them. Diane seemed surprised that I knew about the group and then

told me she was going to the Civic Center at nine o'clock to see them (this was about 7:30 P.M.). She was going to wear a *pants set* made of silk. She described it down to gold trim around the collar and long full sleeves. She was also going to wear a wig (I think she said she had three wigs). I have never seen Diane's own hair. She always wears a black scarf. I expressed an interest in seeing her outfit. She said she would ring my bell before she left, about eight o'clock. I believed her to be telling the truth. I noted it was already seven-thirty and she better get ready. I went upstairs to get supper.

An hour and a half later I heard Dan talking to Diane, Judy, etc. I thought maybe she was ready and was going to walk downstairs and see her. I said to Dan who was downstairs, "Is Diane dressed?"

I had told Dan where Diane was going. Meanwhile he was asking her, "When are you going?" She said, "What are you talking about?" Dan repeated and Diane reiterated her answer. Dan then did not pursue it because he then knew she had lied.

I left with Dan later and talked to her from the window of her house. Judy and Contessa were also there. I started to ask her why she had not gone but stopped in the middle of my question.

The face-to-face play, in which Karen was to counter with a similar speech genre but certainly was not to *believe*, as if the play were some positive version of the fact-world, extended outward. That is, the children could construct a play world that had elements of social organization, a fictive social organization that seemed to hover between the fact-world and the play in which they might achieve their finest social realization. In reading Karen's following field note, the reader can see how the very naming process in the making of fictive social relations was brought, in a discursive way, from the child's play toward Karen's educated register. The note was written on 12 May, ten days after the one just quoted.

Diane told me that if anyone was mean to her, would beat her up, she would tell her club. Then she told me it was called *Omagify Socializers*. Charmaigne was the one who finally was able to pronounce it correctly. It came out as "Omagify Socialists," or "Omagify Socialistics," several times before we finally understood the correct name, the Omega Phi Socializers. It is made up of seventeen girls and they protect each other. If someone gets hurt by some other person outside the club, then the whole club will go and *work* the person. (Diane will kiddingly say to me, "I'm going to work you," meaning, "I'm going to beat you up.") I said, "I'm glad you warned me." They both seemed surprised at my reaction and readily assured me they wouldn't do anything to me. Their reasoning was "You're grown." They said that if they hurt me they could get in serious trouble.

I asked if they could hurt me or Dan or Telemachus. Diane said they could hurt Telemachus, but Charmaigne disagreed. "He's grown," she repeated. I said, "I'm not going to mess with you." And they again said they wouldn't hurt me. They asked if Dan and I wanted to come to a dance they were having. I asked the details. Two or three clubs were going to have a dance in someone's home. They would bring records. They would do the *Tom Jones*, the latest dance. Diane said the *Tom Jones* was almost out of style.

It sounds rather informal. I mentioned that Dan would look funny at an all-girl dance. Charmaigne said there would be boys there too.

The next day, 13 May, Karen came to the shop to see me. In a moment of epiphany—an epiphany that occurred closer to this writing than to the actual encounter—the everyday life of the street was revealed through a negative example by Telemachus to Karen. Their discussion concerned me. Karen wrote:

> This morning I talked to Telemachus and Dan in the back of the garage. He said, "Dan tells me you were never married."
>
> "That's right," I said. "He told me if that ever comes up in public to always agree with what he told someone, that we were never married."
>
> Telemachus then said, "Dan laughs and jokes, but he never plays. He always tells the truth."

In a joking relationship initiated by Telemachus, Karen always struggled to find the basis of the banter. On this occasion, Telemachus spoke telegraphically, without commentary or Cartesian deconstructive work, and put into focus the juxtaposition of our lives, his public one against my corporate-academic one. He glossed, by the transcribed phrase "but he never *plays*," the *genius loci* and how I did not, though I did not realize it, act like a local person. He pointed out that I had not mastered the salient speech genre of everyday social life. The *play* was exactly what Diane performed when she said she was attending the Jackson Five concert. The same play-life occurred when customers and I stood in front of the shop for a few slack moments and talked.

• • •

The study of everyday life is problematic and contains the fundamental contradiction that one way of life, the ethnographer's, is planted within another way of life and attempts through writing to internalize what happens. The aim is to take the mundane life, in this case of the street, into the realm of thought and to distribute it through prose. The ethnographer's way of life includes leaving and returning to the academic setting, no longer having to make the effort to act as one's temporary neighbors do. Since the nineteenth century, the ethnographer has moved in two social directions: outward to study the peoples of a "shattered world" in which "we interviewed the survivors" (Wolf 1980:457), and downward to live briefly with and document the lives of the lower classes, as did Beatrice Webb. These two movements, outward and downward in social space, define the professional motion of the ethnographer who, desiring a career, then returns to the social location left a year or two before.

"Dan laughs and jokes," Telemachus told Karen, "but he never plays. He always tells the truth." It was not the last sentence that seemed important to me, though it was accurate; it was the three words, "He never plays." The pervasive play of public life was systematically blocked by a notion I had that the performances of the self as fiction were, as Karen recorded in her field note, *lies*. With condensed, almost poetic precision, Telemachus remarked on the incommensurate linguistic relationship in which I had professionally placed myself, an absurd relationship. He told Karen in effect that I was not wise to the language of verbal play. On the street or in the shop, one must not stray too far from verbal play. One winter day, Raymond was in the shop, and we were both lying on creepers under a car, pulling the transmission. Telemachus said something to me that I could not understand. Several times I asked him to repeat what he said and several times he did. Then he refused to with an inhaled *ts* of disgust. Raymond said to me, "You done blew de cool." Words in the play must always be cool; if the mutual poise in give and take broke down through incompetence, the coolness disappeared and the dramatic tension of the moment was shot.

In ethnographic inquiry, which we term *in the field* in order to sustain the distance between us and them, there occurs an overlap of at least two everyday lifeways. The structure of an academic department, academic life, and anthropology (or, for that matter, American civilization or folklore or sociology) as a profession informs the ethnographer. Ethnographers do not leave their world behind but carry it very much with them. While the aim of ethnography is to place its practitioners in the way of others, it does so without giving up anything; there is no fundamental change in the ethnographer's culture back home as a result of the field stay. That is, the institutional organization of anthropology, the academic department, and the university are not altered by the contact. The field remains contained.

The dominant elements of my life-world in relation to household, shop, and street at Fourteenth and Carpenter were that my world was wholly incorporated legally within institutions and that the people I associated with every day had no appreciable existence inside corporate American life at all. The American Anthropological Association, the University of Wisconsin that included its department of anthropology, the University of Pennsylvania that included its Center for Urban Ethnography, were all corporate entities. My corporate identity, tacit and outside my consciousness, dominated my mode of relating to others while living there. The conversations I wrote down and the people I talked with, recorded in my field notes, photographed, laughed with, and went places with were captured in order to be placed as prose inside the literature of corporate life.

The corporate principle dominates the life of the West and is the central social institution that made the industrial revolution, indeed modern science, possible (Braudel 1977, 1986; Chandler 1977; Rosenberg and Birdzell 1986). Partially outside it, not fully enfranchised historically, and actively resisted in the present, are the lower classes, especially those classes comprising peoples of darker skin color. The corporate principle gathers up activities, especially in America, and moves to incorporate them into legal institutional structures. Even the well-publicized and peculiar American institution, the voluntary association, is modeled after the corporation. Like the university, Exxon, or the federal government, the voluntary association has a charter, elected officers, a membership, a budget, a set of goals or mission, and enormous demands for external information. Corporations are legitimated institutions built on information from outside themselves. Ethnographers have provided for the (in)corporate(d) West one of the methodologies by which information is captured and made to flow from outside to inside. The corporate principle, pervasive enough in the ethnographer's everyday life to remain largely hidden, has most often set up a discursive space that excluded nonethnographers from having a voice inside the corporate walls. Seminars, symposia, lectures, and publications were made by and for the professional but not those the professional discussed. Corporations are by their very nature inward-looking, self-privileging social and textual constructions. The information at the boundary of the corporation (the ethnographer in the field is a temporary deformation of the boundary) alters dramatically. Telemachus was not transported into the everyday life of an anthropology department. He stayed in South Philadelphia, and his words, inscribed on paper, were taken to a research center and read and reread, transformed from a field text into prose for a profession and, for the *author* (who was no longer Telemachus), into a career. All this was conducted out of sight, inside a socially bounded set of corporate structures (see Said's comments 1983:169).

The street was a world that was completely unincorporated. The people who lived there touched corporate life, but always as if from the outside, across the counter or at the entry level. People went to stores, shopped at private companies, but were not themselves controlling members of public, private, or not-for-profit companies. They were, however, increasingly defined as citizens by the federal and local governments, and thus were brought further into the public corporation of governance.

I have discussed the corporate-noncorporate split in modes of living everyday life because ethnographers should be seen as members of self-privileging corporate entities. To take this into consideration is to acknowledge another way of knowing ourselves. The corporate form of life names phenomena, forms objects, imports information, and inscribes and circulates literate ideas about local peoples. It is a remarkable transformation process, but one that carries a deep contradiction within itself and an implicit domination not restricted to the formation of a canon or artifact collection. In part the contradiction lies in the fact that the corporation evolved as the mode of social organization to colonize the globe both for trade and for the exportation of European populations. The first

American colonies, for example, were all founded as private-sector companies.

Corporate knowing, with its bureaucratic rationalities, demands a highly disciplined labor force, whether manual or intellectual. To know ourselves, and the contradictions inherent in in-corporation—such as the moving of information inside company walls for purposes of a career and an informed profession, the formation of objects we have called natives or savages, the racially different, or the lower classes—we must move, not to points outside humanity that we imagine when inside our institutions, themselves the mountainous heights of the *Übermensch,* but toward others in more intimate, and self-alienating, embrace. Ethnography has evolved as a form of corporate knowledge conducted in part by highly ritualized discourse; within it there lie concealed, perhaps, the desire and the possibility to move beyond the restricted uses to which it has been so often put. Life on the street constantly subverted for me the rationalized knowing into which I had been institutionally socialized. Now I can glimpse the fact that I systematically was blind and deaf to much that happened.

•   •   •

From my point of view in the early spring, performance arenas where play-talk went on were restricted for the most part to the shop, the spaces just in front of the garage and Lombardo's junk shop, the steps to our apartment, and street corners. With each day the stage enlarged until in the midsummer heat, as when Caesar argued with Telemachus over the Coupe de Ville's poor transmission, people were inhabiting the street most of the daylight hours and much of the night.

Proprietary feelings governed certain public spaces. Strangers did not sit on one's stoop. Parking spaces were also, in this sense, owned. Telemachus had to park cars on the street, and in May 1970 the city was full of cars. Finding a parking spot, especially one where the children would not turn the car into a toy, or someone purloin a part, was critical. Customers held Telemachus responsible for autos in his care during the period of repair.

On 22 May I parked a blue Cadillac convertible with a white top up the street in front of a house that belonged to a longshoreman-minister and his family. I then took the keys to the shop and gave them to Telemachus. Later, as I walked up the street, the neighbor's ten-year-old son, Greg, ran out of the house and said to me, "My mother wants you to move the car so my father can park there." I was walking the other way and did not have the keys, so I said

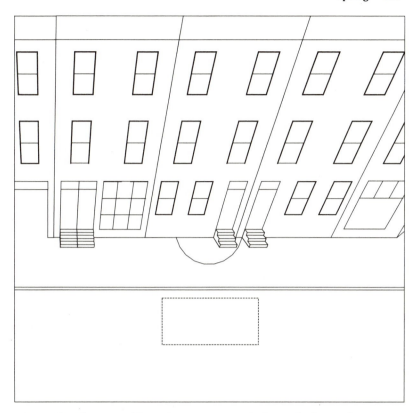

Figure 13. The street with two important spaces in front of a house, the stoop space and the parking space. While these spaces were not in any legal sense owned, they were policed by the inhabitants of the house and considered their *space. Computer drawing.*

to Greg, "Go ask Telemachus; he has the keys." He went back into the house. The next morning the car was splashed with black paint that dripped from the white roof down the window and door. I asked Telemachus who did it. "Greg and Steve," he replied. I went to work removing the paint from the Cadillac.

Jesse, a mechanic that Telemachus and I both knew who worked two blocks away at a gas station, came by as I was cleaning the paint off. Telemachus said he thought the kids up the street had thrown it. Jesse said, "It was probably parked in front of somebody's house," and Telemachus remarked on how much the incident had hurt him. The man who owned the car had come around, seen the paint, and told Telemachus he would not pay for the repair.

Obviously the street and its objects, such as parked autos, were highly used, by children for example, as play-space, and one was not free to park just anywhere. Dramatic reprisals for incursions into sacredly defined space were considered legitimate. The police could be called, for example, as they were when Sonny lay and slept on the stoop of the house where he was staying.

At the same time that space was defined, used, and talked about, and its safety bought through small gifts, an element of culture cut across space, spreading out and animating, in the strictest sense of that word, whoever wished to participate. Music that seeped through doors or windows was everyone's. Music was carried in the form of cassette playing machines by a man (not a woman) walking on the sidewalk, and the sound belonged to everyone who heard it. People moved to sound, even when it came from hidden sources. On 27 May, Karen wrote.:

> Dan has been very sensitive to vocal levels of speech and consequently vocal levels of listening. Franny was sitting on the steps with me at noon. There was the usual noise of trolleys, cars, talking, etc. But Franny began humming along with a song that was playing from the radio in Telemachus's garage. The radio is halfway to the back of the garage. And I had not even been aware that the radio was playing. A similar thing happened yesterday when I was with her.

Musical space is a topic in its own right, and if there was a Durkheimian social fact, it was that popular music, to hear, to move to, to sing eidetically along with, was the collective conscience-consciousness.

> Someday, we'll be together
> Yes we will, yes we will
>
> My love is yours, baby
> All right from the start
> . . .
>
> A long time ago
> I made a big mistake
> I said goodbye. . . .
>
> (Diana Ross and the Supremes)

By the end of May I discovered the formation of instant intimate space wherever one performed to embarrass another. I went over

Figure 14. A radio inside the repair shop created a bubble of musical sound on the street. This was a space that one could move through and, as one did, dance to the music. Or if one was sitting within the bubble, one listened and moved one's body to the rhythm of the music. Computer drawing.

to GI Joe's Auto Supply to buy a gasket for Telemachus, who told me as I left, "Don't tell them where you work. I owe them some money. I would have gone over to pay them but they *loudtalked* me." When he entered the store, the man behind the counter had loudly reminded him of his indebtedness as a way of requesting that Telemachus pay the fifteen dollars he owed.

Public space was also sexually charged space, as evidenced by Sonny talking with Karen and Telemachus avoiding Ivery because of her jealous lover, Babe. If to *see* was to *know* someone, then to *talk with* was to *go with* someone. Once, when I talked with Ivery near her front step, she told me people were *at that moment* talking about us. Male-female talk contained danger and humor, often scripted into the same moment. One way in which humor was generated, if it was not central to the life on the street, was close to it. I heard it from child and adult. The aim was to try humorously to damage intimate ties in order to see what would happen, a ploy akin to Raymond's theft games. Karen wrote on a field note in August:

> This afternoon Godfrey said, "I saw Danny with another girl." I said, "Who was it?" He said, "I don' know, your sister, I think."
>
> Tonight Godfrey said to Dan in front of me, "I saw a man feeling Karen's leg this afternoon." Dan said, "Now you got me mad." Dan pretended to try and cut his throat. I said, "You weren't there when that man felt my leg."
>
> Godfrey looked at Dan and said, "See, I told you!"

After one talked with a person of the opposite sex, one could encounter damaging sexual accusation. One not only was talked about but was confronted humorously with fictitious (or real?) sexual involvements. The humorous accusations of a third party could lead to fights between the man and woman on whom the game had been started.

As spring gave way to summer the theatrical pace of life quickened and lengthened as many people spent more and more of their life out of doors.

5. Summer

The public life of summer rolled over us like a great wave. In June I wrote in the field notes: "People read behaviors in public as if they were a definite language; and this reading seems to be more sensitively done than in other sorts of publics." As the summer unfolds in my rereading of the notecards, I want to show that what resulted was in part a foundation for cultural life, in a sense, a metaphysical pervasiveness, a life of performance in the aesthetically shaped moment. Metaphysics claims for itself the study of the ultimate nature of experience and existence in relatively self-contained conceptual systems. I am not after philosophical truths, but I am after an interpretation and evocation of the street, which is not altogether self-contained, that will stimulate the imagination of the reader. By the end of July, I had a crude verbal map of public space summarized in the field notes, filed at the end of the month and labelled, PUBLICS. "Our publics," the note began, in an explicit contrast of street life with the middle-class life, "seem to be almost all bureaucratically organized, hence they have entrance requirements." The outdoor spaces on Fourteenth and Carpenter, alive with people watching and listening both indoors and out, had no entrance requirements, were not guarded, were not bounded by a corporate charter and selected membership. People moved freely through the area.

In discussing outdoor summer life I want to present the map of its spaces, both fixed and ambient; who appears in those spaces; and what performances or plays take place there. To prefigure understanding I want to introduce an almost metaphysical aesthetics. The central core of life on the street was *motion*, and things that moved aesthetically received decoration and adornment. Heads, arms, feet, and bodies moved and received special aesthetic treatment. Heads, for men, were augmented with hats; hats of all kinds were seen everywhere. The upper lip of men, which moved with speech, was decorated by a mustache. Nearly every man had one, though Telemachus told me that black men were ridiculed by whites in North Carolina for wearing them. Men's shoes were the best, expensive. The auto, a motion machine, was selected not only for the statement it made about oneself but for how it made one feel. The auto was often customized by after-market additions purchased to increase its aesthetic appeal.

Clothing was worn like a mask—a mask not of concealment but of revelation. It was a statement or indicator, not just of self in some abstract way, but of where one wanted to appear as a performer in the public staging. One of Telemachus's part-time mechanics during the summer was a night watchman named Tom. He and I worked briefly alongside one another in the shop in June, and I wrote down a summary of one of my conversations with him.

> Tom gave me a vision of his life. He is buying a house and so is his younger brother. His older brother, however, had fifty jobs a year to his one, he said. The older brother is a welder and has worked on the drydocks at the Naval Yard. He'll leave home for maybe three months but always come home to momma. Tom told him the other day to get himself started on building a wardrobe and since they are the same size to use his clothes whenever he wanted to. His brother came home the other day with a twenty-eight-dollar pair of shoes, a twenty-two-dollar pair of pants, a fifteen-dollar shirt, and a forty-dollar cardigan sweater. Tom said he really looked good and when he went out onto the street all the girls talked to him. *Tom said, "If he'd build a good wardrobe, like I've done, he'd get ambitious."*

Clothing makes the man; the logic, according to Tom, was that if one presented a finely turned out version of oneself and was made social by it, one became, *behind that* (as a result of), ambitious. In other words, one would have performance possibilities to live up to.

The space around the body was a highly visual one that attracted or repelled others, but it was a highly charged proximal space as well. I was talking with a woman whom I knew well and and reached out at one point to touch her shoulder. She intercepted my hand with her eyes, objectifying my hand and arm. I felt as though the whole limb was detached and burned by her intense, visual concentration. I withdrew a scorched stump and never reached toward her again in any intimate gesture, though we were close friends.

It was as if the tension between persons, such as that in the sexual space Telemachus alluded to and even that among persons of the same sex, was created by the pull between the poles of autonomy and intimacy. The autonomy of self was totally pervasive; each self considered other selves autonomous in terms of taste, actions, ambitions, attitudes, and values—"You gotta do your own thing." This powerful distancing—a constant, dramatic, unbalanced force—was set against an always-shifting intimacy made possible by speech and gesture. The aesthetic value of the tension was continually assured by keeping this play of *great distance–no distance* implicit. One did not allude to it as it happened; one had to perform it, reading and responding to every gesture between people present to one another.

One winter day in the shop, for example, Raymond needed to go outdoors and wanted to use the gloves Auston had on. He asked Auston for them, but Auston did not even acknowledge that he had heard, and I began to wonder what would happen. I started to watch very closely, out of the corner of my eye, what Auston would do. Very slowly he pulled off the gloves, placed them on the trunk lid of a car, and moved on about his business. I thought the move was very cool because he showed no emotion; he did not, for example, seem to resent the request. Instead, he said absolutely nothing in what was for me a charged atmosphere. Raymond walked over to the trunk lid, pulled the gloves on, and, not saying anything either, just went out the door.

Autonomy and intimacy were vastly remote poles present to some degree in every interactive occasion; they were bridged by speech, gesture, and play. The autonomy kept a relationship abstract and distant, even as two people became intimate with each another. Intimacy, rather than overcoming or conquering distance and abstraction, seemed actually to evoke them. As a result there was a magnificent sense, among the intimately acquainted, of externality: one could not peer *into* another: the interior remained forever opaque. Rather, through long experience one interrogated the other's *ways* and thus built up a knowledge that was always incomplete and could be surprised by sudden revelations or actions. An old woman remarked how her old husband could go to bed as one person and wake up as another. I had an extended conversation one night with the wife of Maryjane's brother Sammy about how a man could stay out all night and not be *changed* by it. A woman, she asserted, was changed by staying out all night.

The autonomy of the self led to a society of autonomous selves that were radically democratic. Szwed wrote of this as it is captured in jazz: "The rise of jazz was the most stunning of modernisms, becoming a form that carried within it the theory of relativity, surrealism, primitivism, radical democracy, and a new way of *being*, all at once" (1986).

Again, balanced in tension with the externality of all selves, was talk or gossip about another. One did not merely talk about another person in some particular situation; one mimed the other's speech, taking up the voice and manner, in telling the story. Stories were not only told but re-enacted as minor plays themselves. The storyteller, or enacter, then, collapsed the space between the person talked about and the person now telling or performing the story. One could literally, for the moment, wear the persona and speech of another.

In the dramatic realization of the metaphysic of motion and beauty, and the always stretched dynamic distance between intimacy and autonomy, one could ridicule, mime, burlesque, dance, and sing about others in personal or generic situations. The theater of public space was not defined by such a simple relationship as performer-audience, but rather by the ever-present possibilities of humor and death. Fun and danger were mixed; play could become fateful, and intimacy, drained instantly of humor by a gesture, could blossom into sudden death. Humor and death, eroticism and adventure, were bundled together and could develop or diminish spontaneously in given encounters. Humorous performance was played against a serious backdrop of instigator-damaged relationships, of death itself.

Triads were the smallest unit of street performance. It was not the triad of the public fire-eater in Mexico City or the contortionist at the Centre Pompidou in Paris: one performer and two or more members of an audience. It was a triad of two performers playing before the third member of the party who was, for the moment, the audience. And whoever was audience could become player. The performers could impugn a member of the audience, and both players and audience could take turns in the two separate roles during the same theatrical event. Telemachus playing with me in front of two women, or two men *jugging*, as Telemachus and Old Gray Fox did, for the street in front of the shop—these were minor theatrical pieces. The more serious, or should I say more fateful, play was the kind that Raymond instigated—trouble, *starting shit*—when he confronted me in front of Telemachus, knife in each hand, because he wanted, through theater, through the adventurous embrace of danger itself, to make himself feel better. In children's play, three children would rotate parts; two performed against the third, the audience, but were then implicated, as in a theft game, in the next turn at play.

• • •

Karen sat on the step much of the summer. I worked part-time for Telemachus, then off and on sculpted, had bronzes cast, sat on the street, and played cards or checkers or visited far into the night. One of Telemachus's young employees, Charles, who lasted only several weeks, came up to the apartment with his girlfriend one evening. I showed him one of the rather minimalist bronze pieces. Titled SLAB, it was a rectangular box open on one side with a hole at the top. A human figure lay crumpled beneath the hole, as if it had been trying to escape. Charles looked at it and commented, "Now I *know* you're a witch doctor."

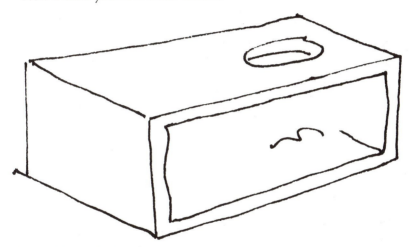

Figure 15. SLAB. Drawing.

As the summer progressed and I took notes, my overriding concern was that I was not acquiring adequate information. I felt as if I were straining to learn, to absorb knowledge, and the effort blunted the ease with which I should have taken life on the street, with its slow rhythms punctuated by dramatic incidents.

The street, with its charged space and fixed zones, felt highly charged with people moving about. The fixed areas included the spaces around the stoops, the spaces inside the houses, and the parking spaces in front of the houses. Outside the immediate street area were school, work, agency, and retail spaces, mostly white, also fixed. The space—one's body in motion, the others one was walking with—included the conversational expanse, within or outside houses, and the leisure regions, such as the bar, the cabaret, the speakeasy, or the street itself.

To say that these were fixed reserves that could be moved through does not capture the ways in which they were personated. Telemachus, I noticed, would on occasion begin talking to and joking with *complete strangers* (the term is from the white middle class), as he did, for example, when he entered for the first time the street life in front of the house of Mary Jackson, his black lover. He was already engaged in performing as he got out of his car because he was with her, and he was able to transform an anonymous space into a far more intimate one for himself by joking with people sitting nearby.

Anyone could appear in a space, but it helped to show intention or to have a reason for being there; otherwise people would take action by asking if they needed help, for example. A stranger passing through could stop and play a game of chess for money with someone who had a board set up beside his stoop. Persons walking through a space were either known or not known. Those who drove through a space in a car and recognized someone familiar on the street honked and waved, perhaps stopped and talked. Men and women walked together, but male-male and female-female groupings were more common. Often several women and their children walked together as a travel group, going shopping or just visiting. Against the house fronts, other people stood or sat. Greetings were not mandatory, although they indicated one's relationships to others. One could see another person every day and still not show visible recognition.

Public space also had its special effects. Ivery claimed to me that she could become invisible and leave the house, and that no one could see where she was going. There was from my point of view an exaggerated sense that everyone saw you, everyone talked about you, everyone on the street kept track of you. Ivery's statement reflected this pragmatic paranoia, and from my experience I would say that in her case the feeling was warranted.

During the winter people tended not to visit one another in their houses. I observed that in cold weather the people who entered a house were either relatives or an individual's best friends, though it would be an exaggeration to claim this would be true for all households. Parties were a different matter. The Omega Phi Socializers did have their party with boys, and we provided the record player and attended. At birthday parties, too, there would be a full house. If there was a small party with couples, like the ones Franny

11. Households on the street. In this scene there are five households represented including neighbors from across the street and people from a boarding house. The mothers are caring for their own children and minding *Little James. (Photograph by the author)*

and Herb had, only those invited tended to show up. But during the summer the household turned inside out, as if there were a large incision in the house and the interior suddenly spilled onto the sidewalk. Photographs show that visiting, rearing children, game playing, arguments, *loudtalking*, private conversations, hustling, skating, rope jumping, woofing, and just sitting and watching became paramount. Music poured from inside houses through open windows, from the garage, and from the corner bar jukebox. The street was totally alive.

It would be satisfying to list all the spaces used by the people I knew, then to list all the performance genres, then to list all the social groupings or individuals associated with each space and each performance genre, and finally to use the subsequent semiotic matrix as the source of thought about local public space. Two other dimensions would make such a matrix invaluable: first, a historical comparison within Afro-America, and second, a comparison with other areas, such as a white working-class neighborhood, also in Philadelphia.

As I read through my field notes and arrange them into categories, I select vignettes that illuminate the summer street.

Spaces

I have an image of everyone making several intimate spaces for themselves from the already anchored intimate locales of street life around the city, the way Telemachus made himself at home on the street where Mary Jackson lived. A vast network of public spaces emerges, tied together by persons who fit into several such zones for longer or shorter durations. The image is of a wholly interconnected, slow-moving fluidity of ever-changing persons in contact through all the black public, residential, and work spaces, held together in large part by frequent or infrequent face-to-face visits and telephone calls.

Rough Theater

This is the theater of noise. . . . Of course it is most of all dirt that gives roughness its edge; filth and vulgarity are natural, obscenity is joyous: with these the spectacle takes on its socially liberating role, for by nature the popular theater is anti-authoritarian, anti-pomp, anti-pretence. (Brook 1968:61)

The profoundly local, rough theater of performance, this large stage of housefront, sidewalk, and street with its intense but almost invisibly achieved visual awareness of everyone, was, in addition to its consummate aesthetic quality with endless improvisations, an economic and legal space. Public and private domains crosscut one another and crosscut the endlessly interconnected households in processes of continuous re-formation. The street was a locus of exchanges between acquaintances and strangers, and it was the legitimate theater for lesser or greater public arguments.

The *Street*

"Out there on the *street*."

Where improvisation and the little *play* re-form anything
Where all players as they are playing are co-authors of the
    script, which unfolds as it is lived in those dramatic moments
Where popular music is compressed theater

Where popular music is the theater of morality

Where sexual joking is the theater of intimacy

Where watching others is the theater of intimacy

Where the least gesture is the theater of intimacy

Where there are breakthroughs into nonperformance, and where those breakthroughs are healed as soon as possible and performance is restored

Where theater is played without authority

The theater of confrontation

The theater of jealousy

The theater of disgust

The theater of theft

The theater of litigation

The theater of heterophony

The theater of pleasure

The theater of gossip

The theater of laughter

Where the greeting "What's happenin' " raises the curtain

Where the stage (inhabited by the audience) is completely round and stretches to the other side of infinity

Where theater begins with costuming

Where costumes create an instant audience

Where a costume defines the role and suggests the lines

Where the play is subtle beyond words

Where motion is the metaphysic of beauty

Where things that move (feet, arms, heads, bicycles, bodies, cars, spirits of the dead) are adorned, decorated, aesthetically enhanced

Play:

    The play

    Playing

    Players

    Playful

    To make a play

    To make a play for

To play with
To play on
Plaything
Spontaneous theater:
The action
The story
The game
Rapping
Word up
To read (someone)
To go into my act
To be in someone's face
To be in someone's chest
He said/she said
Starting shit

Looking

A junkie asked me for a quarter and I gave it to him. I had looked at him. Telemachus said, "Don't ever look at those junkies." Today I avoided looking at him, and he did not ask me for money.

•   •   •

"I really gets turned on by watching peoples' reactions. I studies them and I can tell what they are thinking just by watching them."

•   •   •

Old C.C. was in the bus station last night. He was standing watching people. Although he lived two doors from me, he did not acknowledge me as I passed through the lobby, looking in his direction.

•   •   •

A man had sideswiped a number of parked cars on the street and the trolley could not pass. Local people gathered on the sidewalk to watch the unfolding spectacle. As the driver and passengers on the trolley looked inquisitively at the street, wondering why they could not proceed, the local children challenged them with a shouted word, "*Newsy!*" To be newsy was to attend to events more closely than was warranted.

• • •

Taking a break from work, I went to the bar late in the afternoon for a meatball sandwich. Tucker, whose mother was black and father was Italian, was sitting at the bar. He too did mechanical work, but not for Telemachus. There was a large bulge beside his left eye, and I was surprised by it.

"Hey, man, what happened to you?"

"I was walking down the street with my girlfriend, minding my own business, and a man walking toward us hit me. I asked him, 'Man, what did you want to do that for?' He said, 'Cause you wuz *gritten* on me.' I said, 'I wasn't gritten on you.' He was crazy."

"Did you hit him back?" I asked.

"Naw, I just walked on."

(*To grit on, gritten on*: to stare uncivilly.)

Greetings

When men enter the garage and I say hi, there is no reaction. It is as if no one hears me. If I say, "How are you?" they say, "Awright" and acknowledge me. If my original greeting is "Awright," they say, "Awright, awright."

• • •

A man I did not know appeared in the shop and asked after Raymond, then stood around for a while. Telemachus kept mumbling about "those junkies" and was upset he was there. When Raymond happened by a few minutes later, the man held out his hand and greeted him. Raymond was wearing a pair of black gloves. As he raised his right hand to shake the man's hand, the man looked down at the glove and said, "That's too dirty," and withdrew his hand.

In response, Raymond slowly removed the glove on his right hand. The man offered his hand again, and so did Raymond. Then, hesitating, the man glanced down at Raymond's hand again and said, "That's too dirty too." They both laughed and did not shake hands.

• • •

Two men were walking down the sidewalk together. On the opposite sidewalk a slightly drunk man was making his way slowly up the street. One of the two men called across, "Hey, Catfish. Save your money and let's go to Georgia."

The drunken man responded, "Naw, I ain' goin' until tomorrow." He paused, then repeated himself, "I ain' goin' until tomorrow."

The three of them were laughing.

• • •

Across the street Brother Smith, a tall man of about forty, walked by with an exaggerated swagger. Telemachus said, "He really thinks he's cool. He really thinks he's cool."

Later the man walked back on our side of the street, and he and Telemachus greeted each other. I was sure it was the first day Telemachus had ever seen or spoken to the man, although I had seen him before. I knew he had moved in around the corner. He exuded an intimidating physical presence.

• • •

The same Brother Smith began to tend bar at the corner and one day discovered the cigarette machine was not working. I had found out earlier when I tried to buy a pack of Camels and it would not take my money.

Brother Smith carefully removed the drinks sitting on top of the machine and proceeded to brutalize it. His beating failed to heal it or make it cough up the money, however, and he announced that he was going to unplug it so no one else would lose their money.

After he pulled the plug and the light went off behind the advertising, he sat on the edge of the miniature shuffleboard game. He claimed loudly that only the advertising light, not the cigarette machine itself, was run by electricity.

Pig and Juanita, who were drinking in the bar, disagreed immediately and said just as loudly that the machine was run by electricity. Leanna told them, "Why don't you shut up and go on?" The argument heated up. More people in the bar stood up and formed a circle around Brother Smith, raising their voices either in support of his position or Pig and Juanita's.

Brother Smith brought the argument to a close by shouting even more loudly, "Shut up, shut up."

The litigious voices subsided, except for his. He walked behind the bar affirming his point again and again.

Brother Smith did the same thing on the street when we played pinochle in the evening: he started a big argument, then shut it down. He was very physical, and no one wanted to move those arguments toward a personal confrontation with him.

Musical Space

In warm weather, in the evening, three men stood outside the bar on the corner and harmonized.

•   •   •

People danced in front of the shop to the music from the radio.

•   •   •

A woman told me if she did not hear soul music she became sick.

•   •   •

Sitting on the front step in warm weather, people accompanied any music they heard, even during a conversation.

•   •   •

In every bar there was a jukebox. When someone played it, he or she danced to the music or moved in place to it. Others moved also while sitting in place.

•   •   •

Inside a house, in a woman's kitchen where she served food and drink—a speakeasy—music played from the radio. But Miss Odetta did not allow anyone to dance in the kitchen; dancers had to move into the living room.

•   •   •

Through the middle and late 1960s, soul music and the Motown sound dominated the radio stations and black consciousness in South Philadelphia. Then the immensely successful Delphonics introduced the Philly sound, recorded by Kenneth Gamble and Leon Huff in their Philadelphia Sigma Sound Studios.

In the garage and on the street, people discussed the breakup of Diana Ross and the Supremes.

The Motown music had crossed the color line again as it had in the early 1950s; in the process it produced some classic love-centered popular hits. "Surprisingly, the political ferment of the late sixties did not invoke memorable musical responses on behalf of popular Afro-American musicians. The youthful black market thrived on music for dance and romance; and such music was the mainstay of the late sixties" (West 1984:92).

While there was music of protest and political consciousness, even some written by whites for black singers, the dance and romance popular songs tacitly resisted it by embracing the ordinary flow of life. The sounds on WDAS were public and oriented toward getting on with living. Politicians had their own media; they used newspapers and television. Popular song, coextensive with another form of public consciousness, spoke to those who lived and danced, for the most part, in public space.

> Don't want to love you
> Don't want to make you my wife
> Don't want to see you every day for the rest of my life
> All I want is a one night affair
> ...
> Baby when the night is over
> I don' want to see you no mo'
> All I want is a one night affair

(The O'Jays)

Public and Private

When a woman—and it was usually a woman—wanted to make a steady income, she used her house and opened a *speakeasy*, an illegal, after-hours tavern. The customers were made up of regulars drawn from networks of people known to her and her friends. Strangers, however, could not be kept out, especially when appearing with a friend of a friend.

The speakeasy was one of a number of economic choices that could transform private space. Another common choice was boarding. Most of the row houses on the block were carved into single rooms and apartments. Couples, mothers with young children, and unmarried men rooming together rented apartments. Extended families, who themselves rented their homes, often let a room to an old, single man or woman.

The older people who lived alone tended to board at a woman's house. A woman who boarded people served food and beer for very modest amounts of money, and it was said that any woman who cooked also sold food, usually *platters*. One could, if one wished, exist on these purchased plates of hot food. Telemachus and others in the shop, including me, bought food from one man in particular who delivered what his wife prepared.

Man and Woman

The strong male-female dichotomy underlay and animated the transformations between public and private, street and home.

• • •

As Franny walked in front of Lombardo's junk shop, one of the men there called out, "Hey, Baby!" After that she walked on the other side of the street.

• • •

A woman walked across the street in front of the shop and Telemachus called out, a large smile on his face, "Some day I'm going to marry you."

"You'll have to get a divorce first," she called back.

"That can be arranged."

• • •

Ivery had just swept her steps and was standing in the mouth of the shop. Telemachus joked with her. "Last night when I was going home I saw a woman I was trying to get up with and I asked her where she was going. She said she was waiting for a bus. 'Oh no you're not,' I told her. 'Come with me.' I took her to the Blue Moon Hotel and we wrassled."

"Telemachus," I said, "you didn't say who won."

He laughed and replied, "It was a draw so we decided to have a rematch."

Ivery cut in and asked him, "Why are you talking like this in front of Danny?"

Telemachus told her, "In Wisconsin they never heard of rape."

"That's right," I said.

• • •

Auston and Raymond were standing in the door of the shop as a *fox* walked by. Within her hearing Auston asked Raymond, "Can I have that?"

"You'll have to talk for it."

To the woman's receding back, Auston asked, "Can I talk for it?"

She ignored them completely.

• • •

Two young women were standing in the doorway across the street visiting. Raymond, Auston, and I were talking in the doorway of the shop. The women did not look at us once.

• • •

Telemachus said to a man who lived in the house on the other side of Karen and me, "You can't talk to the kids unless someone says you are going with one of them." By this he meant that you cannot talk to either a boy or a girl without incurring sexual accusations in the gossip of neighbors. Such accusations in the conversational networks trained people's attention on everyone anyone knew.

• • •

Contact between men and women on the street was performance, and although there were no heroes and villains, or winners and losers, the playing was important. Back in the early spring, Greg, the longshoreman-preacher's son, brought his skates to the shop and asked me, since he knew me best, to oil them for him. I did and he tried them out.

It was Saturday afternoon and Auston noticed that Greg's sister, standing nearly a block away at the entrance to their house, was dressed up. Carol was fifteen and attractive, and Auston put a play in motion. When Greg skated by, Auston called him into the shop and told him, "Go tell your sister I want to marry her."

Greg skated away and returned. Auston then said, "Tell her I'm Telemachus's son, he has money, and you and I will be brothers-in-law."

Greg skated off and returned. He told Auston, "She says she already has a boyfriend, and she told me to beat you with this stick."

Greg skated back and forth with messages seven times by his count. On his last trip he said he was too tired to go back and forth any more. "Besides," he said, "she left for a wedding with her boyfriend."

Auston replied, "If you had jumped on her and held her, I'd have given you three dollars, but you only get a quarter." Greg seemed satisfied.

Telemachus, Auston, and I had a good time watching Greg make the trips, though Telemachus and I stayed mostly inside the shop door, out of sight of Carol and her boyfriend. Auston said afterward he didn't think anything of it since he had not talked to her himself.

Children

Little James was two the summer of 1970. In the late summer evenings his mother Joyceann and I sometimes played pinochle on the sidewalk where their building and ours joined until there assembled a sociable group and skilled players. We sat around and drank beer and talked.

Little James was special and received a lot of attention from adults, in part because he was the only two-year-old on the street. He was one of the reasons that households were intimately involved in public space. To press the point, he was one of the reasons that public space was itself an intimate space.

One Sunday morning, without telling anyone, Telemachus put Little James in the car on the seat next to himself and drove to an auto parts store. I went along, bought a Pepsi, and shared it with Little James. On the way home he started to move to the beat of the gospel music on the car radio. Telemachus said, "Look how he's dancin'." James drew his right hand up to his eye. Telemachus noticed and said, "He's smart enough to be embarrassed."

When we returned, Joyceann commented flatly, "Oh, I wondered where he was." Telemachus tried to return James to his doorstep, but he cried and kept running into the garage. Neither my Pepsi or his mother's threats could keep him from Telemachus.

•   •   •

I looked at James and he looked at me. We were standing on the sidewalk. He made a small motion with his hand, opening it slightly, palm out, near his face.

•   •   •

Caesar's wife Juanita (Miz Mamie's oldest daughter) was holding Chavonne Davette on the steps of Maryjane's house. The newborn was wrapped in a white nylon quilt. James looked at Juanita and said, "The baby is Joyceann's."

Juanita looked at James and said, "No, she's mine."

James said, "No, Joyceann's," and he slapped Juanita.

Juanita slapped him right back but not hard. This began an exchange of slaps between them. Finally James lost his balance and fell back and bumped his head. He started crying and his grandmother came to the door.

"What's happening?"

"James is fighting."

•   •   •

Miss Lizzie came up behind Little James and tapped him. Then she said, "Hi." He said, "No," and twisted away from her. She said, "Shut up." He replied, "Go home."

Distance and relation.

•   •   •

Little James was teased on occasion until he cried. When he cried he was called a faggot.

12. Little James on Easter Morning, 1971, standing in front of the apartment doorway. (Photograph by the author)

• • •

A young boy playing with James called him animal names:

You little rabbit
You little monkey
You little spider
You little roach

In harsher games with people his mother's age he was called faggot, punk, dumb James, and so on.

• • •

James said to an eight-year-old, "Kiss my ass." Joyceann heard him from inside the house. She came out, took off her shoe, and slapped him on the rear once and on the stomach once. He cried and she said, "I told you not to say that again."

• • •

Joyceann: I'll break you back if you don't stop.
Little James: Go home.

• • •

Karen was sitting on the steps of Maryjane's house with Maryjane, Joyceann, Diane, and Little James. James kept running into Telemachus's garage. Karen went after him several times, and Telemachus brought him out. Finally Telemachus took him down to Maryjane's and put him on the steps. When James began to run after Telemachus, Joyceann, no play in her voice, yelled after him, "Hey boy, get back here." James returned.

• • •

We were playing pinochle on a hot August evening, the humidity hanging stickily in the air. Norman said to Joyceann, "James'll be something else when he's ten."
"He'll be in jail," she said.

• • •

When James interrupted someone playing cards or checkers he was gently pushed away: "Don't James."

• • •

Norman said, "I'm going to hit you in your mouth."
James repeated, "I'm going to hit you in your mouth."
Norman said, "I'm going to hit you in your stomach."
James repeated, "I'm going to hit you in your stomach."

• • •

A mother told her young daughter, "You as stubborn as you is black."

• • •

An older man said to a young boy, "Nappy head."
"You better go home and comb your hair before you talk like that."

• • •

Joyceann, her own childhood in the remote past, was jumping rope with the young girls on the sidewalk. It was the first time I had seen her on the street since the birth of Chavonne Davette. Two girls whirled two ropes as fast, it seemed, as they could, and they chanted rapidly,

Ball-headed baby
Sitting in the gravy
Mother coming home
With a ball-headed baby.

Joyceann twisted her foot and hobbled toward her doorway claiming, "I was winning! I was winning!"

• • •

Slick Willie, Fast Eddie, Darrell, and Little Johnny, Leanna's four boys, walked by the shop on their way to school. I noticed that Darrell had stitches in his nose.
"How did that happen?" I asked.
Fast Eddie, quick to talk, began a play. "Darrell cheated Johnny, so Johnny hit him with a shovel."
Darrell said it wasn't like that. Johnny was shoveling dirt and caught Darrell accidentally in the nose. Then Eddie, his play broken up at the beginning, began mock fighting, dancing around Little Johnny, throwing punches but not landing them. He said, "I can take you."
Johnny ignored him and looked at me. He raised his hand solemnly, pointing upward with his index finger. Then slowly he drew his hand downward until he was pointing at the ground.
No one said anything more, and they turned and walked away together toward school.

• • •

"C.C." Turner lived in the third-floor apartment on the corner. He was nearing sixty. As he walked by Diane, she said, "There goes old Mr. Baggy Pants." He looked hard at her but did not say anything.

. . .

Children earned quarters by running to the store to purchase goods for adults.

. . .

Privacy

In a summer sidewalk gathering of mothers, children, and visitors, one could create privacy by moving out of earshot of everyone. No one would interrupt the conversationalists. Joyceann and her uncle Sam (mo br) conducted a low, private conversation with ten others nearby, just out of earshot.

Games

The old man across the street set up a checkerboard and waited for someone to come along and challenge him to a game. He was called Sitch, after his longer nickname, Situation. The name was in a way self-generated, because Sitch would say after a demanding checker game, which he usually won, "I've got to get me a little *situation.*" His "little situation" was a nip of whiskey, which he thoughtfully kept nearby.

Freddy, a truck driver, walked by and challenged the old man. There was a ritual flavor to their talk and the language that accompanied the flow of the contest. Their words never wandered outside reference to the game.

"I'm going to make you call me uncle," Freddy repeated again and again. "If you call me uncle, I'll ease off." He was telling Sitch that he would beat him. Freddy lost.

. . .

George, a man of about sixty, often stopped by to play checkers with Sitch. I challenged George to a game, which he won easily. "You're pretty good," I said.

"I was a lot better until a woman messed me up." He repeated that again and again. He lost to Sitch regularly.

. . .

At 9:00 P.M. Telemachus and I locked the shop and walked to his car. Crawford, a friend of Ivery's and often on the street, was standing in the doorway of the Chas. Cafe with a drink in his hand. Telemachus pointed down the street toward the shop and said to

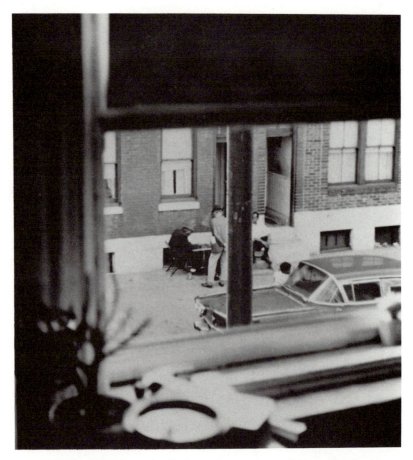

13. The game of checkers. The black people on Fourteenth Street played a game of checkers that used two extra rows of squares on both the side and the bottom. With more counters on the board and different rules than the standard game, checkers became a far greater challenge and very difficult to master. The game was often learned and artfully mastered by young men in prison. (Photograph by the author)

him, "This here's my car, the first one there, and the third one, and the one across the street in the middle up there."

"I've got you covered," Crawford said; then he pointed in turn to each car Telemachus had mentioned. "I've got you covered."

• • •

A man of sixty, tall and gray-haired, stood on one street corner every evening, talking with people and watching the Nixon children half a block away. He made sure that they did not play on the cars and pickup trucks parked in front of their house and would call out loudly to them to stop any activities he thought might damage the vehicles. He constantly watched children and made comments to them, as they did to him.

Two of Ivery's children were standing outside a conversational circle that included this man and Karen. The youngest boy, Patrick, did not have his hair combed. The man said, "They never comb their hair. Old nappy head." He directed his remarks at Pat, who clicked his tongue, rolled his eyes, and turned away. The man always said things like that when the children were with Karen but not properly groomed.

• • •

Karen and I were walking on the street one Wednesday and met Smitty, a man from the 410 Bar. It was not yet summer, and Auston was still working for Telemachus. I was making every effort to do unto others what was being done unto me in order to learn the roles and rules. Smitty was one of the men I had talked with at the 410 Bar, and he told me I was into something being friendly with Al and Trip. He worked at a dental manufacturing company, he said. One night he had pulled out of the left pocket of his sport coat a plaster cast of someone's lower and upper teeth. As he held them together in the air it was as if the skull were missing.

Now, as we drew closer on the sidewalk, we greeted one another. Smitty was holding a brown paper bag in one hand and opened it as we paused to talk.

Inside was hot jewelry, he said, watches and rings in their original packages. He told us how a friend of his who worked on Jewelry Row left the bag in the trash in the back of the store. Smitty was tipped off when the man made a drop.

Smitty then took the jewelry; he would sell it and split the take with his partner in the store. I looked at the price tag on one of the watches. It read $125 but I did not recognize the brand name. Karen and I both told him we were not interested.

Late Saturday afternoon I went to the 410 Bar to get a drink and to see the men I knew; Smitty was there showing one of the *hot* rings to a woman. He told her that she could buy one for herself and one for her boyfriend. She examined the rings for both men and women, holding them up to the wan light from the transoms.

I stood near them and ordered a beer. As the woman tried on a ring in her size, Smitty pulled out one that fit me, a gold ring with a diamond set in it. He said he could let me have it for twelve dollars because he thought it was cut glass rather than a real diamond. I had six dollars in my pocket, so I told him I would give him the six dollars and pay him the rest later. He agreed, and I arranged with Claude, the bartender, to leave an envelope with the balance for Smitty, after I was paid.

After the beer, with the ring in my pocket, I went to the shop to collect my pay for the week. I stood around waiting for Telemachus to acknowledge my presence and pay me. Auston was also waiting for Telemachus to pay him for his week's work.

I showed Auston the ring and he examined it, turning it around in the light from the fluorescent bulb. He asked me how much I wanted for it, and I explained to him who I had bought it from and how it had come from a store on Jewelry Row, playing out the same line that Smitty had given me. He said he might buy it from me, but I could see he remained unimpressed. Then he offered six dollars for it. I said I needed more than that because I spent more than that, to which he replied that he would give me six more dollars on Monday.

Auston walked to the back of the garage where Telemachus was working. He put his arm around his father and then came back. "My dad will pay for it," he said.

Telemachus came up to where I was standing near the door and tiredly asked, "Do you have to have the money right now?" He reluctantly pulled out three dollars and gave them to me. I told him I had to have the money right away because I still owed Smitty. Finally Telemachus came up with a total of five wrinkled one-dollar bills. Auston, looking on, said, "You can have the rest on Monday, or from my dad anytime."

Then Telemachus paid me for the week. I returned to the 410 Bar, put six dollars in an envelope for Smitty, and left it with Claude. I had paid Smitty's full asking price.

Before I could ask for the rest of the money from Auston for the false ring (called a *hook*) I had sold him, he said to me, "I'm mad with you." His voice was threatening and I felt a moment of panic at the implied danger I was now in. The ring I had sold him was no good, he said, and he claimed that he had bitten it and found it was plastic underneath.

"Didn't you know that when you bought it?" I asked.

I could not anticipate his answer and was surprised when he said, "I thought it might be," and went on to add that he figured *that my relationship with Smitty was such that the ring was authentic.*

Smitty's hustle was a form of economic play fusing the play quality of a performance in public space with the necessity for the exchanging that sustains life. It was not the economy of play or the play of economy; it was economic play, transaction performance, encounter play, or, more pointedly, relations play. Relations play was serious, fateful play, demanding, fun, dangerous, and necessary.

Excursion

It was the middle of July. Late in the afternoon I was sitting on the steps of Maryjane's house playing with Little James. I watched Eunice walk down the street; her progress was slow because she stopped and talked, it seemed, to everyone. Eunice was tall and gracious, her mother very reserved, and her daughter very attractive; her sister, I heard, was a New York model, and her brother was in the army.

Eunice was selling tickets. As soon as I figured that out, I knew I wanted to buy into whatever was happening. As she drew closer, she did not avoid me and asked if I wanted to buy tickets for an excursion to New Jersey. I had never spoken with her before and was pleased to be asked. I bought two tickets and made sure of the date, then asked her who was sponsoring the event. She told me it was the CCC. I did not know who or what that was, but by talking about the coming occasion I discovered that the barbershop had just closed on the corner and a new Model Cities neighborhood office had opened. It was called the Community Concern Committee and was apparently devoted to community projects. The excursion was a sendoff, a get-acquainted event, subsidized in part by one of former president Lyndon Johnson's Great Society programs.

The next morning when I went to work for Telemachus I mentioned I had bought excursion tickets for Karen and myself. Telemachus looked concerned and said to me, "I know these people. I know what they are thinking when they get up in the morning, when they go to bed at night, when they go to work, and when they are on the job. They'll kill you for a quarter."

This was not reassuring, and I felt the now-familiar surges of anxiety, probably underlain by the raw fear that was already well known to me.

"Don't drink too much," he went on. "Tell Caroline not to talk too much with them young boys."

I accepted his advice as if he were the Oracle at Delphi and mentioned to Karen what he had told me.

On the warm morning of 19 July we stood at the corner of Montrose and Fourteenth waiting for the buses that would carry us to the park in New Jersey. We waited for an hour, and I recognized several of our neighbors, though most of the faces were new to me. I imagined the others were amazed we were among them, but no one showed the least surprise. An old, former Greyhound bus pulled up with the name ALSAB written near the door. It was as if it were the name of the bus and not the name of the bus company. A second bus pulled up behind, named DEER, and our group split in two.

A huge woman named Miz Mary was in charge of our bus; she took tickets and counted who was on board. Karen and I sat near the front. An old couple who were not getting along well were arguing with each other in the seat behind us. There were children, old people, and teen-agers. The teen-agers sat in back, and as we crossed the bridge into New Jersey they were singing the hit songs from WDAS.

When she wrote her field notes the next day, Karen commented on Miz Mary's relationship with her young child: "She would say to her child, 'Come here baby.' It was in a soft inflection with a lilt in the voice and the stress on the 'Come' not the 'here.' And 'baby' was said 'ba-a-a-bi.' It was pleasant to hear the adults use this term of address to the children. It was very affectionate."

Miz Mary lived with Mr. Joe. On the ride over he and I talked, and he showed me their little daughter, beautifully dressed and her hair impeccably styled. Mr. Joe, I could not help but notice, had a thin scar that ran from the bottom of his left eyelid all the way down the cheek to the jawbone. Mr. Joe's scar looked as if a razor had cut him perfectly, missing the eye by a surgeon's fraction and slicing straight downward. A tear welled up in the little V-shaped cut in the bottom eyelid and oozed out, dampening his upper cheek. He, like Mary, was big; he seemed about fifty years old and was a longshoreman.

We found the park in Williamstown, New Jersey, late in the morning, having gotten a little lost en route, and discovered on arrival that a number of people were there already. The barbecue pit was smoking, the jukebox was playing, and the swimming pool looked inviting. The grounds were arranged as shown in figure 16. I was surprised to see that there were five uniformed guards at the grounds. When I later asked Telemachus why there were

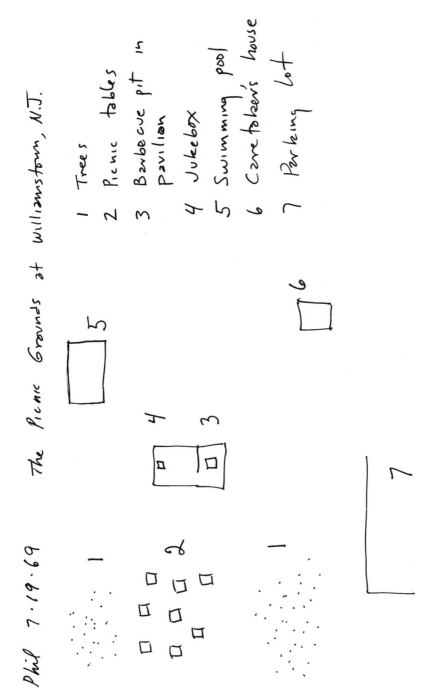

Phil 7.19.69

The Picnic Grounds at Williamstown, N.J.

1 Trees
2 Picnic tables
3 Barbecue pit in Pavilion
4 Jukebox
5 Swimming pool
6 Caretakers' house
7 Parking lot

Figure 16. Picnic grounds, Williamstown, New Jersey. Drawing.

guards, he responded that they would keep people from fighting. It was interesting to see what the guards did tolerate. Brother Smith—the same Brother Smith that swaggered in front of the shop and and tended bar on the corner and beat the cigarette machine—played rough. He threw everyone he could into the pool in midafternoon. His victims retaliated en masse and tossed him in as well. The infrapolice ignored (while watching closely) the universal behavior that swimming pools seem to evoke.

Karen and I swam and lay by the water for a while. Young children played and a few people in their twenties swam. One woman pretended to be drowning and several men pretended to save her. The giveaway to the game was that she could have stood on the bottom of the pool at any time and her head would have been well out of the water. Later in the afternoon, we sat at the picnic tables and waited for the barbecued ribs and fresh corn on the cob to finish cooking. The middle-aged women, friends of the woman who directed the CCC, cooked; the men sang together or talked, and one group of men shot craps for an hour and a half. Some old couples walked into the woods, and the teen-agers danced to the jukebox in the pavilion.

Karen and I stood for a while near the circle of singing men and then, not wishing to return to the pool, sat at a picnic table. I chatted again with Mr. Joe and found it difficult to keep my eyes away from his scar and the casual cascade the tears formed. He, Karen, and I talked politics and argued about whether or not there were more poor black people or more poor white people in the country and what their proportions were. I said that the proportion of poor blacks to the total black population was greater than that of poor whites to well-off whites. He kept asserting that there were more poor whites than poor blacks. We each declared our positions a couple of times. Karen alleged that she agreed with him, trying to minimize our difference and our total lack of discourse. She later wrote:

> I kept interjecting that I agreed with him and tried to make Dan stop pressing his point. Dan then felt that I didn't understand what he was saying, which I did understand. Ultimately Dan realized the fruitlessness of continuing the argument and stopped. The man was convinced of the correctness of his statement and did not feel he needed to qualify it in any way. Dan wanted to qualify it while not disagreeing entirely. It was impossible.

There was no win or lose to the continued assertions of a given position. I had heard Telemachus do the same sort of position taking. Political arguments were less arguments than twin monologues oftentimes. It was like Brother Smith's repeated avowal back at the bar that the cigarette machine was *not* run by electricity.

•   •   •

Brother Smith was a double-faced figure to me: he was unknown, and he was known. I knew him for his swagger, for he walked like many young men in Philadelphia did when moving through public space, up on the ball of the left foot, down on the right, or lowering the right knee with each step. It was an asymmetrical style of walking, sometimes called a *strut*. A woman told me that her boyfriend strutted so hard that once, when she was walking with him and he put his arm around her, she pulled away and said to him, "Ay, man, you crippled or something?" Brother Smith walked like that. I knew his public persona but not which exact house he lived in, who he lived with, or what he had done before he began tending bar on the corner that summer.

I have already mentioned that he exuded a sense of danger, an aura of instant intimidation. He was forty, six feet tall, muscular, and trim. Once he had argued briefly with Franny across the street and had slammed her against a parked car. At the bar one night he had shot at a man named Ike. Everyone mentioned it the next day. Did he hit him? I had asked. No, he did not.

That afternoon I watched the men shoot craps. The play was far too rapid for me to follow, even if I had wanted to. Brother Smith was bent intently over the game, a large sheaf of dollar bills in his left hand. We talked afterward, for he made it a point to talk with everyone and enter all the action—the dancing, the cooking, and the middle-aged men singing a capella. People listening pulled him from the song because he was destroying the close harmonies and subtle rhythms.

"Did you win all that money in your hand?" I asked. "No, I gambled it all away. I love gambling more than anything." He continued, "I take care of my family, but I gamble as much and as often as I can. If I had a million dollars, I'd just gamble with it."

He mentioned how he had been a longshoreman for five years but was trying to cut it loose. He liked being a bartender. He told me he had tended bar one place and a customer had asked him, "Why are you so mean looking?"

"See how you are sitting right now?" Brother Smith had responded.

"What do you mean?" the customer had wanted to know.

"Your back is to the door, and it wasn't before I tended bar here."

Brother Smith added that he protected the virtue of women at the bar. "If a girl against her will is bothered by someone, say, your wife came into the bar, I'd have to say something to him."

He shifted the topic to his recent run-in with Ike. I had not heard parts of the story. Ike was arguing with someone, and Brother Smith, who claimed he was friends with Ike, went over to talk him out of the argument. Ike was so heated, however, that he refused to talk to Brother Smith. "What are friends for if you can't talk with them?" He and Albert, who also tended bar on the corner, put Ike out.

There would have been no problem, he went on, but Ike came back, picked up a brick from the brick sidewalk, and threw it through the bar window. Almost before the crash of glass and the sound of the brick hitting the floor was over, Brother Smith had grabbed his pistol and run out the door, firing away in the darkness at Ike's retreating back.

Since I seemed to be nodding and agreeing with everything he said (what else was I to do—tell him he was wrong?), he backed slowly away laughing and said, "You don't understand, do you?" He continued to laugh and backed further away, and as he narrowly missed a picnic table he turned away saying, "I like to kill people."

I understood nothing; I really did not understand.

•   •   •

After the men quit singing, late in the day, a man came over to where several of us were sitting at one of the picnic tables. He introduced himself as Raymond (not the Raymond who had worked for Telemachus) and told how he lived near us around on Montrose Street. He had sung bass with the Silhouettes in the late 1950s and had traveled and lived with two white girls.

He pointed to Mr. Joe across the table, something I would not have done, and said to me, "I'd rather meet you coming down the street than that black man." Mr. Joe gave no sign he had heard. Raymond wanted to make the point that black people could not get along with one another and could not, as he put it, "get them-selves together."

"The reason the black man cannot get together is that he is always scheming how to get what you have." It was as if he was commenting on, without naming it, the street hustle. If so, he attributed to it a great deal of cultural weight. He may have been claiming that the hustle was a divisive social practice and the source of a failure to achieve social solidarity.

"Wait a minute," I interrupted. "What if you and I were in a bar out in the suburbs and we each had a nice house and a car in the garage and fifty dollars in our pockets. What would happen then?"

"I would still be trying to figure out how to get the fifty dollars out of your pocket."

Karen interjected, "He'd be trying to pay for a car and would need the money."

Mr. Joe from across the table said emphatically, "That's right, that's right." I do not now agree with Karen and Mr. Joe. With hindsight I believe Raymond was making a rather sophisticated cultural critique of hustling in somewhat the same way Stevie Wonder did with "Misstra Know It All."

Raymond and I continued to talk, and Mr. Joe tried to say something. I did not turn to face him and Raymond did not at that point stop his monologue. Mr. Joe said disgustedly, "Aw, he hasn't got time."

•   •   •

In the early evening we bought our dinner of barbecued pork ribs, white bread, hot corn, and beer, served by the women from the Community Concern Committee. After we ate there was talk around the bar, more drinking, and dancing. It was after dark and the bus was not yet ready to leave, so I asked Raymond whether he was leaving right away, and if so, whether we could get a ride back. He assured me we could ride with him, but then time dragged on and it did not seem that he was leaving any earlier than the buses. Karen documented what occurred.

Eight-thirty P.M. While sitting on a stool at the bar, train case by my feet and a damp blanket in my lap, Brother Smith walked up beside me as I listened to the band playing and watched the dancing. He asked, "Are you married?" (I thought he asked this.) I turned to him and retorted, "Yes, I'm married." He said, "Why are you mad?" I said, "I thought you asked me if I was married, not mad. No, I'm not mad. I can't help it if I look like this." He said something about "Why are you sitting here like this" (demonstrating resting his chin in his hands). Dan walked up and stood beside me ready to join in the conversation. Brother did not move over to accommodate Dan's presence. Dan interrupted a couple of times, yet Brother still did not acknowledge him visually or verbally. He did not integrate Dan into our conversation even though he had obviously seen him come up. Raymond came up and stood by, lit a cigarette as I finished my conversation with Brother. Raymond said to Dan, "I'm going to be a little late because I'm going to help clean up around here." Dan replied, "That's no problem, we'll just go home on the bus."

As Dan continued to talk with Raymond, Pop walked up. [Pop was the husband of the woman who ran the CCC. He worked in a turn-key construction company and was the same age as Brother Smith and Raymond.] Pop said, "We've been up all night and we're both tired." Then Pop walked closer until he was standing almost between Dan and me and said, "I've been up all night, I got home at 7:30, slept half an hour and got up. My wife was mad at me for getting up. It took me four or five hours just to get the ice. I drove it to Williamstown, went back to Philly and brought another load of people to the park."

I said, "Wow, I just cannot do that." He just looked at me in disbelief.

Then Albert, who was tending bar, obviously noticed what was taking place. He walked to our end of the bar and, seeing me still seated, said, "The bus is getting ready to go. Let those kids go." I looked around and people were already on the bus and others were preparing to get on.

Dan then said, "Look, we'll just get on the bus and go." Pop said, "You ever smoke, do you like to smoke?" Dan said, "I used to but I don't much anymore."

Then Dan turned to Raymond and asked, "I have tickets for the bus; I think we'll just go home on the bus. The only reason I mentioned going home was I thought you were going home early."

Raymond replied, "I understand, that's alright, I understand." Albert, seeing that we had not yet left walked over to us once again and with a more urgent tone of voice said, "Let those kids go, the bus is leaving."

At that point, I bent down and picked up my train case and started inching past Dan behind him, and Dan picked up the blanket and we left the group. Dan looked back at Raymond and said, "I'll buy you a drink at the bar sometime." Raymond handed Dan his shirt and asked him to put it in his car on the way to the bus.

Monday morning I went down to the shop and worked with Telemachus half the day. During a break in the work I casually stood blowing on a hot cup of coffee and told him about the excursion and what had happened there at the end. "What was going on?" I wanted to know. He squinted his eyes and looked at me and explained that if we had gone with them (meaning Pop, Raymond, and Brother Smith) they would have killed me and raped Karen. I was incredulous. Was his verdict some kind of play on their play? Nothing that evening was ever stated. The way they positioned themselves around us was threatening. Who knows what happened that night, what might have happened?

Trajectories

During the late spring and early summer, Boycie had been in jail. No one could say why he was taken in. Suddenly, in the middle of the summer, he was back on the street. I was never sure at any time where Boycie lived, even when I came to know him better. It was as if he needed no fixed address either socially or psychologically. He clearly seemed at home in the area of Fourteenth and Carpenter and several blocks west of Broad Street. He may have lived at four or five places at once, rotating among them at random. On any given night he might sleep in a room he rented, in a storeroom, at an old couple's house, in his three-quarter-ton Ford pickup truck parked near the Martin Luther King, Jr., Plaza, or somewhere else. Boycie was the consummate public figure. He lived in public, his life was public, and because it was public it was performance. His life—the very contour of his motion through day and night—was theater.

Boycie wore a French beret and army fatigues. In Korea, where he had been an Army Ranger and tank mechanic, he had been badly wounded; his right ankle was twisted and gnarled like hot wax. After the war he had married and fathered children by a *China Doll*, a beautiful, light-skinned woman. The China Doll and his children received his disability check, and he *scrambled* (hustled) on the street for his own means of support. Boycie was a superb mechanic but he drank a lot, which altered his consciousness and reduced his pain, and so did not always complete what he had been commissioned to do.

The day after the Fourth of July, a Sunday, was hot, and the evening darkness brought little relief from the humid heat. Karen and I were watching television, the blue flicker coloring the room. The windows were open to the sounds of the street.

I heard the doorbell and Karen went to the window. Boycie called up, "Is he home?" She told him that I would be right down. I pulled on some clothes and Karen put a leash on the dog. She wanted to walk the dog anyway and had seen who was on the street as she looked out.

Downstairs, Boycie asked me to buy him a drink. Karen overheard me say I would, and without a word the two of us were off. People were on the street. Karen joined Judy and Contessa Sims from next door, who were on the sidewalk talking. I did not feel the same anxiety leaving Karen as I had in February; our friends and our life in public had changed all that.

Boycie and I walked in the direction of the Martin Luther King, Jr., Plaza. It rose against the night sky, ominous on the horizon. We knocked on the doors of six houses, but either there was either no answer or the people did not have beer. We were looking for a speakeasy; Boycie was hungry and wanted to drink beer.

We walked up Christian to Thirteenth Street, then took Fitzwater to Webster, and from there went on to Bainbridge. It seemed to be one of the roughest, most dangerous places in the world, with abandoned houses and cars, empty lots, strewn trash, and often enough, violent confrontations. People, when they were out, were locked in shadow, talking in low tones as we walked by. Next to a bar we entered a house without knocking.

Boycie had grown up in the area and, save the time he was in Korea, had lived there all his life. For him it was home; for me it was a world of unknown dangers.

In South Philadelphia row houses, the first room tended to be the living room. As we walked past the living room, I saw a man sitting there, perhaps dozing, alone in the semidarkness. A child stood on the stairs to my right in the dim light. I looked ahead over Boycie's shoulder into the kitchen where I saw in my line of sight a disheveled man standing with a dime in his hand. Against the back wall of the kitchen sat a forty-five-year-old woman, and next to her was a twenty-five-year-old man sitting silently and holding her hand.

The kitchen was a light green trimmed in pink, like others I had seen. In the middle of the room was a vintage chrome dinette table, the red formica top cracked and peeling at the edges. Behind the table a short man with processed hair was pouring Tokay into a

shot glass, then transferring it, by the shot, into a small beer glass.
A radio over the sink was playing

I know you,
You know me.
One thing I can tell you is
You gotta be free.

Come together,
Right now,
Over me.

(The Beatles)

Our entrance—my presence—had frozen the action. Boycie's
first words, as if meant to free the scene, were, "The white boy
with me is okay."

This assertion did not dispel the tension, which seemed solid and
unyielding in the air. The man behind the table broke it by asking,
"I see you on Pine Street?"

"Yes, I used to live there."

"What're you drinking?"

"Tokay," I said, and everyone laughed. The ice was broken.

He measured shots of Tokay for Boycie and me, and I paid for
us both. We drank them down and Boycie wanted another one. I
told him I only had thirty-five cents left. He turned away from me
and asked the man pouring the shots for a beer. He was out of
beer, so Boycie asked for another shot of Tokay.

Boycie's blue shirt was open in front except for one button. There
were three stripes on the sleeve, an iron-on patch made to resemble
military insignia. The man pouring us drinks, whose name was
Randy, began to argue with Boycie about whether or not that was
a midshipman's blouse. The dispute got louder until Boycie broke
it off by holding his glass out and saying to Randy, "Give me a hit."

"I'll give you a hit," Randy threatened in a serious way; "I'll give
you a Hawaiian Punch." He was referring to a television commercial
in which a cartoon figure asks for Hawaiian Punch, is immediately
hit in the mouth, and falls down. Randy then repeated that he
would give Boycie a Hawaiian Punch.

Boycie pointed to the gallon bottle of Tokay on the floor and
said, "You know what I mean." As Boycie pointed, Randy grabbed
his finger in a three-finger hold, one over, two under. Forcing

Boycie downward he ordered him, "Sit in the chair." Boycie sat on a chrome chair with a marbled green and white vinyl seat.

"Say 'Please.' " Boycie did not say please. He replied that he was using his biceps to put counterpressure on his finger.

"Say 'Please.' " Randy repeated the demand several times, and Boycie, who was hurting, finally said "Please."

Randy poured out the wine, carefully measuring the portion with the shot glass. Boycie downed it and then said, "Another."

"You owe me for the last one," Randy reminded him.

Boycie pointed to the empty glass and said, "You didn't give me the drink." Boycie was drunk, and I was confused by the Tokay, the heat, and their rapid-fire byplay.

"You owe me for the last one," Randy insisted, whereupon Boycie quickly turned and ran out the front door.

I looked at Randy and shrugged, then said goodbye and walked into the dark street. Boycie had disappeared, and I wondered what I would do next. I did not know if I could make it home alive from there.

Across the street, deep inside the shadow, a voice said, "Boycie's here."

I walked in the direction of the disembodied sound. The humid sky was orange-gray with haze and reflected city light, but no illumination reached into the shadows.

"I was *never* treated like that before in there. I been going there since I was old enough to drink." He turned and started walking. I followed. We walked into another house and Boycie asked for beer. The woman who ran the speakeasy said she had no beer but that we could go to Trippin' Inn. It was open and we could walk right in, she said.

We walked to Trippin' Inn on the corner of Broad Street. The lights inside were too bright, making for a strongly shadowed but harsh atmosphere. People were sitting at the bar, and Boycie and I eased onto a couple of stools and sat down. No one looked at us, including the woman tending bar. Boycie, in what sounded like an angry scream, commanded the woman to wait on us, and I saw a flash of rage flicker across her face.

She finished waiting on another person and came over and stood in front of Boycie without looking at him. Boycie ordered two beers and we drank them. Giving me five dollars as we finished, he told me to pay; maybe he thought I was more sober than he. I took the five. Boycie then turned to the man next to him, telling him he should meet me. "I don't want to meet him," the man replied in a growl while staring straight ahead.

Boycie turned to me and said, "You'll see some faggots in a minute." We could see two men walk by the door and windows in drag, wearing heavy makeup and carrying purses over their square shoulders. A man on the other side of the bar put money in the jukebox. A saxophone solo opened the piece and then, as if blown from the instrument, voices sang,

What does it take
(What does it take)
To win your love for me
(To win your love for me)?

How can I make
(How can I make)
This dream come true for me
(This dream come true for me)?

(Jr. Walker and the All Stars)

Boycie was hungry and wanted to find a place that served food, so I paid the bartender. When I started to leave a tip, Boycie told me not to, but when I handed him the change he said to keep it for him. We left Trippin' Inn and angled across the street to a White Tower. Outside the White Tower, standing against the wall, a young man had a radio playing. When we entered the zone of sound, Boycie moved to the music, sketching a dance as we went into the restaurant.

My love is yours, Baby,
All the way from the start
You, you, you,
You possess my soul, now, Honey,
And I know
I know you own my heart. . . .

(Diana Ross and the Supremes)

The restaurant was busy and the counter was full of black customers. We sat at the only two seats available just then, the ones nearest the door. Boycie shouted something at a white woman who was washing dishes behind the counter with her back to us. A moment later, as she came to our end to put two hamburger buns on the griddle, he said very softly, "Could I have a sausage, Hon?" She seemed to hold no rancor—gave no reaction, really—and put the sausage on the hot griddle for him.

A woman had walked in just as Boycie was yelling up the counter to the waitress. I was holding a dollar of Boycie's in my hand to pay for the sausages. The woman stood just a little behind me, waiting to put in her order, and saw the money in my hand. "*You are in the wrong company!*" she said, formally emphasizing each word. "All he wants is your money." I turned slowly back toward her and said in a quiet voice, "It's his money." She turned away from me and said nothing more.

Boycie was sitting closer to the cash register than I was. People who came in to order take-out food stood next to him while it was being prepared. Three young men came in and asked for Cokes to go, and one of them put a dollar down on the counter. Two were watching the street and the third was singing to himself and dancing in place.

When none of them were looking, Boycie picked up their dollar bill. I wondered if he was going to get us killed. They did not notice it crumpled in his hand out of sight. A minute later one of the men asked the waitress, "Did you pick up the dollar?"

"No."

Boycie then handed her the dollar. The man turned slightly toward Boycie and said, "You better watch what the fuck you're doing."

They left. Boycie did not say anything to me. Our order came soon after, I paid for it, and we went out the door with the food. Later Boycie told me that the three were going to rob him, and that was why he took their dollar. "Even if I had no money, they would want to fight me. I'd have to fight them." After Boycie told me that, I had vivid fantasies of violence that made me so rigid my muscles ached.

We left the White Tower and walked south on Broad Street, the large thoroughfare that cuts South Philadelphia in half. I had no idea where we were going and thought that the walking and drinking we did was shapeless. We turned west off Broad Street, moving further from my apartment, and sat on someone's marble steps while we rested for a minute and Boycie finished his sausage sandwich.

A man came out of the house next door, unlocked his car at the curb, opened the door, and eased himself in. Boycie took himself off the step, and went over and closed the man's door as he was situating himself inside. The man looked up at Boycie, and Boycie looked down at him. Their eyes locked for a moment. Neither said anything. We walked on.

In the next block, which was very poorly lit, Boycie paused at the second house. He climbed two steps and opened the door. I started to follow him, then backed away as I made out in the faint light of the street that it was a funeral parlor. *What the hell*, I thought, but I followed him as he tiptoed inside the narrowly opened door. It was at least eleven-thirty, and I found it hard to believe that the door was unlocked. The interior was almost completely dark. I felt disoriented from drinking.

A man greeted Boycie and turned up the lights a little, revealing a woman lying full-length, fully open to view, in a casket. Boycie walked quietly over to her and felt along her arms, then moved his fingers over each jaw. The undertaker turned on a brass lamp over the casket, illuminating her features. Her eyes bulged beneath her closed lids.

Then with a small flourish the undertaker dropped a lace handkerchief over her face and turned out the brass lamp. "You're lucky to see her, I was just going home."

"Is she going south?" Boycie asked.

"Yes," the undertaker said, moving toward the door to make it clear we were leaving, "by train in the morning."

Boycie began to cry and told the undertaker, "She used to live in the room next to mine."

I could not hear what the undertaker said exactly, but it was something like, "It happens to the best of us."

We went down the steps and the door eased shut almost silently. Boycie staggered against the front wall of the funeral parlor. I did not know what to do. I stood there with my head down, trying to find a pattern in the sidewalk.

Boycie wiped tears from both his eyes and said, "Come on, Boycie'll be alright." With that we turned back toward the way we had come, crossed Broad Street, and walked down Christian Street in the direction of the apartment. On Christian Boycie walked up two steps of a row house with me close behind. It was another speakeasy.

Just as we entered a woman's voice rang out angrily, addressing Boycie, "Don' bring him in here."

We kept walking down the hallway. It was a large house. A man sat in the living room asleep, with the television splashing the flickering blue light across his face. Further along the hall I looked into the dining room; two men were sitting at the table drinking. We faced the kitchen then and the woman who had intercepted us with her hard voice.

Boycie told her, "He's my friend." They began to argue. There were only women around the table, and although it was far too late on Sunday to be dressed up, those women were. Another woman's voice cut into the argument Boycie was having.

"There's no such thing as white."

The argument subsided and I realized that Boycie and I had crashed the wake of the woman we had just viewed.

The woman who said there is no such thing as white introduced herself. I told her my name, and there were introductions all around the table. A woman standing by the stove said her name was Odessa. It was her house, her speakeasy. I recognized her. One of the women bought me a drink. Boycie finally found another beer; Odessa had several in her refrigerator.

I said to Odessa, "I know you."

"Where do you work?" she asked.

"At Telemachus's garage, Fourteenth and Carpenter."

She told everyone how she had taken fifteen dollars to Telemachus at noon one day and he told her he would have her car ready at four. "I went back at five and it still wasn't ready. I took the car."

I remembered vividly how angry she was. She began to tell the whole story to the people sitting around the table. Her Plymouth had not been repaired and was still propped up on metal milk crates in front of her door. I had noticed it as we walked in.

Other people told stories about Telemachus and how he messed up people's cars. Through the exchanges I learned that the brother and sister of the dead woman were at the wake. But Boycie broke the pleasant stories, although I did not hear how it began. The woman sitting at the head of the table said to him, "I'm not ghetto like you."

"Bitch," he responded.

Carrying a fresh bottle of beer, Boycie was ready to leave. On the way out he asked one woman for a cigarette, although anyone could see the outline of a full pack in his pocket. She said no, and then the arguing began again. The issue became who was the better fucker. They shouted claims and counterclaims mixed with insults at one another. As he stepped out the front door, Odessa called after him, saying, "Leave the bottle." He said he would sit on the step and drink it. They argued over this, and Odessa gave up and closed the door on us. I went over by a large London plane tree and, shielded by shadow, pissed into the gutter.

"Do you have anything to eat at your place?" Boycie asked.

"Come on, let's find out," I answered.

Karen fixed him a sandwich in our kitchen. Before he started to eat it he dialed his mother and told her he had gone to the funeral parlor to see a woman who sometime in the past had lived in the room next to his. His mother obviously asked him about what sort of shirt he was wearing. Boycie said, "Momma, it hit me then, and I had to move."

He asked his mother for food and after her response he said into the phone, "Just wrap it up and put it by the door." Then Boycie handed the phone to Karen and told her, "Talk to my mother." Karen talked with her briefly and handed the phone back. Boycie hung up. "Black, blackie, black mother...."

Boycie ate the sandwich Karen had given him and I said I would run him by his mother's house in my car. He said okay. The food was by the door when we arrived, Boycie said good night, and I drove home.

TRAJECTORY I

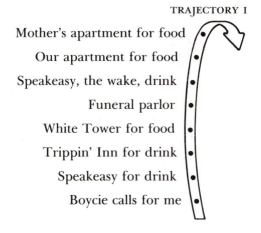

Mother's apartment for food
Our apartment for food
Speakeasy, the wake, drink
Funeral parlor
White Tower for food
Trippin' Inn for drink
Speakeasy for drink
Boycie calls for me

•   •   •

A gray haze hung in the bright, hot air. Boycie and I were drinking sodas in front of Samuel Brothers engine rebuilders, waiting for the head of my Chevy engine. We had the valves reseated because the engine had lost compression; the rings were okay. It was too early in the day for Boycie to have a drink, and as a result our sparse conversation was desultory, the way the humid heat made us feel.

Boycie was looking up and down the street at the traffic. It reminded me of the time he suggested we sit in my car in front of the apartment and look up the noses of the people passing on the trolley. He had a highly developed sense of space. From where we were sitting in front of *Sammy Bruhs* we could look at the Martin Luther King, Jr., Plaza and the area of the speakeasies Boycie frequented.

Boycie waved his arm, encompassing the area of black and ethnic South Philadelphia.

"See all this space?"

"Sure," I said looking at the city panorama.

"I'm fucking all this space."

This was Boycie as public actor—funny, profane, defamatory.

·   ·   ·

Though a quarrel in the streets is to be hated, the energies displayed in it are fine; the commonest Man has grace in his quarrel. Seen by a supernatural Being our reasonings may take the same tone—though erroneous, they may be fine. This is the very thing in which consists poetry. *There may be reasonings, but when they take an instinctive form, like that of animal forms and movements, they are poetry, they are fine: they have grace.* (Keats, quoted in Dewey 1958:32–33)

Boycie displayed poetic grace in the quarrel, but the quarrel was not wrangling; rather, it accomplished a kind of legal work. For Boycie and others a public litigation was an authentic forum where grievances were aired. Public space was certainly an aesthetic space of walking, singing, playing, and dancing, but it was also one of the call to order, one where legal work might be done. And it was as well a space in which one transacted business.

Two months after Boycie and I viewed his dead friend and then crashed drunkenly and argumentatively into the wake for her, he rang my doorbell. It was a September evening and the sun was setting. To my surprise he was driving a pristine Oldsmobile, eighteen years old and in mint condition. He was wearing a flat-crowned, straw Amish planter's hat I had given him, and he looked very stylish. With the old Oldsmobile, he seemed in some indefinable way *archaic*.

In the front seat was a teen-age boy Boycie introduced as Rainbow. There was a radio in the dashboard, concealed under a chemically treated mechanic's cloth. Boycie started the car, lifted the cloth, and turned on the radio. The Jackson Five sang,

Oh Baby I was blind to let you go
Let you go. . . .

(The Jackson Five)

I broke into the music, "Nice car, Boycie."

"It's Sarge's car; I'm fixing it for him." One of the power windows was stuck.

He drove around to the other side of the block and north one more block, then parked the car. There were all kinds of people in the street. The barbershop on that busy corner was closed for the night, but a small grocery store was open, and men with drinks in their hands stood on the sidewalk in front of the bar. Teen-agers and old people were out sitting or standing, talking, laughing, visiting; music pulsed from the bar.

Boycie, Rainbow, and I walked across the street and went into a row house. I was introduced to a man and a woman. There was no furniture in the house, and the radio was broken. A single light bulb hung from the ceiling. Roaches were climbing all the walls in random patterns. I had never seen phalanxes of roaches and was shocked by how stripped down the place was. Boycie poured me a shot into a dirty glass from a bottle of wine that he and Rainbow had been sharing with the couple before they picked me up. When he set his own glass down, a roach, none too steady itself, fell off the wall into it. "Aw man," he whispered disgustedly.

We drank our wine, discussed the absence of music, and began making motions to leave. Rainbow complained that he had money in the bottle, so Boycie picked it up and we left.

We drove over to his mother's apartment across Broad Street. The three of us stood on the sidewalk while he rang the bell. "Hey Momma, hey Momma," he called up to her, then in a softer voice said, "Get your black ass down here," laughing to himself, profaning his *own* mother.

She opened the door in her nightclothes. When she saw me behind Boycie she said that she was not dressed. "Only Boycie can come up; he'll be down in a minute." She was terribly embarrassed and so was I.

Rainbow and I went back to the car, drank from his bottle of wine, and talked. Boycie came out a few minutes later. His mother had come down with him, dressed this time. Boycie asked her if she wanted a ride; she said no. He then interrupted us and asked Rainbow to go to the corner bar for some beer. Rainbow said, "No, I'm rapping." Boycie started the car and we drove away, stopping at Poppa Doc's bar. Boycie and I went in and drank some more wine, he bought a pack of Kool menthol cigarettes, then we drove off. I sat in the back. Rainbow seemed to be insisting that we return to where we had started from, but I could not hear well with the radio playing loudly.

> It's your thing
> Do what you want to do
> I can't tell ya
> Who to sock it to.

> (The Isley Brothers)

I was beginning to realize that something was up. We returned to the house with the high-density roaches. Boycie and Rainbow got out and Boycie told me to stay in the back seat. I was partially hidden and I believe that no one noticed me. We had parked in front of the house Boycie roomed in, which was across the street from where we began drinking. Boycie was attempting to enter his rooming house. When his mother materialized on the sidewalk, I understood why she had come downstairs with Boycie back at her apartment. She now had with her her sister Elizabeth and her sister's husband, Red.

Responding to Boycie's banging on the door and his repeated loud demands to be let in, the landlord appeared in the doorway. Boycie claimed noisily that he had paid his twenty-six dollars rent but was not allowed to enter his room. He said that this was not right, that something was going on here. The landlord, standing on the top step just outside his door, did not reply. People were gathering; some had been on their front steps, others came out of the bar and the houses.

Boycie decided to fight him. He came over to the car, laid his shirt on the fender, and took off his shoes. He returned to the arena, and the landlord stepped slowly from his stoop onto the sidewalk, his right hand poised over his back pocket. Someone yelled out, "He's got a gun!" Boycie announced he wasn't afraid of no gun. The landlord still said nothing. They met on the sidewalk in front of the house and exchanged blows. Boycie was knocked down and lay on his back with his feet raised in the air like an

Indian fighting a man with a knife, insulting the man, attempting to goad him to attack. But the landlord just stood and looked down at Boycie.

Boycie's knockdown did not cause loss of face. The point of his litigation appeared more powerful than his fall to the ground. Furthermore, Boycie was both intoxicated and willing to continue; fortunately the two conditions tended to cancel each other out.

By this time there were between twenty and thirty people standing about ten feet away, silently watching the exchange. As far as the run-in proper was concerned, it was all over. Boycie's mother, Aunt Elizabeth, and Red lifted him off the ground, and Red, restraining him, led him over to the car. Momma fanned him with the Amish planter's hat, saying, "Cool yourself, cool yourself," to which he responded, "Don' fan me, girl."

Boycie told Red not to hold him so tightly, he didn't have to hurt Boycie. Nevertheless, they continued to hold him near the front fender of the Oldsmobile, telling him he could not *go up against the man*. He repeated that he had paid his money, *for real*, that the *motherfucker* wouldn't let him up to his room, that he had *scrambled* all day for that money, and they wouldn't let him take his clothes.

While Boycie was loudly restating his claims, his mother walked over and talked with the landlord. She returned to the front of the car and told Boycie that if he came back sober tomorrow he could pick up his things. She was able to convey this compromise by virtue of her status as his mother. It was after the face-off that she was able to effect or receive from the landlord the outcome of Boycie's suit. The suit was not mediated, adjudicated, or negotiated. After the first contest, however, when Boycie was no longer litigating and the landlord perceived that it was in his best interest to satisfy Boycie, he let Boycie's mother have the result, which was an accommodation.

Boycie put on his shirt and shoes, then asked Aunt Elizabeth for a cigarette, although he had bought a fresh pack at Poppa Doc's. Elizabeth said he had his own cigarettes. He repeatedly asked her for a cigarette, and she continued to remind him of his own pack. He rummaged through his pockets and finally brought one out. By the time he put it to his mouth she had a light for him. It was a pretty example of those tiny nurturant gestures that let people know where they stand with one another. By using the same request, Raymond had tried to restore the order between him and me during our confrontation in Telemachus' shop a year earlier; I had not understood it then.

TRAJECTORY II

To landlord's house: the face-off

Drink at Poppa Doc's Bar

Boycie's mother's apartment

Drink with Rainbow and couple

Boycie picks me up

Boycie drinking with Rainbow

If one party causes a breach in a relationship, the other party may attempt to suture it by providing an intimate hint, attempting to communicate on one level that what may have happened on another level did not have to sever connections between them. Boycie's asking Elizabeth for a cigarette was a request for inclusion, a knock to reenter the social structure at the place he had left it, for he had led everyone related to him into positions they would have preferred to avoid. His request was perhaps the equivalent, elsewhere in America, of asking forgiveness, except that he did not have to humble himself. Instead he was able to maintain dignity, a sign that he was equal to the offense he had committed in involving his relatives as parties to his legal performance. Elizabeth, offering not the cigarettes but the light, acknowledged that she accepted Boycie's request for inclusion in the mundane world. On both sides the litigation frame was replaced by gestures signifying that the ordinary was now restored for people who supported him.

After Elizabeth lit Boycie's cigarette, she spotted me partially concealed in the back seat of Sarge's Olds and wanted to know if I had been there all this time. I said I had. She told me, "Go on home, hon'; don' be around Boycie tonight." I let myself out of the car, and she added, "Nobody'll bother you." I have to admit I wondered then how she knew that. Rainbow asked from across the street if I was leaving. I said yes. He said, "I'll see you tomorrow." I walked the two blocks home.

The day following the argument Boycie returned to my house to have me help him move. It was then, when Boycie and I were discussing the situation, that further issues came to light, revealing particularly why the landlord's silence had seemed so eloquent. They would not let him in his room, he reasoned, because they had taken things from it. A little later he hinted that he had been drinking with the landlord's wife. After suggesting this he let out a high-pitched "hee, hee, hee," which seemed to jiggle everything into focus.

His revelation let me reevaluate what he had done. Boycie was locked out, not on account of back rent, which he did owe, but because he may have been close to making a cuckold of the landlord. He may not have known or may have only guessed why he was barred from his room. What matters at the phenomenal level is that paying the rent did not qualify him for reentry.

The delicacy of the landlord's move in locking the door can be appreciated when it is seen against the possibility that Boycie was caught at nothing more significant than having a drink with the woman. The landlord countered the miniature crime exactly. It meant that he would have to make no public accusation against Boycie and would not have to bring him to court over something he did not like or only suspected. According to local norms, the landlord would have had *no* litigable grounds at all for such action. From the landlord's perspective it was a way of reaffirming his ties to his spouse. Removing Boycie's presence both prevented what is locally considered inevitable—if you drink with a person, you are intimately involved—and erased the possibility that the landlord would have to confront his wife for her lack of cool in handling Boycie's manipulations. In this one rather understated move, much information was conveyed to the landlord's immediate environment.

The immediate environment extended into public space, the public being defined in part as *newsy* neighbors. People's talk was always full of what happened to them and what they witnessed. One reason a litigation could be held in public space was that the public already knew something about the litigants through the effective gossip system, and the particular issues revealed would not evoke more than subdued surprise. In short, the landlord's face was very much exposed to neighbors, who would know about any of Boycie's gambits with the woman.

The outcome of Boycie's public suit was that he and the landlord reached a compromise, full accommodation. It was a successful transition ceremony, a miniaturized status passage; a small tie had been severed and at least one had been preserved. Local relations would adjust accordingly.

It is worth noting what did *not* occur and therefore was not a necessary part of public litigation. There was no confession, no acceptance of blame, no expression of guilt or attempt to assign it; no verbal judgments were passed, and no one meted out any punishments. These mechanisms, familiar enough in Western legal settings, are insufficient to describe the public resolutions of conflict to which I was privy.

Everyone involved or witnessing Boycie's altercation knew everyone else to some degree. This knowledge ranged from knowing that someone roomed in the area to having more substantive dealings with that person, through either kinship or friendship. This meant that most of the people knew something about the usual characters of the parties, and many could probably guess, if they did not already know, what the issues were.

A public litigation might be interpreted as an elaborate statement of an individual's social intention. This takes into account that one was willing to personally sanction grievances that one had. Boycie was willing for witnesses who already knew something to know that he had commitments to honor. The strength of the assertion he made was indicated by his willingness to implicate his body deeply in the proceedings. The landlord as Boycie's opponent had to sustain the intention or bear the consequences. The audience for a variety of reasons read and attended a person's social intentionality.

Members of the audience attended closely and openly all the goings-on. There was no eye aversion or discrete turning away from the litigant's glances. In later conversations about the event, witnesses repeated eidetically what people said to one another during the course of moves and countermoves. The replaying of what went on was a version of the *he said–she said*, and probably fulfills the scientific definition of gossip. Toward the end of narrating what happened, people included what they would have done in the same situation if they had been one of the litigants. The postargument enactment permitted each witness a moral commitment from a safe distance and communicated to the hearer the kind of moralizing that could be differed with, agreed with, or discussed further.

In such intimate locales, one heard, in the course of several days or during one long conversation with a number of people, several personal editorials given on that kind of news. There was no attempt to verify what really happened, since that was self-evident in the quoted recounting. The discussion remained open; what each person would have done had he been in the face-off was given equal status. From these multiple perspectives, listeners gained a kind of detached sense of the original occasion and an assembly of opinions that served as the collective conscience.

There were features of audience talk that returned reflexively to parties eventually. Many of the witnesses were people that we drank with or customers of Telemachus's. From them we would hear a version of Boycie's conduct.

There was a more direct reflexivity in the community discourse between members of the audience and the litigious parties. Mostly this involved the possibility of ridicule. It was conceivable that if Boycie had been locked out and had let his things go, he would have been ridiculed by men who were drinking acquaintances of his and who knew the reasons for the action. The children, too, might have mocked him on the street from a safe distance. Boycie's response would have been acute embarrassment and possibly impotent anger. His litigation, then, stalled off a greater humiliation and insured his future against what would have been taken quite accurately as his social and personal ineffectuality.

There were possibilities less pointed than ridicule that nevertheless could have led to the same results if there had been no litigation. People could have *started shit* with Boycie. To give an example, if one of the landlord's friends had come over to his house armed with the knowledge that Boycie had been drinking with his wife, the friend could have alluded to her relationship with someone, namely Boycie, thus impugning her fidelity to the landlord. After the friend had left, or perhaps while he was there, to the amusement of others the landlord would have had to come to some terms with his wife. A somewhat different litigation might have become public.

The members of the audience, then, have at least two major functions: they provide recountings to one another of what happened, including a mild reflection to the litigants; and, more extreme, they subject those who should have been litigants to more demanding sanctions, effectually paring away their self-images or damaging the substance of their ties with others.

To leave the summary of the staged encounter here would be to miss not the fatefulness *in* encounters but the fatefulness *of* encounters. In the face of ridicule, character and honor have an appreciable way of failing; indeed they sometimes falter with mild aspersions. But, with regard to Boycie's case, I have in mind something talked abroad that was a bit more crucial than reputation alone.

If Boycie had permitted himself to be locked out, without access to his expensive suits and sport coats, he would have signaled much more than a loss of face. He would have conveyed the datum that he was someone who could no longer defend the material extensions of himself against those who could co-opt them. It would have entailed an ostensive shrinkage of his defensible ego. Ridicule would have been simply the first step toward degradation that would include taking his material goods, thereby contributing to the disintegration of his social ties. People could get *next to* him with impunity and on their own terms. If he had it and they wanted it, they could take it. Instead of maintaining an appreciable perimeter around himself, he would have had to permit, perhaps with weakening protestations, incursions against a self he could not keep. Boycie, instead of participating in the war of all against all, would have been the victim of a war of all against one, with the composition of the "all" changing in each skirmish. Showing the willingness to take large losses meant that others would be attempting to realize similar gains.

6. End of Summer

At the end of August 1970, I could not leave. My grant for the conduct of fieldwork was up, but I had no sense that I had done an adequate job of gathering *data*. The financial help from the Center for Urban Ethnography came in two parts: the first year of support was for a field stay, and the second was for writing the dissertation. Although I had completed the year of research, living much of that time on Fourteenth Street, I was certain I was not ready to pick up and leave. I wanted to continue because I knew I needed to remain completely involved.

Though wholly convinced I needed more knowledge, I was now supposed to write; my life split in half. I felt I could not tear away from South Philadelphia, into which more and more of my life had been absorbed. Karen distanced herself from the situation by finding a position in Center City in a sheet music business that she came in time to manage. As a kind of compromise I began during the winter months to frequent the Center for Urban Ethnography and prepare for the dissertation. I moved closer to the everyday life of the American corporation, secretly, for I told no one on Fourteenth Street what I was doing. The notes I took on the social science literature grew into a box of cards like that of my field notes. I examined numerous sources in order to encompass with a literature the life I had led for a year. A third batch of notecards evolved with analyses written on them.

In September of the second year, I wrote, "I can't seem to get my hands clean today." At the time a poet friend, Bruce Renner, was visiting from Columbia University where he was taking his master's degree in writing. He and I had published a book of poems together three years earlier, and we had always stayed in touch through letters. I continued my entry: "Here I am inside these people. I am supposed to be doing fieldwork, I am supposed to be thinking." I went on to write:

At this moment I wish my life were like a very clear piece of paper. That each poem, each sentence, each piece of sculpture were clean, precise. I wish my biography were devoid of actual information. I wish that the documents I secrete, checkbooks, letters, entries in ledgers, shopping lists, were lost or destroyed. Most photographs, except for those taken in very direct sunlight, in black and white, should be burnt. Only a few poems should remain, a painting. Nothing must shed light on this. They must stand. But they must stand by themselves.

Bruce's presence reflected to me an earlier, white middle-class world, and I felt a deep dissatisfaction with myself—a form of self-hatred, I suppose—resulting from being torn between black and white. I cannot explain the feeling; perhaps I can only evoke it.

A month later as cold weather settled in, the street began to close up; public life moved indoors and contracted. In a field note I wrote, "It is getting colder now and people no longer sit on the street. I asked Judy tonight what people do in the winter. Do they go visiting? She said no. She even hates to get up to go to school. What happens? She said they watch TV. . . . Why are they isolated during the winter when sociality is so easy and frequent during the summer?" Then, masking speculation with an assertion, I added, "In a sense individuals do not exist outside these [public, street] events but bide their time, waiting for them to happen. When they do happen, the persons, in concert, carry them off."

In the winter I talked with Goffman and with my advisor at the University of Wisconsin, Arnold Strickon. Goffman suggested that I write an ethnography of the shop, but I wanted far more from myself than simply another field report of a single site, like the study of a bar. Strickon advised me to be experimental. I liked his suggestion and drafted a dissertation so experimental that it was completely unacceptable to my doctoral committee. I threw it away and started over on a second one (which was accepted), all the while reading again through the familiar literatures of cognitive anthropology, face-to-face interaction, ethnomethodology, sociolinguistics, French philosophy, and social psychology in search of a body of ideas that would bestow coherence on the form of life I had lived and the people I had lived with.

Cabaret

Having decided to stay a second year, Karen and I remained on Fourteenth Street and continued to be caught up in local life. I wrote on Friday, 24 October, "This seems to be a particularly benevolent Friday. The sun shone today and the weather was temperate, between seventy and seventy-five degrees." I was walking home from Ninth Street where I had bought some coffee. Mr. Miller, a construction worker who lived around the corner from us on Montrose, saw me and asked me to go with him for a drink. I agreed and we went to the Chas. Cafe. Miss Jane, Mr. Jardine's old lady, was tending bar. A white woman of about fifty-five stood at the end of the bar; she was Mrs. Charles, the owner or wife of the owner, I guessed. All the clients were black. We went to the opposite end of the bar and sat down. Mr. Miller bought me a nip and had one himself. He asked me, although Karen and I had lived in the area nearly a year, "How do you and the madam like the neighborhood?" I said fine, that the people were nice to us. He told me he liked me, I was alright with him. "You keep to your own business and don't bother anyone."

We joked about him beating me at checkers the previous Wednesday evening on the sidewalk in front of Maryjane's house. He said his game was really cards, and then we discussed where I might go to shoot pool.

I remarked to him that I had heard his son Albert was quitting his bartending job down on the corner next to us, so we discussed the difficulties in tending bar and the communications between father and son. He went on to tell me that Albert had studied for the priesthood; "I never discouraged him."

From the other end of the bar White Frank (no one knew if he was black or white) bought me a drink, white lightning, which was 180 proof smuggled from a brewery and sold by the bottle on the street. I refused to drink it and Jane substituted whiskey for it. We had another nip and talked; I was bombed. Finally, Mr. Miller and I left.

We walked toward the apartment and parted ways at Montrose Street. Joyceann was selling tickets on the street. This time they were not for an excursion but for a cabaret, so I bought two. I had heard about cabarets the winter before but had not had an opportunity to buy tickets. I was to discover that the cabaret was an interior musical space that recapitulated local residential space; it was the winter version of the summer street, but wholly enclosed within an evening of musical performance. There was no cabaret season in Baltimore and Washington, D.C.; it was unique to Philadelphia.

The above-mentioned Albert, who was about to quit his bartending job, had lived first on Montrose Street with his mother and father, then had moved above the bar on the corner where he was the bartender through the first year we lived in the area. He was the same Albert who from behind the bar the night of the excursion had urged Brother Smith, Pop, and Raymond to let Karen and me go to the bus to return to Philadelphia. His friendship circle included several other men who called themselves "The Gary D's"; this was a men's social group named after a local black-owned bar, which was itself named after the owner's youngest son, Gary. Albert and his friends sponsored a winter cabaret, as did other men's groups in the area, such as Caesar and the Coupe de Villes.

It was raining fiercely the night of the performance, and Leanna, a neighbor, asked if she and her boyfriend, Big Gregory, could ride with us. We were pleased to have their company. Big Gregory was a club boxer in his early twenties, physically impressive though not very tall. It was only the second time I had talked with him, but we got along very well.

The women sat in back, and Gregory and I sat in front together and talked about cars. He told me the story of the fate of his Cadillac, a present from Leanna.

Some people prepared food and took it with them, but we stopped at Colonel Sanders' Fried Chicken and ordered food to take out. Although there was a bar at the dance hall, most people, including ourselves, brought their own drinks to complement their food.

I dropped Karen, Leanna, and Big Gregory at the entrance and parked the car, unfurling an umbrella against the storm. The streetlights showed a number of abandoned, rain slickened brick houses, their windows empty. The cabaret was in a large hall in a decaying neighborhood.

Inside the entrance was an impeccably uniformed guard who, for reasons that remained elusive, asked all the men to take off their hats. Since men usually wore their hats indoors as a part of their outfits, it surprised me both that he asked and further that the men agreed to remove them. I would not have wanted to make the request.

Albert and his friends of the Gary D Club stood and greeted their friends just beyond the guards; they wore double-breasted black tuxedos and blue shirts with ruffled fronts. When we spoke to them, Albert asked us to breakfast at his parents' house after the night of dancing.

Babe, Ivery's old lover, stood at the bar. I recognized him and recalled that Telemachus feared him. Babe asked me over for a drink. I went, but I could not understand his accent—he was from coastal Georgia—so our conversation did not progress well.

Karen took the food and drink we brought and followed Leanna to our table. The tables were arranged in rows at the edge of the dance floor, spatially replicating our neighborhoods. People who knew one another best—based on the proximity of their houses— sat together. I recognized people we knew from other areas at other tables. Behind us, the older people from our locale sat at a table of their own.

Between our tables and the bandstand was an ample dance floor. The band began to play. There were two saxophones, a clarinet, an electric guitar, an electric piano, and a complex of drums. The lead singer, who played no instrument, sang vocals with the piano player and guitarist.

Most people danced. Albert did, and so did his parents. Those that did not dance sat in their seats, their faces composed like masks, many of them moving to the rhythms of the music. Expressionless, these nondancers watched closely those who performed. Karen and I danced together, and I was impressed that no one laughed at us, for we contrasted with everyone else on the floor, to whom bodily motion was a way of life, was like life itself. It seemed that those who danced were bodies filled with liquid motion. They could choose to move now this, now that portion of the whole, and nothing of the body was alien to expansive movement. By contrast, Karen and I, and I am speaking culturally, were architectonic constructions of discrete parts; when we concentrated on various portions of our bodies, we could move them, even in time to the subtle rhythms, but we did so with little of the expressive grace of the other dancers.

Dances fell into two categories, slow and fast. The slow ones were contact dances; the fast ones were virtuoso performances of sometimes two people, sometimes the whole dance floor. The band was very good. Groups that played for cabarets and other occasions were drawn from a vast pool of talent in much the same way gospel choirs in black churches were. The performers gained experience week after week, and though most of them did not break into the big time of commercial recording success, they nevertheless kept alive performance traditions that were not quite equaled elsewhere in American culture.

A woman I did not know but who was obviously an accomplished dancer was on the dance floor with Albert when the band broke into a formal music I had not heard before. She and Albert danced, and the others gave way until they were the only two left performing together. They faced one another, hands on hips, their upper bodies held slightly bent back, the legs and feet moving to the drummer's mechanical but fast, almost baroque sounding, Bach-like rhythm. When they danced with their heads slightly thrown back and only their lower bodies moving, it was as if they were imitating the dances of the Scottish, Irish, and English, who seem incapable of moving much of their anatomy above the knees.

It was a beautiful, formal mime, and the whole audience relished it. When they were through, the rest of us did not applaud but laughed out loud and discussed our delight in their brilliant performance. They had both evoked and caricatured a kind of European formality. It was as if the musicians had transformed the culture of Karen and myself into a purely pleasurable aesthetic performance beyond irony. Our laughter erupted from their bold mimesis of white dancing style and, by logical extension, of Karen and myself.

Several men asked Karen to dance and she said no. At our table Mr. Ibraheem, who had the misfortune to be attending with his wife, asked Karen to dance; his wife quickly told him to forget it. For a while after the initial flurry of requests no one came over to ask her, and I asked no one to dance with me, not wanting to embarrass anyone with my lack of experience and ability.

Then one imposing man wearing a long, black coat of chemical fur, though it was not cold in the dance hall, walked over to our table. He asked Karen to dance, and impulsively she stood up and joined him. Later she said that he had talked to her the whole time they were dancing and that she had not understood one word he had said. The music was loud, and he had talked in a low voice beneath it.

Later there was a kind of intermission and I went to the men's room. One man I had met had his arm in a sling. He was the quarterback on a pickup football team (the teams were Old and Young, and he was the quarterback for the Old) and had broken it while playing. We were standing with others in a conversational circle. There were various general remarks.

"I got my shit with me," said the quarterback, patting the pocket over a .38 magnum. "I got my shit with me too."

As we were establishing our armaments, a man came up beside me and said, "Excuse me, do you know if anything is happening after the cabaret tonight, like a party..." His voice trailed off. I said that Albert was having something at his house but that I did not know anything more about it. He asked where Albert lived and I told him I did not know. He said, "Thanks, brother" (pronounced *bruh*), and a little later I returned to our table.

The major show was a troupe introduced as African dancers, though I never learned whether or not they were really from Africa or were just imitating African dances. They wore briefs and bikinis made of cloth printed to resemble animal skins. The dancers were highly skilled at what they did. All the numbers they performed were very fast, involved, narrative, and percussive. After they finished there were more slow and fast dances for the rest of us and then a finale.

The last number was passionate and rapid, and more people went up knowing that the end of the evening was near. Soon there was a massive movement of dancers to the stage. I looked around and saw that during the four hours no one seemed to have left; now nearly all were crowding with the musicians onto the small bandstand.

There were no longer a stage of performers and an audience. The people moved with eyes closed, caught up in the sound, and all became one, immersed in a passionate, singular music. Everyone was now a performer. All danced on their own without partners, completely equal, unified in a music that animated each movement and embraced them.

The cabaret, apparently bounded by that passionate and collective final number, was over. It was 2:00 A.M. In order to put on her coat, Karen set down her umbrella; when she reached for it, it had disappeared. She was really angry. I went for the car in the rain and drove it up to the door, and we and Big Gregory and Leanna rode back to Albert's parents' house in South Philadelphia for more drinking and dancing and finally breakfast, which would take us to dawn.

I say the cabaret was over, but in a sense it was not, for many of us from the neighborhood were crowded into the Millers' house. We sat on all the available sofas and chairs, and someone put a record on the stereo, though no one danced. Then through the door appeared the man who had asked me in the men's bathroom what was happening afterward, and right after him entered the big man with the black coat, its fur slick with rain. I could feel Karen tense next to me, and I was getting tense myself, for the newcomers were not anyone that we or, as far as we could tell, anyone else knew.

They settled in and the man who had danced with Karen at the cabaret asked her to dance with him there. She pleaded fatigue and a headache and he turned to the woman next to Karen and asked if she would. The woman was Esther Pierpont, an elegant and publicly reserved person. She was also strikingly beautiful, as were her sisters, her mother, and her daughter. I had noted one Sunday afternoon, when she and her sister, daughter, and mother were returning from church, the languid, regal way they walked.It was as if *they were the pageant*. These were very cool, very controlled people. Esther, without ever glancing at the tall man, stood up and the two of them did a rather cold dance. Then she sat down, never having looked at him. By then I was hoping that the smell from the kitchen meant breakfast was being served. I went to check but it was not yet ready.

On my short walk I reflected on the fact that although Karen was with me and was wearing a wedding ring, the man in the black coat was not reading the tie-signs. Was their dance back at the cabaret also a sign in a language I did not know? Alarmed, I wondered what exactly was going on. We had already had some difficult encounters, and I did not want this situation to deteriorate into something once again beyond her control or mine. He asked her to dance again while I was in the kitchen, and when she replied one more time that she had a headache or some such, he made a joking remark about it in that terribly low, almost inaudible voice.

We all sat for a few minutes listening to the recorded music, and everyone watched everyone else without moving their eyes or showing awareness that anything was amiss until the air crackled with tension. And then the platters of food began to stream from the kitchen: hot ham and eggs, fried potatoes, fried tomatoes, steaming grits with butter, and white bread. It was enjoyable. Karen and I ate, obviously too quickly, and ran into the rain, around the corner, down the street to our apartment. Drenched without the umbrella, Karen cursed again what she considered a quick, clever theft back at the dance hall.

The cabaret had reframed the public space of street and household, containing both within musical space. Men and women dancing together marked the unity and harmony of the sexes that tended in the household to be opposed. The evening progressed alternating between slow and fast dances, and there was contrast between the domestic and the exotic performers. With the final number, however, all contrasts and discontinuities gave way as the dancers poured onto the performance stage and became one with the instrumentalists and vocalist. Locality and spatiality, male and female dissolved within the unity of a heated, transcending finale; the music embraced everyone and held them intimately, briefly within itself.

. . .

During the second winter of our stay I did no sculpture, no art, no poetry. I worked for Telemachus a little, off and on. Karen and I went out with neighbors Herb and Franny to the Latin Casino to hear Dionne Warwick in concert, and we attended another cabaret given by Caesar and the Coupe de Villes. After the cabaret we went to a private club for drinks and more dancing. The sound system was broken and people began to leave. Karen worked evenings with Godfrey on his reading and days at the music business. I went to the center, read books and articles, and analyzed field notes.

. . .

On a cold spring morning I heard Telemachus at the shop at six-thirty. Later, when I went down, he told me what had happened. He had awakened at three-thirty and tossed and turned for a while, but he could not go back to sleep. In the dark he stood up and dressed. His wife awoke as well and started in on him. "She said what she wanted to say and I said what I wanted to say." Before the dawn light he walked out of the house and got into his car to drive to the shop. Mae followed him out and asked him to open the window of the car. He asked her why she wanted him to open the window. "Because I said so!" She hit the glass with a brick and Telemachus began to drive the car away. She threw the brick, then, and it hit the back window although the glass did not break.

"I can't concentrate; let's go see a show Saturday night," he suggested.

We did go to the movies but it was on a Wednesday evening and took another couple along. One of us that went that night was soon to die.

"That sounds good to me," I said.

The scene between Telemachus and Mae began over what had happened at the wedding of one of their daughters. Both Angie and Mary had attended the wedding, but whereas Mary had sat discretely in the back and left before the crowd, Angie had gone to the reception. Telemachus's daughters and wife said that she had watched his wife. "Angie really blew it, she stared at Mae." Telemachus did not realize what was going on at the time, but the women had become increasingly upset. "I'm ready to give Angie up," he continued. "She is really stupid. . . . She doesn't know how to act." Mae had ended up crying. Telemachus had tried to tell her that he was not giving Angie money, but he could not tell her that it was the other way around.

Telemachus's nephew, Jerrold, who was standing with us, said, "No, you couldn't go into all that now."

"I tried to explain," Telemachus went on, "but she just won't listen. No matter what I say she just won't believe me. Angie has done more for me than anyone else in my life."

Later Jerrold said to me that the whole incident was not just Angie's fault; part of the blame, he said, was Telemachus's.

Jerrold went to work for Telemachus over the winter and Judy Sims had her first affair with him. She had not yet graduated from junior high school.

Death on the Street

"Things are getting much better," I wrote on 1 May, 1971, as summer and warm weather approached for the second time since we moved to Fourteenth Street. "Bruce and Julie came down to stay with us for their remaining days in the East." The creative writing program at Columbia had ended for the year, and Bruce and Julie with their daughter, Ona, drove through Philadelphia for a weekend visit on their way back to Wisconsin. Ona, seventeen months old, was learning to talk. Bruce showed me poems he had turned in for one of his writing courses. I read through them; some were familiar, some new. I especially like one that captured a burning sadness (Renner 1982:4).

> like the voice of a shadow
> you wear your clothes
> in my throat.
> Turn me toward you
> with your swollen arm,
> long and whole.
> Your smile covers my terror
> at the world;
> a blanket of rice
> and onions,
> as majestic as bone—

your finger crooked
inside my face;
your eyes, bread
for the winter
that has not fallen
as far as your breast,
to the nipple:
a bitter foam, it burns
quietly into me.

The poem evoked for me memories of his first wife, Ilse, who had committed suicide; Karen and I had known her, and indeed the lines had been written about her. She had sent a letter to her psychiatrist announcing her intention and then had turned on the gas of her apartment range. By the time the doctor received the letter she had been dead for days. I told Bruce I liked the poem better than anything he had done. It was not an objective assessment; the poem just spoke emotionally to me against the background of my knowledge of Ilse. But it is not Ilse's death that I refer to in the section title, Death on the Street. For me, with hindsight, the poem prefigures the events that followed my reading of it, and it provides an implicit contrast with the death that was then still to come.

Bruce and Julie arrived from New York early in the day, and after supper I suggested to Julie that we go next door to have a drink. Bruce was bathing Ona and getting her ready for bed, and Karen did not drink. Joyceann had needed money recently, and as the weather warmed, she had opened a speakeasy on the first floor of their house. Her clients were her mother's friends and her own, and their relatives. She announced its opening by appearing in the doorway of the house on weekend evenings wearing a housecoat.

Julie and I went next door and Joyceann gave me a big greeting. She seemed positively delighted when I introduced her to Julie and told her, "Julie can *drink* some of that stuff." Julie could, too. I had seen her bolt vodka and pepper until she passed out.

We sat in the dining room around the table. Pop was drinking with us. He talked with Julie while I looked sideways at the furnishings and the photographs on the sideboard. There was a good movie at the theater that night, he said. Julie declined his invitation, and when he asked for her phone number she told him she was passing through and would be gone in a day. Joyceann seemed pleased that men were talking to Julie and laughed as she set a six- or seven-ounce pitcher of whiskey in front of her, "I'm going to come and get you tomorrow!"

We drank for a while and the conversation was slow until Caesar came in, already high, and proceeded to perform for everyone. He was wearing a lime green Italian knit suit and sweater combination and very dark sunglasses. Joyceann's mother's boyfriend, Paul, who had moved in the year before, had left behind another family. His son from that earlier union and a friend came in just after Caesar to see the German shepherd dogs that Paul kept in the basement. As they passed through the dining room, Caesar made a big play to include them. "I don't know you, but I'd like to know you; come on and have a drink." They declined.

I had not seen Paul's son before, and I knew that the families of men and women who had affairs could get to know one another. I was curious what would happen here and watched Paul's son's face to see how he would react to Caesar. Paul's son looked directly at Caesar and smiled openly, responding to Caesar's well-performed charisma, although he delicately refused Caesar's expansive invitation.

For a few moments Caesar and Joyceann discussed publicly something that had come up between them that involved Joyceann and Caesar's wife, Juanita. They finished their private-public discussion, and he then turned to include everyone, announcing that last week he had had such a good time because he had seen all his friends at one time. He delivered a monologue on seeing one's friends, and then Chavonne Davette, ten months old, who had been sleeping all that time on the couch in the living room, woke up.

Caesar noticed immediately and exclaimed, "It's because she heard my voice."

Joyceann told us that Chavonne could sing with her, harmonize and everything.

"That's because when you were carrying her, you came to hear me sing and I gave to her essence," Caesar said. He walked into the living room, picked her up, and talked to her in a delicate voice, calling her nicknames like Shiny and Punkin'. Despite Chavonne's sleepiness he carried her to the head of the table where he had been sitting and set her on the edge, holding her in a sitting position and moving her in time to the music playing from the radio. I could see she was moving with him.

"She doesn't seem evil," he remarked, "but she's too quiet."

"She needs some time to wake up," I commented.

"No, she's been quiet too long."

"Let me see you teeth." She firmed her lips and would not let him in her mouth.

"You're beautiful," he told her.

" She knows what I'm saying, she understands everything I'm saying."

He took her in his arms and began to talk about her brother Little James.

"One day Pig and I came down to the house and Little James was on the street. James said hi to Pig but didn't pay any attention to me. Three or four times he said something to Pig and ignored me. I thought maybe he forgot my name or something. That night we came back and James said, 'Hi, Caesar.' I was surprised. Pig tried to get him to say something but James ignored him and said, 'I'm going to sleep now.' He just turned over on the couch, pulled the blanket over his head, and went to sleep."

I said, "Today he had a bag of peanuts and he gave one to everyone on the street but me."

"I'll bet tomorrow he'd give you one," Caesar added.

"Tomorrow he'd give me the whole bag!" Caesar laughed when I said that.

• • •

Bruce and Julie returned to Wisconsin for the summer. Two days later I walked out of the apartment onto the street to find Ivery Sims and her daughter Judy standing there. I pretended to ignore them. Judy asked me pointedly, "Aren't you speaking?"

I looked at her and said, "I can't, my ventriloquist died."

"I don't mean to be calling you," Ivery said, "but come here a minute." I walked over and stood with them. "People said, 'You shouldn't be in that boy's face like that.'"

She was referring to the week before. I had been in front of Telemachus's shop and had asked her to talk with me. She had gone upstairs and brought a book down so she could sit on it on her stoop while we talked. The book was checked out from the library and was about Helen Keller's life. There was even a page of braille in it so those with vision could see and feel what blind readers used. When she came back she had said, "Right now people are talking about us; I don't care what they say." Despite the facts that I was her son Godfrey's godfather, that Karen and I took the children in the car with us, and that we had them up to the apartment repeatedly over the last year, I had a pervasive feeling that there was no room for Ivery and me to speak publicly with each other as though we were in a sexually neutral zone.

I had the same feelings during an encounter with Joyceann one day at the end of the block. She was walking home with James and Chavonne and I was walking home as well, so we were going the same way to nearly the same destination. When I fell into step with Joyceann, it was as if I had stepped into a mine field. She broke step with me, turned away, pretended to hesitate, making me feel as though I had committed an antisocial act by trying to walk the rest of the block home with her. There was no way I could accompany her, and she would not speak with me. The public space was so defined, so charged with gossip and sexual innuendo, that our walking together, apparently, was too intense. At the same time we could sit in front of her mother's house and begin a card game with no problem. Walking together was far different than sitting together.

Ivery now wanted to know about the movie I had seen with Telemachus on Wednesday evening. "Was that with a fourteen-year-old boy?" Telemachus had asked Karen and me to accompany him, Angie, Tommy, and Linda to see *Sweet Sweetback's Badasssss Song*. Karen had pleaded a migraine headache and so I had gone with the four of them. Tommy was a customer and had brought his car in for repairs on a couple of occasions. He was pleasant and humorous, and the five of us had had a good time. I had no premonition that he would be killed that summer.

I began to tell Ivery the plot of the movie, but she was bored with my retelling and changed the subject to a far more dramatic and local event. "Did you hear about Shirley getting stabbed?"

"No!" I said, in shock. Judy was surprised too. The news was completely fresh.

"Mamie sneaked up on Shirley and stabbed her in the back. She is in critical condition in the hospital and Mamie is being held without bail." Mamie was the raw-boned, light-skinned woman, the mother of Pig and Juanita, and thus Caesar's mother-in-law. Her son Bubu had fathered Little James, and she had rented her top floor to Ivery and her children for two years. It was as if I were in the middle of the neighborhood for the moment.

Since Judy had not heard, she wanted to identify everyone: "You mean Big Shirley? . . . You mean Ruth—Miz Mamie?"

The topic of the conversation swiftly changed to talk about Godfrey who had fought with Miz Mamie's youngest daughter, Eve. It was only later that I learned from Karen that Miz Mamie had stabbed Shirley—her own daughter—because she wanted Shirley to care for her own children. Mamie was tired of them being put on her, and her sanction was to physically damage her daughter.

• • •

Now the threads of the story begin to come together: the theme of death prefigured in the poem, the talk with Ivery, the date with Telemachus, Angie, Tommy, and Linda. A month and a half after going to the movies with Telemachus, Angie, Tommy, and Linda, on the evening of 16 June, Karen and I left the Broad Street Diner, where we had gone for coffee. It was a hot night, and we rolled down the windows of the car. I drove north on Broad Street and turned right on Christian Street. In the second block there was a crowd on the north side of the street, as well as police cruisers and a police wagon. I noticed Judy and Contessa, though it took me a minute to realize that they were standing with Ivery who was wearing a new wig.

Karen put her head out of the car and said jokingly to them, "Go home." Ivery replied immediately in a more serious tone, "We're going to. Don't go inside yet." I parked the car, and Karen went upstairs and turned on the television while I walked up the street toward the crowd. Ivery, Judy, and Contessa were still standing there in front of the Chas. Cafe where Ivery most often drank with her friends. Babe, her former lover, was standing in the doorway. "Don't speak to me," he kidded with me. I told him I did not know him without his hat and with a new haircut. He danced for a moment to the jukebox inside. "Now I know you," I told him.

I was anxious to find out what had happened, so I urged Ivery and her girls to tell me why the police and the crowd were there. Not wanting to go into it in front of anyone else, they told me to wait a minute. Judy said, "I'm going to get me some corn chips." From inside the cafe Babe threw a bag of chips to the door. Judy picked them up, and she and Contessa shared them as we walked toward the apartment. As we left the entrance, the three of them all started talking at once.

"I was talking with Miz Mary, you know, Fat Mary," Ivery finally prevailed. "She liked my wig and said she was going to buy one like it. We were standing there talking and this man came to the house. He told her old man, Joe, he was going to kick the door down.

"Mr. Joe ran upstairs and stuck his gun out the window and blew the man's brains out. They're still out there on the street."

When we arrived in front of our apartments, I said to Ivery to come on up and tell Karen. She was eager to, and the four of us walked up the stairs. It took a minute or two to unravel the story that Ivery had herself pieced together. She and Babe were walking on Christian Street when Tommy, who lived next door to Mr. Joe, called Mr. Joe out from his house. When he came to the door, Tommy told him he was mad at him for calling the police on Tommy's children. Apparently Mr. Joe's children and Tommy's children had been fighting earlier in the evening, and Mr. Joe had called the police. When Tommy arrived home after work and learned that Mr. Joe had called the police on his children, he began to drink in preparation for an argument of the kind Boycie had had with his landlord the summer before.

Apparently Tommy called Mr. Joe onto the street and hit him when he came out. Mr. Joe then went inside and slammed the door. Unsatisfied, Tommy began to kick the door down. Mr. Joe then went upstairs and called down to Tommy on the sidewalk. Tommy, seeing that Mr. Joe had a rifle pointed out the window, called loudly up to him, "Go ahead and shoot, I ain' afraid of no gun." Mr. Joe pulled the trigger but missed Tommy.

"At that," Ivery recounted, "the children were running everywhere. I tried to haul ass myself, but Babe said he was going to stay and see what happened."

Tommy yelled up again for Mr. Joe to shoot, repeating he was unafraid of a gun. Joe did not miss the second time and blew Tommy's brains out on the street. Tommy's wife then emerged from her house and put a towel over the remains of Tommy's head.

"Miz Mary could have stopped that. When Mr. Joe went inside and upstairs, she went in after him; she should have tried."

Ivery now mimicing Miz Mary's walk in front of us as she stood in the living room, continued, "After the shooting Miz Mary disappeared out of the back of the house." Then Ivery voiced concern she would be called on as a witness because she was talking to Miz Mary just before the shooting.

Ivery said she then walked across to the Chas. Cafe and sat at the bar shaking. Crawford, one of her drinking partners, asked her what was wrong. "I never seen a man shot to death before," she told him.

After Ivery's story, some of it enacted, especially the parts where she tried to run from the scene and her shoes flopped off, I called Telemachus to tell him what happened. I was sure from the description that Tommy was the same Tommy that with his wife Linda had gone with us to see *Sweet Sweetback*. Ivery claimed that Tommy was a cousin of Maryjane's next door, just at the moment Telemachus said the same thing to me on the phone.

Telemachus did not know who Mr. Joe was, so I told him Mr. Joe was living with Fat Mary and described the long scar through his bottom eyelid, down his cheek, mentioning that I had gone on the expedition with Mr. Joe and Mary last summer. Telemachus still did not know who Mr. Joe was for sure; he had never been a customer in the shop.

I wrote in my field notes, "The whole event shocked me very much. I felt numb and terribly anxious about the whole thing. I knew the litigants, better in fact, than Ivery and many of the people around there."

After I hung up the phone I heard Ivery telling Karen that she was going to the doctor's tomorrow to pick up some pills; she repeated, "I never saw a man shot before." Judy and Contessa, by contrast, seemed unmoved by the event, though they throughly enjoyed the action, the talk about it, the concern.

"Mr. Joe's killed two other people," Ivery asserted.

"I know he likes to start shit on the street when he's bored," I told her. She agreed he did.

"Mr. Joe's kids had their heads out the window and saw him shoot the man," Ivery said.

The next day, 17 June 1971, I bought the *Evening Bulletin* and read, under the headline "Man Slain in Dispute With Neighbor,"

> Thomas Chaney Jr., 32, of 1221 Christian St. was shot to death about 10 P.M. yesterday climaxing a feud with a neighbor.
>
> The neighbor, Joseph Wiggins, 54, of Christian St. near 12th, called police after the shooting and surrendered, homicide detectives reported, and was charged with murder.
>
> Earlier in the evening, detectives said, Wiggins had summoned police to Chaney's home to stop fighting between children of the two families. When Chaney arrived home at 9 P.M. and learned of the police visit, he confronted Wiggins. The men fought and argued briefly, the police said, and then Chaney returned to his house. Wiggins was upstairs with a .30-.30 hunting rifle when Chaney taunted him from the street. He fired one shot into Chaney's head, police reported.

Before I read the paper, the morning after Tommy was shot, I was wakened by a woman on the sidewalk calling up to Joyceann in her second-story window right next door. The woman retold the story, then placed herself in Mr. Joe's position and asserted that she would not do what he had done; she would think first. "She put herself, first person, into the litigant's shoes," I wrote, "and said what she would and wouldn't have done." I heard Joyceann agreeing with her, saying, "That's right, that's right," and had the image of a hundred stories being told by a hundred men and women who had been in the crowd the previous night, each taking up his or her own position inside Mr. Joe's social location, and reshaping the event with a personal moral perspective.

•   •   •

Three days after the shooting there was another death, this one closer to home.

On June nineteenth, 1971, at about nine-thirty, Dan and I were lying in the front room on our bed watching television. We heard the bell buzz in the kitchen only because Jenny aroused and started pacing and whining. Knowing that it probably would be the children we quieted Jenny and continued watching television. A few minutes later we heard Poof and Pat yelling, "Dan!" "Karen!"

We still did not want to go to the window to tell them that tonight we wished to be alone. It seemed strange at the time, however, that they would shout to us. They never had before. We continued watching the television but during the next few minutes I thought I noticed some reddish or yellowish light outside the window. The opaque shades hid everything except the intensive light that crept around the corners. I noticed this but didn't mention it to Dan.

A few minutes later I asked Dan to look out the window. He looked out the window, turned to me and said, "You might as well get dressed." At that point, I looked out and then realized why the children had been screaming our names outside the house. Moon and Ivery had both been alcoholics and in resultant bad health for years. I slipped on my jeans and a shirt. There was already a very large crowd of people, all of whom were very noticeably quiet.

Every eye was looking at the door where one policeman stood leaning over the entrance. There was a red rescue squad truck with a red light flashing. Just after I had left our steps two men evidently from the rescue squad descended Ivery's steps with a large tank of oxygen. They appeared to be routinely tucking it back into its place in the truck. I knew I couldn't walk to anyone and ask a direct question. So I just pulled together a questioning look and noticed Leanna. She acknowledged me slightly and knowingly remained her allowed distance from the steps. Leanna only knew Ivery as a member of the block of Fourteenth Street, her reputation, and her children. She had no claim at this time for any right to pursue any intimacy with the family or the house. But her acknowledgment of me was by no means a brushoff. She was showing her respect by keeping her distance both from Ivery's doorway and by her absence of talking.

I believe it was a relief to the crowd when they saw Dan and me come from our house. We had rights no one else had in the whole community. We had been intimate with the children all last summer. When Ivery had travelled to Virginia to visit, we had fed the children. And through our relationship with them we had claim to Ivery and her house.

I walked over to the step after the rescue men came down and noticed Pat and Poof in the doorway that framed the long hallway leading up the stairs to the second- and third-floor apartment. Pat was crying behind the open door. The policeman stood there and watched the crowd. I saw Poof further down the hallway. I softly asked Pat what was the matter. He didn't resist me but couldn't tell me anything. The policeman allowed me entrance under his leaning arm across the doorway. I put my arm around Pat and repeated my question. Poof had already started up the stairway. I then followed with Pat up the stairway that I had used no more than five times in the entire year and a half I had lived next door.

Situation, from across the street, was sitting in the kitchen at the end of the table with his forehead in his hand. He glanced only with his eyes toward me as I tried to sense where the emergency was. Without saying a word I started toward the front room where I saw first Moon and to my right a policeman; on a single bed lay Ivery. The bed was in a different location than I had remembered. It was now tightly shoved in a corner to my right as I entered the room. She was lying there, head on a pillow, eyes half-opened, arms folded across her stomach and legs gracefully angled in parallel fashion filling up the small bed. I looked at Moon and mumbled something. Moon looked at me and said, "It's Ivery. She's gone."

Upon first glance I was not sure. She looked as if she could have been ill. Upon second glance I recognized from the lack of movement or breathing that Ivery had not had a "seizure" but she was DEAD.

I took Pat, without telling him directly that she was dead, downstairs. Poof had already gone downstairs. When I reached the street I told Dan to take Poof and Pat up to our place. I then started to hunt for Godfrey. I started wandering through the crowd, which had swelled to 150 people. Everything was still. The only thing that disturbed the silence was my repeated question to each of the children that I knew, "Where's Godfrey?" "Have you seen Godfrey?" (I was told that he went up toward Montrose Street.)

An occasional person would reach for my arm, draw me close to them, and ask, "Is it Ivery?" I would shake my head yes and answer, "Yes." Then they would ask, "Is she gone?" I would reply, "Yes, I think so." At that point I didn't want to be spreading an incorrect story, and it had not been reconciled in my mind that she was not sleeping. The conversation upstairs with the police did not include the word *dead* and I had never been certain of the word *gone* used in connection with the dead. After I circled the entire crowd, sent people searching for Godfrey down Montrose, I came back to Ivery's and heard Godfrey was inside. I looked up and saw Godfrey looking out the window. I asked Dan to go up and get him. Dan went up to the third floor without ever entering any second-floor rooms except for the hallway. Godfrey was standing in the middle of the room wandering. Dan brought him down with us. Godfrey said little. The policeman asked me this time if I were taking the children. I told him I lived next door and we would take the children. That was fine with him.

At that point Dan was upstairs with the three boys, the television on, and a Coke on the kitchen table. I went downstairs to find Judy and Contessa. I was told they were swimming. They had come home around nine o'clock to get their swim suits. Dan and I had taken the kids wading at the Philadelphia Museum of Art and I assumed that was where they were. I decided I would wait at home in case they were on their way and Dan, if he went after them, might miss them.

Dan put the three boys in the car and drove across town to Catherine Street where Sims stayed with Ike and Pauline Presley. Fifteen minutes later Dan returned without Judy and Contessa. He discovered that the girls had gone to a YMCA. After discussing the situation down on the steps with Elizabeth's mother, and with Frances butting in, Elizabeth's mother looked at me and asked, "Is there a phone I can use without paying a dime?" Dan said she could use ours and she charged upstairs with Frances saying, "I should go up and help her." No one wanted Frances, but Dan and I didn't have the nerve to handle it like Franny, who would have told her outright. [Frances was considered to be a little demented. Telemachus told me that she had once taken her mother's panties with come in them and claiming they were hers accused two of Raymond's brothers of raping her. He said she was crazy and warned me away from her.]

Elizabeth's mother got on the phone and called the Y at Eleventh and Lehigh Streets. She had decided it would be right to call and tell the children to meet us out in front. I spoke to Contessa after Elizabeth's mother had her paged. I told Contessa to meet us out front and that Dan and I would be over to pick them up in not more than half an hour. After hanging up Elizabeth's mother decided it would be quicker if the police took me over because Dan didn't know where Lehigh was and she could not explain it. She got on the phone again and asked for the Seventh District Police. She knew what police district Eleventh and Lehigh happened to be in. She requested a car be dispatched down to the Third District and carry me to the Eleventh. I was told to wait at Twelfth and Carpenter for the car. Ten minutes later a car arrived. Meanwhile, Elizabeth's grandmother came and stood next to me. Since I talked she remained with me until the car came. If I hadn't been willing to talk she would have just left, because she never asked me one question.

When the car came I got in and told them where I wanted to go. The policeman driving looked back and said, "I have to call in and *confirm* the call." He turned the corner and was on Carpenter when the message came back, "Take her to a cab stand." I said, "All this time and this is the message." He said he couldn't help it. I said, "Let me out."

I then went up and told Dan and we got into the car with the children and finding directions from a man on the street started for Eleventh and Lehigh. The two youngest boys were interested in the sights, City Hall, etc. Godfrey was removed and distant. When we arrived the girls ran to meet us. Tweety, a new girlfriend from across Broad, was with them. I told them I had some bad news for them. "Your mother's gone."

Judy asked, "Is she dead?" and I said, "Yes."

Judy and Contessa started sobbing. In a few moments Contessa asked, "Was she shot?" I told her no, and then explained what happened. Judy asked hysterically, "Where'll we live?" I told her for now she could come with us. And then Tweety said, "You stay with me." The girls cried most of the way home, and the three boys were stunned. The reality of death was sinking in.

When we arrived home four women we had not met were waiting on the front step. They were four sisters, and Sitty was the spokesman. They wanted to know where the children would stay. I said the three boys will stay with us and Judy and Contessa are old enough to go where they want. Judy had been thinking about staying with Tweety and Contessa could stay with Tweety if she wanted to. Sitty said she knew Tweety, she lived very close to her. No one was at home at night. Tweety's mother worked nights at the Naval Hospital. I said fine, we'll take the girls too.

Sitty and her three sisters came upstairs as we proceeded to notify the relatives. We decided to call the relatives in Norfolk, Virginia, first because Grandma Sims, who was closer, had an unlisted number. She lived in Norristown, just north of Philadelphia.

When Dan dialed, we asked Judy to talk. Judy took the phone calmly and said, "Hello, this is Judy, Judy, Judy Sims, your granddaughter." She then handed us the phone and said, "I don't know what to say." Sitty grabbed the phone and said, "Hello, this is one of Ivery's girlfriends calling. Ivery's dead. She died tonight."

Sitty held the phone away from herself and looked at it for a moment, then she exclaimed, "She hung up. She said, 'Thank you,' and hung up.

"She's probably shocked, waking her up in the middle of the night and all."

Well, I was shocked! Dan told me later that he was not surprised by her reaction at all. "One of Ivery's girlfriends" as an identification only served to put her in the same class as Ivery, which evidently Mrs. Knight [her mother] knew all too well. [With the increased acuity of hindsight, I would say that my earlier explanation to Karen was moralistic in a white middle-class way and wide of the mark. I suspect now that Mrs. Knight wanted very little involvement with the responsibilities associated with the death of Ivery in Philadelphia.]

Later we tried to call Mrs. Sims. Because her phone was unlisted, we had to call the Norristown Police and tell them there was a death in the family. They dispatched a car to her house and asked her to phone us.

Within half an hour Mrs. Sims returned the call and I spoke to her. I explained to her who I was and then I told her. I elaborated on the incident and told her I had the children and not to worry. She then spoke with Judy [who she had reared until Judy was eight years old]. She told Judy that she would be down and get them tomorrow. I spoke with her again before she hung up. She asked if Ivery had been drinking. I told her the details slightly more frankly. She told me I should tell the children to be good and to say their prayers.

June twentieth, 1971, a Sunday. Dan and I got up around nine o'clock since we did not know exactly when to expect Grandmother Sims. We all ate pancakes, cleaned the kitchen, and prepared ourselves for her arrival. Dan came up the stairs shortly before noon. I was lying on the bed. He said, "We have company."

I was so shocked by the youth of the two women who had arrived that I couldn't imagine who it was. It certainly must be some other relatives. But they introduced themselves as Mrs. Sims and Mrs. Butler, Mrs. Sims's niece. They were well-dressed, conservative with subdued demeanor, and spoke standard broadcast English [unlike our neighbors on Fourteenth Street]. We went through the entire story again. I was alone with them. The boys were with Dan downstairs and the girls had left to see some of their friends. Eventually Poof and Pat wandered into the house. Grandma Sims did not know them at all. I introduced them and they left and Godfrey came up. Mrs. Butler said she had not seen Godfrey since he was little and asked Godfrey if he remembered her. Godfrey shook his head yes. The children so far were very quiet around the two adults. Mrs. Sims asked Godfrey to come over by her so she could look at him. He did so. A little later the girls came up. Judy and Contessa were amazingly quiet with a polite, not necessarily distant greeting, but very soft modulations in their voices. Meanwhile Mrs. Sims had been telling me, before the girls had arrived, something that Dan had predicted. Mrs. Butler told me, acting as spokesman for her aunt, that Mrs. Sims wouldn't be able to take the children because of her health. In fact when the policeman came last night she was afraid that it was Mrs. Sims' health. Mrs. Sims had been in the hospital off and on. Mrs. Sims looked at me and said, "You know, I have C.A." I had no idea what C.A. was and nothing could come to mind but cancer or heart trouble. But I didn't know which to favor. So with the knowledge that she had no plans to take the children I didn't know what to expect. Mrs. Butler elaborated that she had four children of her own and didn't have any room for more. In fact, she would like to have spent the day with us on Sunday but she had to get back to her family. When Judy and Contessa came they went over and changed into their new clothes. They had just returned from the laundry (they had not been visiting their friends) with Dan. We had wanted them to get their clothes clean for their grandmother. The boys went next door with the girls to change to their clean clothes. They all thought they would be going back to Norristown with their grandmother. Judy had expressed all along that her grandmother's was where she wanted to go and Contessa concurred.

While the children were changing, our talk became more frank. She was most concerned about Simsie, Ivery's oldest boy in Philadelphia. Of course he had not lived at home since we had known the family. She was very dismayed at the fact of the family being split. She was questioning why he was gone. It took some digging back but I remembered that it had been over Babe. Babe had beat Ivery, and Sims joined in to protect his mother. That irritated Babe. There were consequent fights and it came to the point where Ivery had to choose between Babe and Sims. Her choice was that Sims would live with Pauline on Catherine Street. However, to the welfare people, Ivery put on the front that they were all living together. Ivery gave part of her check to Pauline, for Sims.

Mrs. Sims looked at me and said, "Now you know me, I'm frank, you listen to me, now I'm speaking. Sims should be with the rest of the children. He'll feel all alone and left out if he's not with the rest of them. He's at that age."

I agreed but I informed her that I did not know him very well.

A good deal of the remainder of the conversation was around what the family from Norfolk should be doing. I had had a conversation earlier in the morning with Mrs. Knight [Ivery's mother] which I related. She would definitely be coming up. That call was made earlier and Mrs. Sims was extremely upset that Mrs. Knight had not called back to let me know definitely when she was coming. I thought it was too early for Mrs. Knight to know anything more than when she had talked with me, but Mrs. Sims absolutely disagreed. She wanted and expected that they would take more responsibility. After all, it was Mrs. Knight's family. Mrs. Sims asserted she didn't have any right to make any decision. She didn't "want to horn in." The next thing she wanted to know was where Liz was. [Liz was Ivery's mother's sister's daughter, nearly the same age as Ivery. Liz lived in North Philadelphia, but had never visited Ivery as far as we knew and had never been visited by Ivery.] Why, if Ivery knew her, wasn't she over here. As far as Mrs. Sims was concerned that was "family" and she should be over here.

Mrs. Butler indicated her desire to go home and so they decided to leave but to keep in contact with me. Judy and Contessa did not know until the two ladies went over to the Sims apartment. Mrs. Sims told them to take off their good dresses, and at that time the children discovered they were not going home with her. Later Godfrey said, "We got dressed up for nothing."

I was surprised by who did *not* help the previous night. Franny did not come out of her house. Miz Mamie, with whom they had lived on Montrose Street, made no appearance. Maryjane and Joyceann did offer a bedroom for one night, but it was we who went over to the apartment and brought a large mattress to our place for the children. They all slept on it like pieces of a jigsaw puzzle.

Ivery's death coalesced women—both friends and relatives—who began to push events toward the burial and, most importantly, toward placing the children. Neither the children nor the relatives considered us viable candidates to be foster parents for the children until they were grown up.

Ivery's mother, Mrs. Knight, had put things into motion from Norfolk, but not through us. She had called Liz, her sister's daughter, Ivery's cousin, in North Philadelphia. Not long after Mrs. Sims and Mrs. Butler left, Liz appeared at our door. She was near Ivery's age, in her late thirties, and lived with Earl, a man somewhat her senior. His family, it was rumored, owned several houses, and Liz lived with Earl in one of them despite opposition from his family. The house was well furnished, unlike Ivery's apartment. Her son Anthony lived on the third floor of the house, above Liz and Earl; Anthony's wife was pregnant and nearly at term. Drag racing was Anthony's avocation, and he showed me pictures of the machine that he and his friends prepared. As we came to know Liz, the difficulty of fitting Ivery's children into her life loomed large.

Liz visited briefly with us and spoke to several people on the street including Maryjane, who was minding Little James. Then, in what seemed a hurry, she swept up Godfrey, Pat, and Poof and returned to North Philadelphia.

On Monday she initiated funeral arrangements and began the legal work necessary to transfer the children into her custody. By talking on the phone and running back and forth in her car, she quickly came to know Telemachus, who was interested in the fate of the children. He had helped feed them when Ivery had traveled back to Norfolk for two weeks the summer before. Phone calls flew between Liz and Telemachus, and Liz and us.

On Tuesday the children were with us again while Liz attended to necessary details. Telemachus took off work at five and asked me to take him someplace. When I told him I had no gas in the car, he said, "Drive around the corner." We did, and he gave me two dollars for gas and slid some other bills in my pocket. "Don't tell me what you have in your pocket," he played; "I don't want to know." He said, "Drive up to South Street," and we headed that way. "I know a place where they serve some barbecued ribs."

On the way he commented, "I don't know what I'd do without South Philly." He was reminiscing, and in his talk he asked me, "I wonder how many peoples would come to my funeral?" I was, of course, ignorant of such matters and said I did not know, indeed I did not know who attended funerals. That was one of the things ethnographers wanted most to know. Then I wondered aloud, in a question symmetrical to his, how many would come to mine; "probably two or three," I added.

"It's surprising how many friends you've made down here," he told me. "Some you don't even know are your friends ask about you."

I was surprised and felt warmly included in a larger world that I barely discerned.

In our apartment kitchen Telemachus, Karen, the children, and I relished the ribs and laughed and joked through the evening. Liz called during our feast to tell us how the undertaker was charging $350 for the embalming and the viewing, and $75 for the burial. She said he knew the city only allowed $250 and $50 respectively. I told Telemachus that I thought the undertaker was trying to get over on Liz, to which he readily agreed, telling us how at his father's death last year, a greedy aunt had tried to get his father's social security to bury him with. She thought that with the man's sons so far away they would not hear of her maneuver and she would pocket the money.

Afterward, when I walked Telemachus down to the street, he told me he had talked with Liz earlier in the day. He was worried about the *layout*. He thought it ought to be in South Philadelphia, not North Philadelphia, because Ivery's friends were down here. The layout was scheduled for a morning and he objected to that because it meant no one who worked could go to it. He was also concerned because the children, as we all knew, did not have adequate clothes, especially the young boys. They had not attended school over the winter because they did not have clothes for it. They were barely dressed and were seriously embarrassed by their ragged appearance.

"I'll ring your doorbell in the morning," he said on leaving, "and we'll take up a collection." I had only a vague idea of what taking up a collection for Ivery would entail.

"Really strange." I wrote the two words at the head of a notecard for the following day, Wednesday. "Complicated by the unreality of heat."

Telemachus, as he had said he would, rang my doorbell at 7:45 A.M. I had slept half-dressed, because I had come in from the center at five-thirty that morning, so I was downstairs quickly. It had been a blistering hot night and the day just grew hotter. It took extra effort to breathe in Philadelphia's humid heat.

Right away I could tell Telemachus was infused with a rare enthusiasm. It was in his voice, his intensity. He greeted me and then asked, "Do you have a cigar box or shoe box upstairs?" I said, "Sure," and ran back upstairs for a cigar box that I kept small things in. I brought it down and found him in the back of the shop looking for one of his garage letterheads and some scotch tape to fasten it on with. He instructed me to cut a hole in the top of the box so people could put money in.

We started north, stopping first at the Chas. Cafe, where Ivery did most of her drinking and where she and her friends hung out. It was an age-graded bar, its customers all men and a few women in their late thirties and early forties. I had been there twice before and usually felt uneasy., Today was different. I wrote in the field notes, "I felt little of the usual self-consciousness.... There was some kind of fantastic rapport in this solicitation and giving." At the same time, however, both Telemachus and I felt moments of anger and disbelief. The Chas. Cafe was owned by one Charles, a white man. I did not know if he was sick or dead, but he was never there. His wife, who did not tend bar, sat somewhere in the place and seemed in some sense to preside over it. When Telemachus asked her for a donation and explained that it was for Ivery's children, she turned her head away. Ivery had drunk up most of her welfare checks in that bar and the woman could not give! I was speechless, but Telemachus was not surprised. Again I was incredulous when, as we moved around the bar, Babe just sat and watched us; he gave nothing. As we left and began walking, Telemachus began to criticize the white woman for not contributing to Ivery's children's relief. I mentioned Babe, and Telemachus just shook his head and made noises of disgust.

We then turned down small Montrose Street. Telemachus asked all those who were out in the humid air to contribute: "Could you spare a penny, nickel, dime, or anything? We're trying to get together something for Ivery's kids, some shoes and clothes, so they can go to her funeral." I carried the box and Telemachus did the talking.

Crawford, who had been Ivery's main drinking companion, fell in step with us. He was the one who would call up to her window early in the morning, asking her to go for a drink. His features were delicate, he was not tall, and he dressed during cooler weather in thrift-store tweed sport coats. I thought of him as a misplaced professor. He was wickedly funny, the funniest man I met during fieldwork, and I thought he would be marvelous to drink with, although I never did. One night Ivery's "ghost"—her old man, Moon—had attacked Crawford on the street. No one knew what the issues were, although we all knew Ivery drank with Crawford and lived with Moon. At the moment of contact the whole street erupted to stop them; people on both sides pulled them apart.

Telemachus made his request, then Crawford explained some more. If a person would say, "Who Ivery?" Crawford would explain, "That thin gal that used to walk up and down Fourteenth

Street." People generally commented on the helplessness of children.

No one turned away. No one avoided us. Miz Jane, the *old lady* of a man I knew, smiled and kept her head out of the window and watched us make our way up the street toward her. At the Chas. Cafe a man had told us to go ask his wife for money. As we later drew close to her, Telemachus announced, "Your husband sent us."

"I know what you're here for," she replied.

"What's that?" Telemachus asked.

"Ivery," she said. Then she added, "He took all my money." She paused, then said "Wait here." She walked several doors away, found her purse, and returned and gave us some money.

We walked on, the three of us. Crawford asked some men he knew, but we did not, if they would give. When people replied that they had no money, Crawford said, "I'll put in for you," and each time reached over and slid more change through the cutout on the top of the box. In ninety minutes we had collected forty-seven dollars in bills and change. I was very much surprised at the considerable amount, since people had little to give.

When we returned to the shop, Liz had arrived and was standing in silence with Babe close by. Liz and Telemachus wanted to discuss the arrangements for getting people to the funeral, which was to be the next evening, Thursday, five days after Ivery's death. As Telemachus and I walked up with the box, Babe began to announce that all the furniture and other items upstairs were things that he had put there. I looked out of the corner of my eye at Telemachus to see what his response would be to Babe this time, since I remembered vividly that he had avoided Ivery a year and a half ago because Babe was then her old man, and an insanely jealous one at that. Telemachus was looking down and away from him, his expression verging on disgust, but he did not speak. I kept my eyes averted too, embarrassed because we had been at the bar an hour and a half earlier and Babe had pointedly given us nothing. "If the kids need anything," Babe went on to his unwilling audience, "just let me know. I work nights up there at the bar." By this time he had his hand on Liz's back.

"I don't like how free you are with your hands," Liz blasted him.

After Babe left, Telemachus said, "We couldn't say anything with loudmouth around."

Although Telemachus wanted me to keep the money and see it dispensed, he offered it to Liz and told her it would help with clothes and shoes for the children. She expressed her thanks. The viewing was not a little more than a day away.

Telemachus and I had described a square in our route, enclosing a space where he felt comfortable, and we had picked up Crawford's zone of familiarity as well. The area included a block either way from the repair shop. Interestingly, Crawford had urged us to collect at the Blue Moon Hotel, where Ivery used to work. It was four blocks beyond Broad Street, and Telemachus had declined by saying that he knew no one over there. The truth of the matter is that there were many people who knew Ivery in that vicinity and would have contributed. Her boy Sims, for example, lived with Pauline and Ike Presley several doors away from the hotel. I was sure that everyone on the street there knew about Ivery because I had gone over with Godfrey on Saturday night to tell Sims of his mother's death. At that time I was broadly greeted on the street by name, Danny, and people I had never seen before talked with me. I seemed to be known in the sense that Telemachus had meant when he said more people would show up at my funeral than I knew.

Ivery did not really have a funeral. The layout was changed to the evening, but it remained in North Philadelphia, and Karen expressed her shock that none of the relatives from Norfolk came up to view her. Thursday evening we drove up to the funeral home with a car full of neighbors. When we arrived we walked into a room with chairs arranged in front of a cheap casket, the top half opened to reveal Ivery's face and shoulders, a bust of the dead. The children were there, dressed up. Telemachus had also brought a car full of neighbors from our area. There was no one else—just Liz and the children, the people Telemachus brought, and the people we brought. All the way up and all the way back Crawford cracked jokes and tried to start something between the couple who were riding with us. "Katherine, didn't you used to live around here? Didn't I see you up here the other day?" We were all laughing at his joking.

I sat and looked at Ivery's face for a minute and at the Sims children patiently quiet, sitting in a row next to Liz and Earl. Ivery's layout contrasted with that of Telemachus's son, Auston.

Here I flash forward in time. Karen and I moved away at the end of the summer to Wawa, Pennsylvania, in the country. It was on Wednesday evening, 1 March, that I wrote in my journal,

Telemachus called and said, "I had to try and find you 'cause you didn't try and find me." He then told me that Auston strangled in his sleep Monday night. The layout was to be Friday night and the burial Saturday morning. He went into an elaborate monologue on how women come in and attempt to comfort his wife. Mae would cry and they would say, "Crying is good for you." Telemachus said he starts joking when it gets too heavy, it gets peoples' mind off it for a minute. Like the old people say, "You stir shit, the worse it stinks." Joking makes a person forget his troubles instead of pushing him down.

On Friday, 3 March, I wrote,

We got there twenty minutes after the service started. We were put in an adjoining room; the crowd was large and we were part of the overflow. Over the loudspeaker we heard some very well done organ music and vocal songs. The minister spoke eloquently. After the service Karen and I and two men in the room with us were escorted through the other room to view the body. I noticed that the minister had a reversed collar. Auston looked like pure wax. Karen noted that the body was higher out of the casket than funerals she had attended. Like he was floating. His penis was visible beneath his pants, a rather unusual part to display based on my nonblack experiences. The family went out and entered a limousine that would take them home. Karen and I were struck by the incongruity between the character of the deceased and the occasion that he had wittingly or unwittingly launched. There was a momentous grandeur at his death that his desperation as a living person never matched.

There was no grandeur for Ivery, whose viewing was a moment of solemnity bounded by the dizzying and surgical humor of Crawford in the car. We drove south after the wordless, musicless ceremony, to South Philadelphia. Telemachus had arrived ahead of us and was buying drinks at the bar nearest our apartment (not the rude Chas. Cafe).

"Take your time with this one," Telemachus announced loudly, "cause there ain' gonna be another." Everybody laughed, and the bartender poured drinks. Crawford walked in and asked if he was included. Then Moon entered and asked if he was included. Telemachus said yes to both. Telemachus was joking and laughing with everyone. When he finished his drink he left, as did Karen, for she was very tired. Mr. Jardine, Franny's father, asked me to have a drink with him and I did.

After the drink I left and walked the three doors to the apartment. Telemachus and Karen were still talking on the sidewalk. He was saying that he had given money to Liz at the layout, and Karen said that she had as well. "That's good," Telemachus told us, "because the one hundred dollars we gave her will start things off." He went on to add, "I knew things were alright when I saw the boys dressed up." They had worn white shirts, blue short pants, and new shoes. It was the first time any of us had seen them in good clothes. Telemachus continued, "If I live to be a hundred I'll never forget Danny." Later Karen told me that he could not get over that I had collected money with him.

It seemed to me that Telemachus's status was changing in the area. He had taken an initial role in feeding the children, as I mentioned, while Ivery had traveled to Norfolk a year before; he had given money to other children on the street, especially Leanna and Big Gregory's; he had taken a visible role in helping the children financially for their appearance at the layout; and now he was promised that he would manage, beginning in July, Tony's garage across the street. He was generous with the money he made. He bought things for people, and I had even seen him win at numbers and walk down the street distributing portions of his take in small amounts to people he knew.

The viewing had been on Thursday night. On Sunday, Ivery's brother and other relatives arrived to stay for a day at Liz's house. We went to meet them, since they did not come to South Philadelphia. Ivery's mother was not with them. Liz complained that when they were children, Mrs. Knight had left Ivery and two siblings on the street corner with only an apple in their hands. I do not know the truth of the story, but in any case Liz did not have kind words for her.

In one sense, Karen and I were now a part of Fourteenth Street; the irony was that what had helped make us a part—the Sims children—was now removed. Our new sense of competence and involvement was coupled with a growing alienation because the children were no longer living next door. A month later we moved into the house of Karen's employer in Wawa, Pennsylvania, to care for it while his family traveled to England. The transition was a major trauma. I had begged quarters with Boycie in the shadow of the Martin Luther King, Jr., Plaza so we could drink for an evening, and suddenly, within a matter of minutes and within twenty kilometers, Karen and I were in a secluded agricultural valley in the house of members of the East Coast upper class— there was inherited wealth on both sides, and the house was architect-designed. I was staggered by it. I felt spatially as if I had, during the two years in South Philadelphia, fallen through the thin but real and numerous striae of American social structure, to the very bottom. I felt as if I were at the bottom of a racially polarized society, lying on my back looking at times upward to the distant middle class. Then suddenly we were swimming in Karen's employer's pool, and one of the hangers-on at the house, a friend of one of the sons, was shooting heroin in the bedroom he seldom seemed to leave. It was too bizarre for words. I was reeling from the contrast between scarcity and what that home represented. We had tried to put our clothes away in one of the dressers in the master bedroom only to find it was full of papers, of trusts, of sources of an unseen wealth that had been taken for granted for generations.

Karen and I were in the country less than a year before we moved back into the city to a white working-class neighborhood. We kept in touch with the children and we visited South Philadelphia, but with decreasing frequency. Liz had tried and been urged by everyone to keep the children together, but Sims never made the move and continued to live with his friend Ike, and Judy and Contessa kept returning to South Philadelphia. Judy had, as Liz pointed out, "a taste of life." Over the following winter, she and Contessa moved into the Martin Luther King, Jr., Plaza with the mother of the young man who fathered Judy's daughter. Finally Liz gave up the younger boys as well, and they went into an orphanage in West Philadelphia. Sims became a traveling cosmetics salesman.

• • •

It seems strange, even alienating, to call life in South Philadelphia, with black people, with one's own countrymen, *fieldwork*. But when I left the street, even my mode of documentation changed. Life for the ethnographer is a life arbitrarily set apart. Embarking on new genres, I began to keep a daybook of writing, of observations I was making. The style of the notes changed as did what I put in them. My life changed. I was no longer doing the empirical research of cultural science. I began to document a life that I had left behind two years before but was now profoundly alien to me.

Wednesday, 2 January, 1972

I have been reading the Northwestern University Press version of Husserl's *Krisis* papers, edited in German by W. Biemel. In my dissertation I am attempting to ground my work in a way acceptable to Husserl's insights. . . . I suspect that one thing entailed by attending Husserl's phenomenology is a more radical empiricism. . . . I am writing using an extended anecdote. The highly analyzed extended anecdote, embedded in lived events, situated, becomes a kind of paradigmatic situation. It is seen as internally exemplary. Then it becomes immediately comparable to the professional reader's own experience. There is an implicit fundamental comparison going on between the analyzed anecdote and scientists' experiences. . . . Although the high analysis would suggest universality, one will be easily able to recognize those various personal touches that create autonomous, locally constituted reality.

There are up to the writer all sorts of choices about how explicit to become in the presentation. But presenting situations brings problematics of its own—the motivatedness, hence reality of the "characters."

Wednesday, 2 February, 1972

Met with Dell Hymes and John Szwed at the Center for Urban
Ethnography to discuss anthropology and literature. Suggestions
for reading included *The Dollmakers*, *Nomads of the Long Bow*,
Vasilika, *Passage to India*, etc.

Hymes talked about novelists and ethnographers: (1) What
constitutes a good description of what happened? (2) How do we
know what genre we are reading? (3) What counts as narrative?
(4) What is the *criticism* appropriate to each? (5) What are the
common, the different features of a style, genre, being
convincing, etc.? (6) Are ethnographies as so far written the only
or best genre for communicating ethnographic knowledge? (7)
What do anecdotes *represent*?

Concern at the center is running high over questioning the
bases of ethnographic practice (see Hymes 1972).

Friday, 25 March, 1972

I stopped by the shop to see Telemachus before picking Karen up at the sheet music business. I saw Joyceann standing on her stoop. She asked, "Why are down here?" I said, "To kiss you." We kissed on the lips and it felt good. She said, "Telemachus is leaving in two weeks. Tony's eased him out and Little Johnny is back again."

Boycie came up and we hugged each other. Franny called me over and we talked for an hour. She showed me Herb's new Volvo. We talked mostly about our families.

Tuesday, 2 May, 1972

Karen had lunch today with Judy Sims, who wanted to hear that she should stay with Liz. The crisis is that she has no friends at Gratz High School and wants to be in South Philadelphia with the ones she has.

Tuesday, 30 May, 1972

Twelve days ago I sent my committee members my
dissertation [second version] at the University of Wisconsin. Now
I am here and they are each meeting with me to remark on it.
—worthy of the dissertation and degree
—not social scientific enough, too poetic

Monday, 5 June, 1972

Fighting with Karen; assault and counterassault. It goes on for hours. We are then left with the veneer of everydayness. Her grievances seem to have no emotional hold on me, they have drained away, there are new definitions of the state of affect, a new ethos...

Wednesday, 14 June, 1972

Worked all day on revisions of the dissertation.

Saturday, 5 August, 1972

Franny asked Karen to a Tupperware party at her house. Saw Boycie on the street when I took Karen to Franny's. I'm going to meet him at ten-thirty. I bought a Famiglia Cribari Cianti in minor celebration of this portended event. I have the grotesque urge to tell him I read a paper that included him at the American Association for the Advancement of Science.

Tonight I noticed thousands of scars in both eyebrows. How did he get them?

Saturday, 26 August, 1972

Solotaroff, editor of the (formerly *New*) *American Review*, in a
rejection note mentioned I was imaginative; and although he
thought the short stories I'd sent, including *Truckstop*, were
unfinished, he did request something ethnographic if it were
suitable for the *A. R.* It made me think that if ethnographers
borrowed from the New Journalism their sensibilities would have
to become hip, inside (in a hip way), and they would have to
acquire a slightly ironic tone, mockery, embedded in the
personal point of view, so that they could market their
observations for the shock value, debunking, revealing,
emphasizing a particular scene. That way the usual readers of
one's magazine or book would be guaranteed something wholly
new to them or a wholly new way of seeing presented in the
writing. This aim cuts across the one anthropologists typically
have. I'm not sure that ethnology, per se, can emerge from New
Journalism *Ethnography*. Or if it should. New Journalism
Ethnography would have to be ironic, critical, moral in tone, and
might wholly give way to superficial residency by the
anthropologist cum journalist, and to pseudo-accounts. The
politics of the journalistic piece is much different than that of
the scientific ethnography; each has its defensible canons of
authenticity, but the two will never be quite happy with one
another.

Sunday, 21 April, 1973

Picked up the Sims children in South Philadelphia. Judy is about six months into her pregnancy. Had Ginos chicken basket and thirty-one flavors ice cream. We talked about everyone we knew in South Philadelphia and what they were doing.

This morning while Karen and I were talking I heard her speak but saw words emerge from her mouth formed of discrete letters, made of neatly carved transparent ice and with highlights. They melted about three feet in front of her, forming puddles on the floor.

Wednesday, 23 May, 1973

Karen and I have decided to separate. I am flying to Kentucky and my parents' house today. Later she will return to Wisconsin and attend summer school.

On the way to the airport we sat apart in the front seat of the truck until ready to turn onto the Schuylkill Expressway. Then she slid over. I almost began crying. I wanted to put my head on the wheel and shed water or something. (The roar of this plane is godawful; I can't concentrate on my writing.)

Wednesday, 5 June, 1973

It was a daydream. I was lying in the sun in the backyard of my parent's place around noon, taking a break from revising. This pretty well captures how I've felt. I had my head against the matted grass. I imagined small bugs, maybe ants detached my face from the hairline, in front of the ears, under my neck. Each of them, perhaps a hundred, lined up and held a tiny handful of skin. They each began walking outward, stretching my skin away from my face like a rubber mask. It stretched further and further. Their activity failed to damage me in any way. My whole body sank slowly into the ground as I expanded hugely. The pores of my skin began to open, growing larger as my skin grew. Little blades of grass began poking through the opening holes of the pores. As I expanded, I sank deeper and tufts of grass appeared where the flat blades had been in my pore openings. My skin then melted with the earth; the light skin with the dark earth. The earth, where it could be seen beneath the grass was a dark cream color, a miscegenation, and perfect blending of dark and light, soil and flesh. For a moment there was no outline of my body. There was only the flat back lawn. Then subtly protuberances appeared. The giantly spaced apart (covering the whole back yard) toes pushed through just a little. My nose, distantly, was emerging, a soft hillock, a ways away; two shoulders' outlines could barely be discerned. The upper part of my stomach and hips, upper thighs, softly rolled into view. I became slowly transformed to earth and man, continued to grow, to have a giant physical, human-shaped integrity. I would eventually be able to get to my feet, to stand. I would tower over the planet. (Rose 1982)

2 August, 1973

Dear Dan:

I'm sitting in the kitchen of Elna and Elwyn Cooper here at the farm, where I have set up my office while your Mom is over at the trailer of Grandpa and Grandma Walter's. We arrived here from Kentucky about 9:15 Tuesday evening, and will be staying until Monday or Tuesday of next week....

•   •   •

While this week has been a glad one in certain respects, it has been a very sad one, knowing that your home has broken up. Not only as your parents does this bring us sorrow, but remembering that I performed the wedding ceremony it gives me added pain that those marriage vows have been broken and that home which was so hopefully proclaimed there is now in shambles. Your Mom and I would certainly like to talk to you more about your tragic loss in this area. Let us keep in touch about this problem, for there have been those who broke up their home and then re-established it, by remarriage. Your cousin Kathy Rose had this experience. They are now living together again near Pontiac, Mich....

•   •   •

With love and prayer,

Dad

america   as much a problem in metaphysics as
it is a nation earthly entity an iota in our
galaxy   an organism that changes even as i
examine it   fact and fantasy never twice the
same   so many variables

          •   •   •

confess I am curiously drawn   unmentionable   to
the americans   doubt i could exist among them for
long however

Robert Hayden (1978)

References Cited

Abrahams, Roger D.
1966 *Deep Down in the Jungle*. Hatboro: Folklore Associates.
Abrahams, Roger D., and John F. Szwed, eds.
1983 *After Africa: Extracts from British Travel Accounts and Journals of the Seventeenth, Eighteenth, and Nineteenth Centuries Concerning the Slaves, Their Manners, and Customs, in the British West Indies*. New Haven: Yale University Press.
Barbusse, Henri
1908 *Hell*. Translated by Robert Baldick. London: Chapman and Hall, 1966.
Barthes, Roland
1967 *Elements of Semiology*. Translated by Annette Lavers and Colin Smith. New York: Hill and Wang.
1972 *Mythologies*. Translated by Annette Lavers. New York: Hill and Wang.
Bourdieu, Pierre
1977 *Outline of a Theory of Practice*. Translated by Richard Nice. Cambridge: Cambridge University Press.
Braudel, Fernand
1977 *Afterthoughts on Material Civilization and Capitalism*. Translated by Patricia N. Ranum. Baltimore: Johns Hopkins University Press.
1986 *The Wheels of Commerce: Civilization and Capitalism, 15th–18th Century*. Translated by Sean Reynolds. New York: Harper and Row.
Bree, Germaine
1980 Michel Leiris: Mazemaker. In *Autobiography: Essays Theoretical and Critical*, ed. James Olney. Princeton: Princeton University Press.
Brook, Peter
1968 *The Empty Space*. New York: Avon.
Bulmer, Martin, ed.
1982 *Social Research Ethics*. London: Macmillan.
Chandler, Alfred D., Jr.
1977 *The Visible Hand: The Managerial Revolution in American Business*. Cambridge: Harvard University Press.
Clifford, James
1983 On Ethnographic Authority. *Representations* 1:118–46.
Davenport, Guy
1981 *The Geography of the Imagination*. San Francisco: North Point.

Dewey, John
1959 *Art as Experience*. New York: Putnam.
Dickens, Charles
1842 *American Notes, Pictures from Italy*. New York: Dutton, 1908.
Drake, St. Clair, and Horace Clayton
1962 *Black Metropolis: A Study of Negro Life in a Northern City*. New York: Harper and Row.
Drucker, Peter F.
1979 *Adventures of a Bystander*. New York: Harper and Row.
Dubois, W. E. B.
1899 *The Philadelphia Negro*. Philadelphia: University of Pennsylvania Press, 1967.
Ellison, Ralph
1984 Interviewed by James Thompson, Lennox Raphael, and Steve Cannon in 1967. Reprinted in *An American Retrospective: Writings from Harper's Magazine 1850–1984*. New York: Harper's.
Flink, James J.
1975 *The Car Culture*. Cambridge: MIT Press.
Foley, Eugene P.
1966 The Negro Businessman: In Search of a Tradition. *Daedalus* 95:107–144.
Frake, Charles O.
1964 Notes on Queries in Ethnography. *American Anthropologist* (Special Publication) 66 (3), pt. 2:132–45.
Fusfeld, Daniel R., and Timothy Bates
1984 *Political Economy of the Ghetto*. Carbondale: Southern Illinois Press.
Geertz, Clifford
1966 Transcript of the Conference. The Negro American. *Daedalus* 95:297.
Glassie, Henry
1982 *Passing the Time in Ballymenone: Culture and History of an Ulster Community*. Philadelphia: University of Pennsylvania Press.
Glazer, Nathan
1969 The Missing Bootstrap. *Saturday Review*, 23 August.
Goffman, Erving
1959 *The Presentation of Self in Everyday Life*. Garden City: Anchor Doubleday.
1963 *Behavior in Public Places*. New York: Free Press.
Goodenough, Ward Hunt
1961 *Property, Kin, and Community on Truk*. New Haven: Yale University Publications in Anthropology 46.
1964 Cultural Anthropology and Linguistics. In *Language in Culture and Society*, ed. Dell Hymes. New York: Harper and Row.
Hannerz, Ulf
1969 *Soulside*. New York: Columbia University Press.
Hayden, Robert
1978 *American Journal*. Staunton: Effendi Press.

Heidegger, Martin
1962 *Being and Time.* Translated by John Macquarrie and Edward Robinson. Oxford: Basil Blackwell.
Husserl, Edmund
1913 *Ideas.* New York: Collier, 1962.
Hymes, Dell
1981 *"In Vain I Tried to Tell You:" Essays in Native American Ethnopoetics.* Philadelphia: University of Pennsylvania Press.
Hymes, Dell, ed.
1972 *Reinventing Anthropology.* New York: Pantheon.
Knorr-Cetina, Karen, and A. V. Cicourel
1981 *Advances in Social Theory and Methodology: Toward an Integration of Micro- and Macro-Sociologies.* Boston: Routledge and Kegan Paul.
Langland, William
1367–70 *Piers the Plowman.* Baltimore: Penguin, 1966.
Leiris, Michel
1986 A Special Section: New Translations of Michel Leiris. *Sulfur* 15.
Levi-Strauss, Claude
1974 *Tristes Tropiques.* Translated by John and Doreen Weightman. New York: Atheneum.
Liebow, Elliot
1967 *Tally's Corner.* Boston: Little Brown.
Lynd, Robert, and Helen Merrell Lynd
1937 *Middletown in Transition.* New York: Harcourt, Brace, and World.
Malinowski, Bronislaw
1922 *Argonauts of the Western Pacific.* New York: Dutton.
Milner, Christina and Richard Milner
1973 *Black Players: The Secret World of Black Pimps.* New York: Bantam Books.
Montaigne, Michel de
1960 *The Complete Essays.* Vol. 2. Garden City: Anchor Doubleday.
National Commission on the Causes and Prevention of Violence.
1969 *Violence in America: Historical and Comparative Perspectives.* Washington, D.C.: U.S. Government Printing Office.
Northrup, Herbert R.
1968 *The Negro in the Automobile Industry.* Philadelphia: University of Pennsylvania Press.
Price, Richard
1983 *First Time: The Historical Vision of an Afro-American People.* Baltimore: Johns Hopkins University Press.
Rabinow, Paul
1977 *Reflections on Fieldwork in Morocco.* Berkeley: University of California Press.
Raper, Arthur F.
1936 *Preface to Peasantry: A Tale of Two Black Belt Counties.* Chapel Hill: University of North Carolina Press.

Reed, Ishmael
  1970 *Catechism of d neoamerican hoodoo church*. London: Paul Breman.
Rein, Martin
  1969 Social Stability and Black Capitalism. *Transaction* 6:4–5.
Renner, Bruce
  1982 *Song Made Out of a Pale Smoke*. Berkeley: Epervier Press.
Robbe-Grillet, Alain
  1965 *Two Novels by Robbe-Grillet*. Translated by Richard Howard. New York: Grove Press.
Rosaldo, Renato
  1980 *Ilongot Headhunting, 1883–1974: A Study in Society and History*. Stanford: Stanford University Press.
Rose, Dan
  1974 Detachment: Continuities of Sensibilities among Afro-American Populations of the Circum-Atlantic Fringe. *Journal of Asian and African Studies* 9.
  1982 Daydream #7356. *Dreamworks* 2:312.
  1983 In Search of Experience: The Anthropological Poetics of Stanley Diamond. *American Anthropologist* 85:345–55.
  1984 Experimental Writing and the Dispersion of Ethnographic Methods and Genres. Paper read to the American Anthropological Association Annual Meeting, Denver, November.
  1986 Transformations of Disciplines through Their Texts. *Cultural Anthropology* 1:316–26.
Rosenberg, Nathan, and L. E. Birdzell, Jr.
  1986 *How the West Grew Rich: The Economic Transformation of the Industrial World*. New York: Basic Books.
Royal Anthropological Institute
  1951 *Notes and Queries on Anthropology*. London: Routledge and Kegan Paul Sahlins, Marshall
  1976 *Culture and Practical Reason*. Chicago: University of Chicago Press.
Said, Edward
  1983 *The World, the Text, and the Critic*. Cambridge: Harvard University Press.
Sartre, Jean-Paul
  1963 *Being and Nothingness*. New York: Pocket Books.
Sayers, Gale
  1972 *I Am Third*. New York: Bantam.
Schutz, Alfred
  1962 *Collected Papers*. Vols. 1,2. ed. Maurice Natanson. *The Problem of Social Reality*. The Hague: Martinus Nijhoff.
Silk, Gerald
  1984 *Automobile and Culture*. New York: Abrams.
Szwed, John F.
  1972 An American Anthropological Dilemma: The Politics of Afro-American Culture. In *Reinventing Anthropology*, ed. Dell Hymes. New York: Pantheon.

1986 World Views Collide: The History of Jazz and Hot Dance. *The Village Voice*, 26 February.

West, Cornell
1984 Out of Motown. *Semiotext(e)* 4:91–94.

Whyte, William Foote
1955 *Street Corner Society*. Chicago: University of Chicago Press.

Wolf, Eric R.
1980 The United States: The Cultural Predicament of the Anthropologist. In *Anthropology: Ancestors and Heirs*, ed. Stanley Diamond. The Hague: Mouton.

Songs

The Beatles, "Come Together." Maclen Music, 2654.
The Impressions, "Choice of Colors." Curtom (Buddha), CR1943A.
The Isley Brothers, "It's Your Thing." T Neck, TN 901A.
The Jackson Five, "I Want You Back." Motown, M1157.
Jr. Walker and the All Stars, "What Does It Take." Soul, S–35062.
The Moments, "Somebody Loves You Baby." Stang Records, ST5003.
The O'Jays, "One Night Affair." Neptune Records, N–12, ZTSC–142014.
Diana Ross and the Supremes, "Someday We'll Be Together." Motown, M1156.
Nina Simone, "Black Gold," RCA Victor, LSP–428.
Stevie Wonder, "He's Misstra Know It All," Tamla, T326VI.

Acknowledgments

The computer graphics were designed by Reza Ghezelbash on the Intergraph Vax 751 from drawings by the author.

The University of Pennsylvania Research Foundation graciously granted funds for photographic and computer work.

Dean Lee Copeland of the Graduate School of Fine Arts made funds available for an earlier draft of this book, then titled, *EVENTS*, as did the National Institute of Mental Health (MH #30962–01).

SBK Entertainment World granted use of the following: "Come Together" by John Lennon and Paul McCartney, copyright ©1969 by Northern Songs, Ltd. All rights for the U.S., Canada, and Mexico controlled and administered by Blackwood Music Inc., under license from ATV Music (Maclen). All rights reserved. International copyright secured. Used by permission.

Thanks to Mrs. Robert Hayden to quote from *American Journal*, to Bruce Renner to quote from *Song Made Out of a Pale Smoke*, and to Warner Bros. Music to use "Choice of Colors" by the Impressions.

Index

University of Pennsylvania Press
Conduct and Communications Series

Erving Goffman and Dell Hymes, *Founding Editors*
Dell Hymes, Gillian Sankoff, and Henry Glassie, *General Editors*

Erving Goffman. *Strategic Interaction.* 1970
William Labov. *Language in the Inner City: Studies in the Black English Vernacular.* 1973
William Labov. *Sociolinguistic Patterns.* 1973
Dell Hymes. *Foundations in Sociolinguistics: An Ethnographic Approach.* 1974
Barbara Kirshenblatt-Gimblett, ed. *Speech Play: Research and Resources for the Study of Linguistic Creativity.* 1976
Gillian Sankoff. *The Social Life of Language.* 1980
Erving Goffman. *Forms of Talk.* 1981
Dell Hymes. *"In Vain I Tried to Tell You."* 1981
Dennis Tedlock. *The Spoken Word and the Work of Interpretation.* 1983
Ellen B. Basso. *A Musical View of the Universe: Kalapalo Myth and Ritual Performances.* 1985
Michael Moerman. *Talking Culture: Ethnography and Conversation Analysis.* 1987
Dan Rose. *Black American Street Life: South Philadelphia, 1969–1971.* 1987
Charles L. Briggs. *Mexicano Verbal Art.* 1988
J. Joseph Errington. *Structure and Style in Javanese: A Semiotic View of Linguistic Etiquette.* 1988